Bringing the Empire Home

Bringing the Empire Home

Race, Class, and Gender
in Britain and Colonial South Africa

ZINE MAGUBANE

The University of Chicago Press
Chicago and London

CONTENTS

ACKNOWLEDGMENTS

This book marks the provisional end of an intellectual journey that began some years ago. Because of the wide variety of contexts in which its various parts were composed and presented, an enormous number of people contributed, both directly and indirectly, to its eventual completion. Fellowships from the Center for Advanced Study at the University of Illinois at Urbana-Champaign; the Center for African Studies, also at the University of Illinois at Urbana-Champaign; and the Illinois Program for Research in the Humanities made the project possible. I am also very fortunate to have a wonderful group of friends and colleagues who have provided much intellectual support and stimulation along the way. I am particularly grateful to my fellow members of the "support group"—Michael Goldman, Zsuzsa Gille, Rachel Schurman, Anna Marshall, and Winnie Poster—who provided intellectual stimulation and a lot of laughs. Paul Tiyambe Zeleza is a great friend and intellectual mentor. Emily Ignacio provided countless critical references and much-needed work breaks. The book also benefited tremendously from comments and suggestions made by David Theo Goldberg and Bernard Magubane.

I owe my greatest debt of gratitude to Patrick McCabe. Were it not for his infinite patience, culinary expertise, witty repartee, and constant interruptions, none of this would have been possible.

CHAPTER ONE

The Metaphors of Race Matter(s):
The Figurative Uses and Abuses of Blackness

"Woman," John Lennon once said, "is the nigger of the world." The Irish have been called the "blacks of Europe." Norman Mailer (1959) stirred up tremendous controversy when he penned an essay suggesting that blacks are more sensual than others and function as the "female" of the human species.

These amalgams of well-known and well-worn stereotypes demonstrate how our ideas about race, class, gender, sexuality, and nation are deeply implicated. In each case *blackness* functions metaphorically and as shorthand for social marginality. Why is this the case? What is it about *blackness* that makes it such an elastic signifier—able to signal pain as well as pleasure, disfranchisement as well as resistance? The fact that these analogies make sense even though they require us to suppress, and therefore accommodate, enormous contradiction indicates the complex and ever changing nature of our cultural and social constructions of race, gender, and class difference.

In the interest of a better understanding of these dynamics, *Bringing the Empire Home* explores how, over the course of a period roughly spanning 1800–1900, images of blackness—of black bodies, black labor, black leisure, and black suffering—became metaphorically incorporated into English discussion about everything from poverty to the extension of the franchise. I aim to demonstrate the tremendous diversity of ways in which blackness was used and became incorporated into English political and social life. The premise that guides this book is that figurative language, whatever form it takes and although it is frequently used unthinkingly and imprecisely, *matters*—particularly when we are speaking about race and blackness. Wilbur Urban (1951: 176) put it quite well when he stated that "We abuse words and concepts when we use them metaphorically—that is in other senses than they are ordained for. However, it is quite clear that if we do not use them metaphorically, we shall not use them at all." Figurative language matters precisely because of what it can tell us about the intentions of the individuals who deploy it. "Language symbolizes or represents not just the referent, or object of the word but also the intentions of the speaker" (Urban 1951: 117).

By no means am I the first person to have noticed that the language of racial difference, particularly blackness, functions in a figurative manner. Authors like Jean and John Comaroff (1992) and Anne McClintock (1995) have done interesting work on the manner in which blackness was made to serve a purely analogical function, such as when the poor were compared to African savages or English women were compared to African men. Other scholars have looked at how people have historically pointed to aspects of blackness or the black condition in order to dramatize or highlight a problem facing another, unrelated, community. David Roediger (1991) has written eloquently on how "white worker" developed as a self-conscious social category mainly through comparison with blacks, thus giving birth to and bestowing meaning on concepts such as "wage slave." Yet another interesting body of work looks at how racial difference functions as a negative pole against which to construct an identity by way of contrast. Ann Stoler (1995), for example, has done innovative work on how the construction of "bourgeois sensibilities" and the making of a European self implicitly and explicitly referenced colonialism and the colonies.

What, then, given all the important work that has already been done, could I possibly say that adds anything new or interesting? The purpose of this text is to supplement, rather than supplant, the type of work alluded to above. Indeed, many of the processes of analogical association that I reference and discuss have already been referenced or discussed by other scholars. What makes this book unique is that it brings together a discussion of the figurative uses of the language of blackness, especially in reference to black people in South Africa, with another exciting body of knowledge, produced largely by economic historians, about the historical development of the rhetoric of capitalism and the poetics of economics, and the emergence of conceptual abstractions like "the economy" that are associated therewith.

The economist Deirdre McCloskey has written a number of interesting books showing how "economics and other human sciences rely on metaphors and stories" (1990: 1). According to McCloskey, it is in the definition and study of problems that stories and figurative language have been instrumental for the construction of conceptual categories and abstractions:

> The nineteenth century invented the talk of a "social *problem*," an "economic *problem*," and the like, problems which finally the Great Geometer in London or Washington is to solve with compass and straightedge. The economic his-

torian Max Hartwell speaks often of the rhetoric of British parliamentary inquiries in the nineteenth century as defining problems where no one had seen
them before. It is not always done with mirrors, of course; this or that condition worthy of correction does exist. But in any case it is done with words.
Someone who has persuaded you to speak of inequality of income as a problem has accomplished the most difficult part of her task. (1990: 155)

Mary Poovey has argued that institutions like the Bank of England and
the stock exchange, "along with the discipline by which they were detailed
and naturalized—political economy—constituted the first of many concrete
forms in which individuals encountered and imagined the economic to exist" (1995: 6). Poovey, like McCloskey, maintains that delineating what constituted the boundaries of a particular problem was a critical component of
the process of carving out conceptual entities like "the social" or "the economic": "The emergence of the social domain involved the specification of a
set of problems that was related to but not coincident with political and economic issues" (1995: 8). Thus, "social" topics like education and crime were
separated from "economic" problems like the balance of trade and "political" topics like the franchise by fiat of a particular type and style of rhetoric.
Ellen Meiksins Wood, who is both an economic historian and a Marxist, has
done perhaps the most innovate work in this regard, analyzing the dynami-
cally interdependent histories of capitalism and economic theory. She places
the "disaggregation of domains" that Poovey discusses and the "rhetoric" of
economics that McCloskey writes about within the context of the dynamic interaction of two processes—the historical development of capitalism and the
evolution of the economic theory that supports it. In this way Wood is able
to reflect on what she terms the "rigid conceptual separation of 'the economic' and 'the political' which has served capitalist ideology so well" and
thus "understand exactly what it is in the historical nature of capitalism that
appears as a differentiation of 'spheres,' especially the 'economic' and the
'political'" (1995: 19). Douglas Dowd, another Marxist economic historian,
likewise remarks in his *Capitalism and Its Economics,* "just as economics came
into being with capitalism, so did the notion of 'an economy'" (2000: 13).

It appeared to me that these two exciting bodies of work could usefully
be brought together. Most economic historians, even extremely talented ones
like Wood and Dowd, tend to forget that "the political and institutional histories of 'the centre' and its outer circles [are] mutually constituted" (C. Hall
1996: 70). Therefore, they have not examined the role that images, stories,
and rhetoric from the colonies and about colonized people—particularly
Africans—might have played in the drawing of boundaries between differ-

ent kinds of knowledge, in the social construction of conceptual entities, and in the creation of a poetics, of economics. Likewise, although many post-colonial theorists have analyzed the process whereby certain populations, particularly the poor, were racialized, they have not specifically concerned themselves with looking at the connections between this process and the rigid separation of social life into the spheres that characterized bourgeois political economy. Thus, the aim of this text, which is located at the inter-section of these two bodies of work, is to bring these two areas together.

Outline: The Shape of Things to Come

In chapter 2 I look at how the authors of the classical texts of political econ-omy explained the transition to capitalism. I show how the ways in which women figured in these texts authorized a commonsense separation of the political and the economic. The ideological treatment of women's bodies— how they were described, analyzed, and depicted—provided a means for constructing "the economy" as something determined by disembodied nat-ural forces rather than by power relations. My argument is that the manner in which female bodies were described functioned as a rhetorical maneuver that effectively wrote the exploitation of female bodies and women's labor out of the narrative of the transition to capitalism. At the same time ex-ploitation of females was being written out of the narrative, so too was the fact that the balance of power between the individual capitalist and worker was determined not by natural economic forces but by the political con-figuration of society—that political power was an essential condition of capitalist appropriation. In this way, "economic" and "political" factors came to have the appearance of belonging to totally separate and disconnected spheres. Chapter 2 thus places women's bodies at the center of the struggle between classes, showing how control over women's bodies and women's labor was a central determinant of the political configuration of society as a whole and therefore critically affected the disposition of power that ob-tained between the individual capitalist and worker.

In chapter 3 I continue in the general vein of looking at how embodiment articulates the evolution of capitalism and colonialism. Here I focus, how-ever, on representations of colonized male bodies, examining how they provided a stock set of images and metaphors for reconstituting public knowledge about the destitute in England. Political economists used images of nomadic African bodies as a way of explaining, and thereby rationalizing, the allocation and control of labor in a capitalist society. The rhetorical uses to which the idea of nomadism was put contributed to a view of society wherein the social relations in which "the economy" was buried—in other words, the social relations that actively constituted it—came to be seen as wholly external to it. The discourses produced by political economists compared English male workers with "nomadic races" in order to conceal the fact that politically derived control over the mobility of labor was a critical tool for controlling the labor process and thus increasing surplus in production.

Although men's bodies are the focus of the chapter, it is through this discussion of men's bodies that it becomes even clearer that the power relationships between classes that conditioned the nature and extent of exploitation were significantly influenced by women's economic agency, which was an important determinant of the balance of class forces. The concerted ideological effort on the part of elites to use colonial imagery and analogies to demonize poor households for their "unnatural" gender organization is shown to be yet another means whereby the wealthy were introducing new forms of political power into the production process while, at the same time, claiming to be removing any political influence from the economy.

The chapter concludes with a discussion of how defenders of the poor and working classes sought to replace the body of the nomadic African with that of the enslaved New World African in analyses of English poverty. Black bodies became the cornerstone of English debates about the cultural status of labor as working-class radicals compared themselves to slaves in an effort to dramatize the ways in which capitalist ideology made the activity of labor and its attendant virtues the attributes of the employers of labor rather than of laborers themselves. The radicals' efforts to undermine one of the ideological cornerstones of capitalism failed, however, because white workers attempted to elevate the cultural status of labor without rehabilitating the cultural status of blackness. Thus their efforts further entrenched, rather than overturned, the reification of spheres that characterized the discourse of political economy.

In chapter 4 I turn from the discussion of individual bodies to an examination of the concept of the "social body," a conceptual abstraction that was produced alongside other conceptual abstractions like "the economy" and "the civic sphere." I document how the ability to manipulate racial discourses, and specifically the social meanings attached to different ideas of race, determined who would have the power to define what problems threatened the social body and, thus, who would be given the authority to fix them. The civic sphere was a site for conflicts both between the middle and working classes and within the middle classes as men and women competed for the right to be the exclusive caretakers of the social body. Over the course of the middle decades of the nineteenth century, middle-class women became increasingly vocal in their attempts to carve out an independent space for themselves in the public sphere. They did so not by constructing arguments around gender equality, but by formulating an alternative discourse around race and social problems to that used by male reformers. Female reformers were far more likely to promote a cultural, rather than biological, definition of race precisely because the former allowed for the formulation of social problems and their solutions in terms that put women and their particular set of problem-solving skills at an advantage. In the course of delineating these struggles, I aim to examine how the notion of an autonomous civic sphere of social action came to occupy such an important ideological place in capitalist culture and to show how the full conceptual differentiation of civil society required the simultaneous emergence of the idea of an autonomous economy.

In chapter 5 I turn from a discussion of how the racial Other abroad was put in the service of constructing the domestic Other to consider how and why images of racial Others were used by middle-class women and elite sections of the working class to articulate their own experiences of political exclusion. The chapter thus documents an important shift in how the bodies of racialized Others were incorporated into metropolitan social debates. I specifically focus on the effect the Anglo-Boer War had on images of "native" bodies and on those bodies' subsequent deployment in metropolitan discourses about citizenship. Because the Anglo-Boer War shaped public and parliamentary discussions of the extension of the franchise, the meaning of citizenship, and the limits of liberal democracy in much the same way as the 1865 Morant Bay Rebellion in Jamaica shaped public and parliamentary discussion of the 1867 Reform Act, it is an ideal location from which to trace some of the sources of the politically exclusionary impulses that got written into the universalistic theoretical framework of liberalism.

I explore how three different social groups in Britain used African bodies and the Anglo-Boer War as dual vehicles for representing their own political marginality. First, I examine the writings of trade unionists and other working-class radicals who used the African body to launch a critique of capitalist property relations and denounce the cynicism of a system wherein socioeconomic inequality and exploitation coexisted with "political" equality. While the trade unionists offered a radically new conception of democracy as encompassing the right to expand democratic control over production, they did so by deploying a discourse on African suffering that cast Jewish men and women out of the body politic. Hence, the model of democratic participation they offered, while ostensibly free of class bias, had exclusionary racial politics written into its very foundation. I next examine the writings and speeches of pro-war suffragists. These women used the Anglo-Boer War and the suffering of Africans as a vehicle for proposing a model of citizenship that, while more gender inclusive, was also more restrictive, in that the balance of class power was purposefully excluded from being a criterion of democracy. Here we get some insight into the ways in which the conceptual framework of liberal democracy can, while expanding its parameters of inclusion, nevertheless maintain the invulnerability of the economic sphere to democratic power, thus making the separation of the economic and political spheres not only a conceptual abstraction, but a real fact of life.

In the final section I look at the actions of the pro-Boer suffragists, who used the war as the pretext for promulgating a model of citizenship that stressed the consent of the governed as the main criterion for defining democratic citizenship. The way in which they imagined the ideal consent-granting subject effectively erased the concerns and claims of African people while whitening the Boers. This analysis of the ways in which the suffragists used the Anglo-Boer War as a signal moment for concretizing the ideal of consent enables us to see how it was that a liberal democracy could become more gender inclusive even as it was becoming more racially exclusive, as well as how the political exclusion of certain groups got written into ostensibly inclusive and universal political principles.

In the next two chapters I turn my attention from the enunciations and actions of the dominators to those of the dominated. In this way I hope to avoid the error of other postcolonial studies that, in the words of Ruth Frankenberg and Lata Mani, simply take a detour through "the Other" in the interest of, once again, recentering the Western Self. "Only this time, it is not the Other as 'ourselves undressed' so much as 'ourselves disassembled'" (1996: 355). Laura Brown observes that "productive and important as it has been for critics of colonialism, the category of the 'other' . . . sometimes precludes finding a place for the voice and struggles of the native in the massive and complex edifices of power that seem to surround and contain all resistance" (1993: 32). In the final two chapters I therefore seek to provide a place for hearing the voices of the Others and seeing how they struggled against the powers that sought to contain them while, hopefully, avoiding the pitfall of simply "endowing the enslaved with agency as some sort of gift dispensed by historians and critics to the dispossessed" (Hartman 1997: 54). I have tried to read between the lines of missionary accounts, newspaper articles, and travel writing in order to get some idea of what concepts like whiteness and blackness meant to colonized Africans. Clearly, as I read against the grain I cannot in any way hope to fully recover the experience of the dispossessed, and I might inadvertently reconfirm the authority and hegemony of the very documents I am trying to deconstruct. Nevertheless, it is worthwhile to try to piece together some notion of how the dominated experienced and resisted domination, while recognizing that the accounts one relates are still very deeply implicated in the politics and processes of domination. In other words, "the effort to reconstruct the history of the dominated is not discontinuous with dominant accounts or official history but, rather, is a struggle within and against the constraints and silences imposed by the nature of the archive" (Hartman 1997: 11).

In chapter 6 I thus attempt to reconstruct what the white image might have represented in the minds of Africans. I argue that Africans always maintained a highly critical stance on whiteness, and I identify three mechanisms through which Africans unmasked and unveiled the power of the English: the politics of refusal, whereby Africans simply refused to accept the renderings of the world and their place in it offered by the English; the politics of bearing witness, whereby African people used the renarrating of history as a way of decentering whiteness and critiquing white supremacy; and the demythologizing and desacralizing of whiteness, whereby Africans exposed and rejected English claims to superhuman status.

In chapter 7 I consider what blackness might have represented in the African imagination. I focus on the diamond mines of Kimberley, South Africa, where images of African Americans, gleaned partially from the minstrel stage and partially from visiting gospel troupes, provided African people with a means for thinking about and thinking through the diverse meanings of blackness. The chapter traces how images of African Americans became deeply intertwined with images of leisure, public visibility, personal adornment, and consumption, examining the connections between citizenship, consumption, and social power. The chapter concludes with a discussion of how middle-class African men used images of African Americans and ideologies taken from African American activists to simultaneously resolve the dilemmas of citizenship and of manhood. Because cultural and political reclamation became so deeply implicated with the recuperation of black manhood, many of masculinity's most problematic features were unthinkingly adopted and encouraged in the name of racial progress. I conclude the chapter by exploring a curious paradox that lay at the heart of black political culture. Femininity provided both the pole against which men defined and asserted themselves and an ideal set of behavioral parameters to guide the conduct of a properly cultivated man. Thus, the definition of a true race man devolved, in part, from the expropriation for black manhood of some of the virtues traditionally associated with white upper-class femininity.

Postmodernism, Postcolonialism, and the Critique of Ideology

A recent trend in scholarship, postcolonialism or colonial discourse theory, has attempted to challenge the theoretical assumptions that have traditionally underwritten studies of race and colonialism (Comaroff and Comaroff 1992; Gilman 1985; C. Hall 1996; McClintock 1995; Pieterse 1992). Taking their inspiration from Edward Said, postcolonialists seek to bring metropole and colony into a single analytic field. They abjure the idea that the *post* in *postcolonial* in any way means "past"; their aim is to unsettle the idea of an impermeable boundary between the metropole and the colony. As Stuart Hall explains in his essay "When Was the Postcolonial? Thinking at the Limit," "What 'post-colonial' certainly is *not* is one of those periodisations based on epochal 'stages,' when everything is reversed at the same moment, all the old relations disappear for ever and entirely new ones come to replace them." Rather, Hall argues, postcolonialism is a method of analysis that "obliges us to re-read the very binary form in which the colonial encounter has for so long itself been represented. It obliges us to re-read the binaries as forms of transculturation, of cultural translation, destined to trouble the here/there cultural boundaries forever" (1996: 247). Arguing in a similar vein, Anne McClintock maintains that "imperialism is not something that happened elsewhere—a disagreeable fact of history external to Western identity. Rather, imperialism and the invention of race were fundamental aspects of Western, industrial modernity" (1995: 5).

Postcolonial theory, particularly that which deals with colonial discourse analysis, owes a strong intellectual debt to postmodernism, poststructuralism, and cultural studies. Deepika Bahri explains that "one of the most significant reasons for the exponential expansion in postcolonial discourse is the host climate generated by the development of postmodern theory. . . . Postcolonialism's truck with postmodernism demonstrates a strategic mobilization of some of its principles and conscious abjuration of others" (1996: 151). Thus, postcolonial theory has come in for many of the same critiques as postmodernism and cultural studies. Bryan Palmer captures the essence of these critiques with his complaint that: "An ironic consequence of postcolonial deconstructive writing, with its understandable refusal of the Orientalist metanarrative, and its unfortunate textualization of imperialist plunder and indigenous resistance, is the further silencing of those marginalized 'others,' whose differences are celebrated, but whose umbilical link to *class* formation on a global scale is twisted in the obscured isolations of cultures and countries" (1997: 69, emphasis in original).

Reading the critiques that Marxist scholars make of the work of post-modernists and postcolonialists—and vice versa—one is tempted to dismiss out of hand the possibility that the two theoretical positions could ever be reconciled. The critiques coming from both sides seem to rule out the possibility that we could fashion a theory that makes productive use of insights from both. However, as with most battles between opposing theoretical viewpoints, the tendency of pundits on both sides of the divide has been to caricature the arguments of their opponents. Thus, scholars from the various "post" schools represent Marxists as being not only mesmerized by the "base-superstructure" model, but also so hopelessly reductionist as to have no appreciation whatsoever of the power of language, culture, and ideology. Likewise, reading some critics of postmodernism and postcolonialism, one might believe that all adherents of those schools are so hopelessly enamored of Derrida that structure, politics, and oppression are nothing more than discursive constructions. However, as Ania Loomba reminds us, while "minority intellectuals and feminists have felt affinities with post-structuralists, there have also been sharp debates *between* them. . . . For feminists, but also for others, the sweeping divide between a 'Third World Marxism' and a 'First World' postmodernism is extremely problematic" (1998: 252). But even if we acknowledge the sometimes overblown nature of their attacks on each other, the question still remains as to whether it is possible to combine Marxist and postmodernist approaches. Are they philosophically incompatible? Can an analysis that purports to take the modalities of consciousness seriously still truck and barter with materialist analyses of ideology?

It is helpful to start with the points of commonality between the two approaches. First, both see knowledge and consciousness as historically conditioned. Steven Best and Douglas Kellner explain that "post-structuralists criticize the claims of structuralists that the mind had an innate, universal structure. . . . They favor instead a thoroughly historical view which sees different forms of consciousness, identities, signification, and so on as historically produced and therefore varying in different historical periods" (1991: 20). This idea is not so far from what Marx expressed in *The German Ideology* when he wrote, "each new class which puts itself in the place of one ruling before it, is compelled, merely in order to carry through its aim, to represent its interest as the common interest of all the members of society, that is, expressed in ideal form: it has to give its ideas the form of universality, and represent them as the only rational, universally valid ones" ([1846] 1970: 66).

Second, both Marxists and postmodernists see language as a terrain of power and domination. "One of the main features of imperial oppression is control over language," the authors of *The Empire Writes Back* tell us (Ashcroft,

Griffiths, and Tiffin 1989: 7). Marx likewise asserted that, "the individuals composing the ruling class possess among other things consciousness, and therefore think. Insofar, therefore, as they rule as a class and determine the extent and compass of an epoch, it is self-evident that they do this in its whole range, hence among other things rule also as thinkers, as producers of ideas, and regulate the production and distribution of the ideas of their age" ([1846] 1970: 64).

Finally, Marxists and postmodernists agree that processes of signification and material production are deeply implicated. Marx argued that "German philosophy is a consequence of German petty-bourgeois conditions. . . . Neither thoughts nor language in themselves form a realm of their own, they are only *manifestations* of actual life" ([1846] 1970: 118, emphasis in original). Likewise, the editors of *The Postcolonial Studies Reader* tell us that "material conditions and the relationship to questions of ideology and representation are at the heart of the most vigorous debates in recent post-colonial theory" (Ashcroft, Griffiths, and Tiffin 1995: 7).

Thus, the schools are in agreement about the important role of consciousness in human life, the socially mediated character of knowledge, and the role knowledge plays in the exercise of social power. Major differences exist, however, in their conceptualizations of power, the relative weight they give to property relations as compared to discursive structures, and their understanding of causality as it relates to the relationship between social structures and consciousness.

For Marxists, power ultimately derives from the degree of control social actors exercise over productive property: the social power of the bourgeoisie, Marx wrote, "derives from its property" ([1846] 1970: 94). Much postmodern theory conceives of power in a more Foucauldian sense: power, Foucault argued, "is never localized here or there, never in anybody's hands, never appropriated as a commodity or a piece of wealth" (1980: 72).

Further, although a basic agreement exists on the fact that language is a terrain of power, postmodernists tend toward the position that power relations are constructed in and through the practices of knowing humans, who classify, measure, discipline, and categorize them. Foucault argued:

> To analyze the political investment of the body and the microphysics of power presupposes, therefore, that one abandons—where power is concerned—the violence-ideology opposition, the metaphor of property, the model of contract or of conquest; that where knowledge is concerned—one abandons the opposition between what is 'interested' and what is 'disinterested.' . . . One would be concerned with the 'body politic' as a set of material elements and

techniques that serve as weapons, relays, communication routes and supports for the power and knowledge relations that invest human bodies and subjugate them by turning them into objects of knowledge. (1979: 28)

Marxists, on the other hand, see power both as an expression of class interests and as something that emanates from control over private property. Thus, it is not through processes of classifying or knowing humans, but through the exploitation of their labor-power—the transformation of humans into so many sellable units of time—that people are rendered powerless and subject to control. Marx argued that "Capital cares nothing for the length of life of labour-power. All that concerns it is simply and solely the maximum of labour-power, that can be rendered fluent in a working day. It attains this end by shortening the extent of the labourer's life as a greedy farmer snatches increased produce from the soil by robbing it of its fertility" ([1867] 1967: 264).

Finally, a major split occurs between the two schools over the hierarchy of causes to which historical events can be attributed. For Marxists, class struggle and the organization of productive relations play a central role in the movement and determination of history. History, Marx wrote, "is nothing both the succession of the separate generations, each of which exploits the materials, the capital funds, the productive forces handed down to it by all preceding generations, and thus, on the one hand, continues the traditional activity in completely changed circumstances and, on the other, modifies the old circumstances with a completely changed activity" ([1846] 1970: 57). Postmodernists, on the other hand, analyze history as a series of discursive differences and tend to avoid the issue of causality. As Best and Kellner explain, the archaeological approach pioneered by Foucault differs from a hermeneutical approach because "the surface-depth and causal models utilized by modern theory are overturned in favour of a postmodern description of discontinuous surfaces of discourse unconnected by causal linkages" (1991: 40).

These differences are not insignificant. Nor, however, are they insurmountable. I maintain that taking signification, language, images, and representations as serious objects of study and analysis does not mean that we must accept the assumption that social interaction is only or even primarily discursively constituted. Cornel West has argued that racism must be understood as both a structural system of economic dispossession and a cultural system that inflicts "ontological wounds" by means of beliefs and images that "attack black intelligence, black ability, black beauty, and black character in subtle and not-so-subtle ways" (1993b: 18). In order to analyze these processes, which demand a theory as complex and agile as the historical developments they are called upon to explain, West adopts what he calls a "genealogical materialist" approach. While rejecting Foucault's evasion of the role of ideology in the practice of domination, West retains the idea of a genealogical approach that examines "the discursive and extra-discursive conditions for the possibility of racist practices" (1993a: 268). He reminds us that we must resist the methodological inclination to explain all social phenomena as the product of a single factor. Thus, he explains, "decisive material modes of production at a given moment may be located in the cultural, political, or even psychic spheres" (1993b: 266).

Three key premises guiding this book, then, are that language is a terrain of power and domination; that hierarchical relations have a tremendous influence on language and speech; and that all relations, including economic relations, are expressed or have to be expressed in thought. Therefore, all economic relations have an ideological dimension, and issues of language and meaning are not simply ephemeral or secondary. As V. N. Volosinov argues in *Marxism and the Philosophy of Language*, "the sign is an arena of the class struggle" (1986: 23). Thus, language is one aspect of a multifaceted nexus of social relations, and human beings struggle over language and signs as part of their efforts to secure their conditions of existence.

CHAPTER TWO

Capitalism, Female Embodiment, and the Transformation of Commodification into Sexuality

In this chapter I examine the economic relations that serve as a backdrop and context to the trope of female beauty. Specifically, I focus on how and why the body of the "native" or colonized female body became a locus for the intersection of capitalism and aesthetics. My specific concern is with how aesthetic representations of the female body, and related gendered propositions about "human nature," became a way of articulating private propositions about sexuality to the global historical politicoeconomic enterprise of colonialism. This is an ideological process I have chosen to term the "transformation of commodification into sexuality."

In demonstrating that the makers of capitalist ideology always deploy specific notions of embodiment, which, in turn, contain within them specific codes for how these bodies are racially and sexually identified, I also wish to highlight the connection between the aforementioned process and the ways in which the economic and the political come to be conceptualized as separate entities in capitalist ideology. My argument is that the rhetorical and ideological maneuvers that wrote the exploitation of female bodies and women's labor out of the narrative of the transition to capitalism simultaneously made invisible the fact that the political configuration of society as a whole determined the disposition of power between the individual capitalist and worker. Indeed, the former is the ideological precondition of the latter. Thus, the ideological treatment of women's bodies in these texts is strongly connected to a particular way of viewing "the economic" in capitalism as the product of disembodied forces, rather than as a set of social relations.

Concepts of gender always have to be reconciled with some notion of embodiment. A similar claim might be made for understanding racial and class imagery as well. Thus, in this chapter I take a close look at how the bodies of racial "Others" are described in colonial texts, especially those produced by travel writers and missionaries. My primary concern is to look at the ways in which these texts explain how precapitalist societies make the transition to capitalism. My argument is that the position assigned to women in these accounts is strongly connected to mechanisms by which the coercive impulses of capitalism were rationalized. The bodies of "native" women are a figure of profound significance in these texts, and it is in discussions of these bodies that the inconsistent and contradictory assumptions about the relative balance between freedom and coercion in capitalist society come most strikingly to the fore.

Many of the texts I reference in this chapter were produced by evangelicals, who played a key role in popularizing theories first developed by political economists. It has become fashionable to dismiss any text that suggests that the missionaries played a significant role in facilitating colonial conquest as "reductionist" (see Bank 1995; Bredekamp and Ross 1995; Elbourne 1991; Ross 1986). Elizabeth Elbourne, for example, argues that the "undue stress on the missionaries as 'really' the agents of capitalism . . . makes converts appear like the duped and agentless victims of processes beyond their control" (1995: 65). I disagree. One can acknowledge the creative uses that indigenous communities made of Christianity without losing sight of the structures that the missionaries were part of and that they helped to create. James Cochrane provides, I believe, a more compelling analysis in *Servants of Power*, wherein he argues:

> What requires elucidation is why missionaries (and the Church) did their best to inculcate a way of life which bears no necessary relationship to biblical Christianity, and what this had to do with three important principles advocated by most missionaries: the "dignity of labour" as an end in itself; the importance of obedience to constituted authority (meaning British and not the African authority); and, economic individuation. . . . Notwithstanding any legitimate evidence of humanitarian behaviour or racial tolerance in missionary relations to the indigenous peoples, or their positive contributions . . . [we cannot] refrain from judging the contrary evidence in the disastrous impact upon the indigenous peoples of a systematically applied racial (colonial) capitalism from which the missions cannot be abstracted. (1987: 38)

In the texts of classical political economy, the transition to capitalist social relations is always depicted in terms of freedom and choice. The ideology of the invisible hand, for example, obscures the fact that coercion might be integral to the workings of capitalism. The bodies of "natives," especially if they are female, however, have the potential to expose the centrality of force to the workings of capitalism. The ways in which the authors of these texts dealt with issues of embodiment and the body, especially when discussing female bodies, reflects how these contradictions were culturally managed. It is precisely because these bodies were sites of ideological crises that through descriptions of them the authors of these texts, and by implication their readership and thus society at large, were able to ideologically displace the contradictions of "free market" capitalism. Aestheticized representations of the female body thus enable the interaction of seemingly incompatible discourses.

Scotland and the Cape Colony: The Ideological Connection

This chapter focuses on the transformation of commodification into sexuality in two colonial contexts—Scotland and the Cape Colony. I have chosen these two locations for several reasons. First, the people of Scotland were among the first victims of the expansionist impulse of the English, who sought not only to bring under their sway all territories not already theirs, but also to make the indigenous populations of these territories into cultural and racial Others. As Michael Hechter explains in *Internal Colonialism: The Celtic Fringe in British National Development*, "It must not, however, be assumed that colonial development is to be found only in those areas subjected to nineteenth-century overseas imperialism. Simultaneous to the overseas expansion of Western European states in the fifteenth and sixteenth centuries were similar thrusts into peripheral hinterlands," like Ireland and Scotland (1975: 31). Indeed, it was in the context of the expansion into Scotland that many of the practical models and ideological strategies we associate with overseas expansion were developed and refined—including but not limited to monopolization of commerce and trade, creation of economic dependence and underdevelopment, and eventual cultural and social marginalization of colonized populations, usually expressed in racial terms.

There are a number of marked similarities between representations of the Scottish Highlanders and representations of the indigenous people of the Cape Colony. Occasionally the two groups were directly compared with one another, as when Samuel Johnson decried the habitations of the Highlanders for being "as filthy as the cottages of Hottentots" (1775: 41) and John Barrow declared that the social organization of the Xhosa resembled, in its fundamentals, that of the clans of the Scottish Highlands ([1801] 1968: 202). This is significant because, as Mary Louise Pratt (1992) has pointed out, when we can identify similarities in the conventions and writing strategies associated with colonial expansion, similar dynamics of power and appropriation might well be at work. Indeed, important parallels can be drawn between the experiences of the indigenous people of the Cape Colony and those of the Scottish Highlanders.

Second, when considering the deployment of colonial imagery in Scotland and South Africa, the strength of this connection between the practical and rhetorical effects of internal expansion on overseas expansion is made even stronger by the fact that the vast majority of missionaries and travelers to the Cape Colony were originally from Scotland. "The new British empire of direct rule over alien peoples was forged in large part by Scottish administrators, soldiers, merchants, and missionaries" (Keegan 1996: 90), and the Scottish missionaries and travelers who came to the Cape Colony were personally influenced by the experience of witnessing Scotland's transition from feudal to capitalist social relations (Comaroff and Comaroff 1992; Crais 1992; Ross 1986). According to Jean and John Comaroff, their experiences in Scotland shaped the "moral terms in which they were to deal with other Europeans and with the 'savage' on the frontiers of empire" (1992: 187). Scottish political economists, such as Adam Smith, Sir James Steuart, Adam Ferguson, and Francis Hutcheson, had a tremendous intellectual influence on evangelicals, and concepts derived from these writers were the source of many evangelical pronouncements. John Philip, a middle-class Scotsman and chief official of the London Missionary Society at the Cape, explicitly acknowledged the influence of the Scottish humanists when he pledged to avoid the mistake of formulating policies as if "Adam Smith, Ferguson, Malthus, Ricardo, etc., had never blotted paper" ([1828] 1969: 378). Thus, if Barbara Fields is correct, that when it comes to observations about human bodies our ideological context, rather than our sense perceptions, guide us as to "which details to notice, which to ignore, and which to take for granted" (1982: 146), the importance of looking at Cape colonial images in tandem with Scottish images becomes even more apparent.

Women as the Embodiment of Productive Relations: The Meanings behind the Trope of Female Beauty

When we look at representations of what, at the time, were considered native female bodies, it quickly becomes apparent that both males and females are embodied, but the female body undergoes a negative metamorphosis over time, from a state of beauty to one of visual offensiveness. Furthermore, in these narratives the ability to perceive beauty is completely dependent upon one's visual sense. Beauty is vested in the corporeal and can be read off the surface of the body; it is a function of the symmetry of features and forms. Thus, what strikes us first in these narratives is the complete repudiation of the Platonic ideal of beauty on two counts. First, according to the Platonic ideal, beauty does not "take the form of a face, or of hands, or of anything that is of the flesh." Second, beauty is not subject to temporal change. Plato held that real beauty is "an everlasting loveliness which neither comes nor goes, which neither flowers nor fades" (Plato 1950: 221a). The writings of Edward Topham, who traveled through the Highlands in 1776, are a striking example of this repudiation of the Platonic idea of beauty. Topham described the women of the Highlands in terms that strongly emphasized both embodiment and temporality. "The bloom of young desire lasts but for a day; the flower is no sooner expanded, than it begins to wither, and often dies long before its season of coming to maturity. You rarely find a woman above twenty tolerably inviting" (1776: 83). His fellow traveler Thomas Pennant also found the "common women" of the Highlands "in general most remarkably plain," with a "natural hardness of features" that soon "acquired an old look" (1776: 131).

John Barrow echoed the sentiments of Topham and Pennant about the fleeting character of Scottish female beauty when he described Khoikhoi women, the indigenous women of the Cape, as being beautiful for only a very short time: "Their charms, however, are very fleeting. At an early period of life or immediately after the first child, their breasts begin to grow loose and flaccid and as old age approaches become distended to an enormous size. The belly protrudes and the posteriors swell out to incredible dimensions" ([1801] 1968: 157). Khoikhoi men, in contrast, were described as "small," "delicate," "graceful," "neat," and "by no means void of symmetry," and their bodies were not viewed as subject to temporal changes. William Burchell, a naturalist and Barrow's fellow traveler, also described San men as "well proportioned," "symmetrical," and "firm" without reference to change over time. When it came to the subject of women, however, he lamented that "If the women of most nations find the season of beauty short-lived, it may among Bushwomen, with more than equal justice, be termed momentary" ([1822] 1953: 415).

In these narratives, to be an embodied female is not simply to be helpless in the face of the ravages of time and parturition, however. To be an embodied female is to be, literally and figuratively, a physical extension and manifestation of the system of productive relations. In these narratives, social relations of production became related to embodiment—a way of thinking that can be traced back to the writings of Adam Smith, who "believed that unproductive workers had personal characteristics of which he disapproved" (Perelman 2000: 185). *Productivity* in these narratives is a highly loaded ideological term masquerading as a neutral social scientific concept. To be productive was not simply to produce things of value or to live in relative comfort. Rather, it was to depend on the market to gain access to the means of life and to specialize in the production of commodities for the market.

Being productive also meant manipulating the organization and instruments of work, particularly human capital, in order to enhance the productivity of labor. Hence, Mary-Anne Hanaway maintained that "the Scotch are insensible of what degree of improvement their country is capable." To this she attributed the fact that she had "seldom seen a pretty girl among the lower class which is so frequent in England" (1776: 162). Likewise, the corpulence of the Dutch frontier women, Boers as they were called, was also blamed on the fact that they were content to live without improving the productivity of either the land or the servants they employed. John Campbell, for example, claimed that "a great majority of the white inhabitants are corpulent, especially the females" ([1815] 1974: 347). "If a Hottentot is brought up in the service of a Boer," he explained, "he has so many fellow servants and the Boer so little work to perform that very little labour falls to the lot of an individual. A farmer's servant in England has more actual labour to accomplish than is assigned to six servants of an African Boer" ([1815] 1974: 92). These sentiments were echoed by a number of other travelers (see Latrobe [1818] 1969; Robertson 1819; Stravorinus 1798).

The ways in which dependency was defined were strongly conditioned by prevailing notions of what constituted productive and unproductive labor. Adam Smith defined laborers as unproductive if they were dependent on the aristocracy, a slave master, or a feudal lord because this type of labor was, for the most part, not embedded in market relations. The same charge was leveled at these laborers' employers or masters. Smith's ideas strongly conditioned how the Dutch women at the Cape were viewed. At first glance, it might appear that the Dutch frontier women were despised simply for being slave masters. However, on closer examination it is clear that their corporeal excess was not solely attributed to the fact that they had a multitude of black and brown bodies to serve them, but rather, to the fact that these servile black and brown bodies did not engage in market-oriented production. Whereas the Dutch frontier women were uniformly described as corpulent, the wives and daughters of the Dutch bourgeoisie, whose families were equally dependent upon slave labor to produce wheat and wine for the export trade, were described as having "small and delicate forms." Far from being condemned as slaveholders, the men of this class were praised not only because they spent the vast portion of their days "employed in the concerns of trade" but also because they made "money matters and merchandise engross their whole conversation" (Barrow [1801] 1968: 49–50). Even the condition of the servile black and brown bodies, particularly if they were female, was a function of the social relations of production. According to John Philip, because their Dutch masters did not "feel the interest in them which they do in a marketable property," young Khoikhoi girls "exhibit much stronger marks of degradation and wretchedness than the young slaves of their own age" ([1828] 1969: 183). Thus, the social relations of production determined whether even the most servile and exploitative of relationships was to be positively or negatively evaluated.

Self-Provisioning and the Gendered Division of Labor

What united Scottish peasants, Boer frontiersmen, and African people was the fact that, even subsequent to conquest, they were able to gain access to the means of life and reproduce themselves without engaging in wage labor or becoming dependent on the market. In other words, these societies were marked by a high degree of what Michael Perelman (2000) calls "self-provisioning." Dr. Samuel Johnson observed that in the Highlands "the produce of the land is not conveyed through the labyrinths of traffik, but passes directly from the hand that gathers it to the mouth that eats it" (1775: 135). John Barrow explained that the Dutch frontier farmers had no use for money because they were content to "exchange with others their cattle for as much as may be necessary for the family consumption" ([1801] 1968: 84). The Reverend John Campbell described Khoikhoi society in similar terms: "If a Hottentot obtains barely enough to support nature he is satisfied and can sleep contented in his sheep skin, under any bush" ([1815] 1974: 92).

Women's labor in the subsistence economy was instrumental in determining whether men engaged in wage labor. Hence, most aesthetic evaluations of women made some reference to the gendered division of labor within the household. Edward Topham, who, as we saw above, described Scottish women as both "large and lusty" and "coarse and masculine," attributed their deplorable appearance to the fact that women's economic participation allowed the Highland farmers to indulge their "general contempt for labour" (1776: 43). Mary-Anne Hanaway agreed that "female beauty depends much on delicacy and the hard and laborious part which the women take in this country when young accounts for their being coarse and dis-agreeable" (1776: 135). Joseph Mawman, who chided the women of the Scottish Highlands for their "short and brawny" physiques and "tarnished complexions," attributed their unprepossessing features to the fact that "the management of the land and cattle were delegated to women," which obvi-ated the need for male wage labor (1805). "Here that ascendancy, which amongst refined nations the delicacy of the sex generally acquires from the gallantry of civilization, is totally disregarded. . . . The men seem fully to ex-ercise that authority, which their superior strength bestows. The females we saw constantly bustling about their habitations, or carrying immense loads of fish; their lords often sauntering about, never without shoes or stockings" (1805: 94). Stephen Kay, a Scottish missionary at the Cape, was clearly draw-ing on this intellectual tradition when he maintained that "as in most barbarous nations, the lot of the *abafazi* (women) is hard indeed. . . . When young, they are in many instances beautiful (laying aside the prejudice of color) but the hard labour which they commence as soon as they enter the married state, and which may be regarded as a kind of bondage, soon destroys the charms which nature may have gifted them, and they become, at an early age, even disgustingly ugly" (1833: 141). Robert Moffat, another well-known Scottish itinerant at the Cape, also maintained that the "unpre-possessing appearance" of African women was due to the fact that they were "the drudges of a haughty husband who spent the greater part of his life lounging in the shade, while she was compelled, for his comfort as well as her own to labour" (1844: 251).

The trope of female beauty thus came to have meaning within a very spe-cific economic context. There was a strong connection between the creation of a widespread wage-labor relationship and the gendered division of labor within the household. Women's labor was the crucial deciding factor in the process whereby independent workplaces were joined together into an ever-expanding set of market relationships and the workplace was separated from the household—in other words, the social division of labor was created. It was at the junction between female industriousness and the social division of labor that the narrative conjoining of female embodiment and economic reproduction took place. Under the conditions described above, men and women alike engaged in wage labor only sporadically—a state of affairs that was not at all conducive to capital accumulation in England. Thus, in order to understand the social conditions that precipitated this particular constel-lation of ideas relating to female embodiment, it is necessary to undertake a brief analysis of economic relations in Scotland and the Cape Colony and their relation to capitalist accumulation in England.

The Economic Context of the Trope of Female Beauty: Labor and Capital Accumulation in Scotland and at the Cape

Capital accumulation in the English textile industries, as well as by those bankers and financiers who invested in textile production and agents and dealers acting on behalf of commercial institutions like the British Linen Bank, were critically dependent upon the transformation of the Scottish peasantry into a pliable and pliant reserve army of labor. As the economic historian Robert A. Dodgshon explains:

> From the agent or manufacturer's point of view, the Highlands were an abundant source of cheap labour. This fact was often proclaimed in support of their claim for grants and loans from agencies like the Board of Trustees for Manufacturers and the British Linen Bank. The former started its operations in 1727 and the latter in 1746. Both were extremely active in the Highlands, providing forward loans for dealers and investing directly in heckling stations, spinning schools, and equipment like spinning wheels. . . . Such investment was concentrated in areas where labour was plentiful but cheap. (1981: 313)

Capital accumulation in the textile industry was also dependent upon an adequate supply of kelp, which provided the alkali needed for the rapidly growing textile industry. "Without kelp, scarce timber would have been burned for potash" (Perelman 2000: 143). Kelp gathering was an extremely labor intensive activity, and from the 1730s onward, English industrialists looked to Scottish peasants to provide the fifty thousand units of man power the industry annually demanded.

Thus, a national division of labor developed between England and the Celtic regions, whereby the majority of manufacturing, processing, and distributing functions were performed in the metropolis, while the hinterland was in the subordinate position of supplying materials and cheap labor. Scotland was a dependent supplier of raw materials for British industry. This state of affairs, which required that Scotland's peasantry be put to productive toil, could not come about as long as Scottish peasants were able to support themselves through extramarket activity.

Conditions were not very different in the Cape Colony. Under British rule, the Cape's international trade was decisively reoriented toward Britain and its empire. According to economic historian Susan Newton-King (1980: 172): "The prosperity of the colonial economy was of great importance to the metropolitan government because of its contribution towards the colonial budget. . . . Indeed, the Cape's commercial value was not negligible; by 1820 its total exports had reached a value of nearly £195,000 while its imports, including imports of capital, were worth approximately £367,000" (1980: 172). British merchants at the Cape had substantial commercial and financial connections in England; indeed, many of them were agents for English firms. Financiers based in London were critical to the development of Cape commerce, as they provided credit, financial services, and manufactures for trade. By 1830 over fifty London mercantile houses had interests in the Cape trade. In addition, "the London merchant community, together with the banking, insurance, and shipping interests of the City at their back, had considerable influence with officials of the Colonial Office and maintained allies in parliament" (Keegan 1996: 50).

If the local mercantile elite and their English counterparts were to accumulate capital and prosper, the colonial economy had to be developed in such a way as to improve its productive and revenue-generating capacities. Profitable enterprise required that labor relations be restructured and that indigenous people be integrated into the larger colonial economy. In particular it meant dealing with the labor shortage that prevailed in the colony for the first three decades of the nineteenth century. As Newton-King explains: "There is considerable evidence in contemporary documents to show that, at least by the end of the second decade of the nineteenth century, the colony was facing a generalised labour shortage, which was more serious in Cape Town and the western districts than elsewhere" (1980: 171).

On the one hand, the transformation of the prevailing social relations of production required that a very specific set of actions be undertaken by both the state and the accumulating classes with a vested interest in social change. On the other hand, the producers of political economy in its various guises, including authors of evangelical tracts and travel writings that dealt substantively with matters of economy and society, were operating under a very strict set of rules as to how these social transformations should be narrated and represented. The prevailing fashion in political economy was to deny any role to government in stimulating economic development, to see economic progress as a neutral affair guided by market forces, and to deny the existence of class conflict and exploitation. Political economy sought to detach theory from any real consideration of the human beings whose labor was expected to create the wealth of the nation. However, "at every turn their lives obtruded themselves, insisting on inserting question marks at the end of [their] confident expositions" (Thirsk 1978: 152). It is at this juncture between the personal lives led by individuals and the demand to produce economic theory that private propositions about female beauty and sexuality were articulated to the world-historical enterprise of colonialism. This is the process I term the transformation of commodification into sexuality.

The Transformation of Commodification into Sexuality

Economic historian Mary Poovey has argued that the conceptual entity or domain of knowledge we refer to as "economics" or "the economic" is "an imaginary entity governed by a specific rationality—in this case, the logic and procedures by which productivity and financial security are thought to be ensured" (1995: 6). She further explains that over the course of the eighteenth and nineteenth centuries the economic domain was gradually specified as separate from the political, theological, social, and ethical domains. This was a process that "entailed the negotiation and eventual redrawing of the boundaries between kinds of knowledge, kinds of practice, and kinds of institutions" (1995: 7). Those things that fell under the domain of the economic were those left to the operations of a free market, within which individuals appeared as independent and self-regulating agents. Those things that fell under the domain of the social, however, "could be subjected to government oversight" (1995: 11).

In theoretical expositions of political economy, the transition to capitalism is represented as falling completely under the domain of the economic, and nonmarket forces are not acknowledged as necessary for hastening the process of capitalist accumulation in the countryside. These texts contain nary a mention of Game Laws or Vagrancy Laws, which criminalized hunting and unemployment, respectively. Nor is there any mention of the myriad of other state-sponsored initiatives that were used to separate rural people from their main sources of sustenance, adding considerable force to the pressure to submit to wage labor. Rather, reformers continually pointed to the "natural" desire of human beings to truck, barter, and exchange as well as the "natural" longing in every human being to have money and to purchase commodities.

The concept of "human nature" also informed—and continues to inform—economic theory. According to economic historian Douglas Dowd (2000), all economic arguments are ultimately supported by some theory of human nature. Ironically, the eighteenth century writings of the Scottish humanists, which had such a profound influence on the Cape itinerants, were themselves critically informed by a previous generation of travelers and naturalists who had produced narratives about the indigenous people of the Cape. Naturalists like Francois Le Vaillant, Peter Kolbe, and Anders Sparrman produced well-read narratives about the indigenous people of the Cape, especially the Khoikhoi and the San. These narratives, especially Peter Kolbe's *The Present State of the Cape of Good Hope,* published in 1719 and translated into English in 1731, were frequently cited by Scottish humanists. Kolbe's text was particularly useful because of his "insistence on the commensurability of Khoikhoi and European societies" (Pratt 1992: 44). Adam Smith frequently cited Kolbe's text. In both *The Wealth of Nations* and *Lectures on Jurisprudence,* he cited it as a basis for his assertion that the social division of labor should be understood exclusively in terms of the anthropological principle of the natural disposition of human beings. According to one economic historian, "Smith attempted to use the experience of the New World as an object lesson in the virtues of laissez-faire" (Perelman 2000: 277).

Thus, the very theories that were employed in the analysis of African societies were based on previous travelers' evaluations of those societies. Paradoxically, indigenous people were often accused of failing to measure up to the standards of "human nature" that were developed from observations about their own societies! For example, John Philip, a Scottish missionary at the Cape, used Adam Smith's writings and conjectures on human nature to support his contention that the mere "sight of a shop" at a mission institution operated as a "most effective stimulus to industry" ([1828] 1969: 365). A few decades earlier, Samuel Johnson had argued that once the Scottish Highlanders became "acquainted with money and the possibility of gain" they would voluntarily submit to wage labor. "A shop turns the balance between good and evil," he opined (1775: 211). Similar views were echoed by countless other missionaries and travelers to the Cape and the Highlands (see Barrow [1801] 1968; Hanaway 1776; Latrobe [1818] 1969; Newte 1791; Percival 1804).

Yet, the social practices of indigenous people continually demonstrated the incoherence and instability of this idea. These narratives are shot through with images of male bodes that refused to voluntarily submit to the demands of wage labor, no matter what the inducement. Edward Topham remarked that the men of the Highlands were "very idle." He complained that the average Highland farmer was "content to wrap himself up in his plaid, throw himself at his length on the ground and lie there totally unconcerned while his wife and children are busily employed in getting the scanty harvest which the barren nature of his land allows him" (1776: 43). The Reverend Robert Moffat also lamented the fact that the African man was content to "spend the greater part of his life lounging in the shade" (1844: 251). The pages of these accounts are likewise brimming with images of men oblivious to the temptations of money. The Reverend John Buchanan related how the

Scottish peasants would prefer living in a "hardy and wild but independent state" to submitting to the rigors of wage labor and purchasing finished commodities. "They would willingly live on fish and vegetables with a little sea water . . . even without potatoes provided they were allowed to shelter in some hut raised by their own hands" (1793: 205). John Barrow also lamented the fact that the Dutch frontiersman, although "placed in a country where not only the necessities, but almost every luxury of life might by industry be procured, has the enjoyment of none of them" ([1801] 1968: 77).

How, then, were these societies going to transition to capitalism when their members seemed utterly lacking in the natural propensity to "truck, barter, and exchange"? It is here that the female figure came to play a central role in the constitution of free-market capitalist ideology. It is important to note that the "natives" described in seventeenth- and eighteenth-century travel narratives, from whence the classical theorists derived their model of *Homo economicus*, were exclusively male. In "Kolbe's travel descriptions, Khoikhoi society emerged as almost exclusively male. In the text, as in the illustrations, the women were never in the foreground, and their sexual characteristics were hardly noticeable" (Abrahams 2000: 110). As a result, in the classical economic texts, *Homo economicus* is also depicted as male. All this changed dramatically in the eighteenth- and nineteenth-century texts that derived their logic from this earlier generation of treatises. What distinguishes the second generation from the first is the fact that in the latter, women, far more than men, are depicted as having an innate desire for accumulation. In these texts women are portrayed as the prototypical consumers, with women's clothing standing as a synecdoche for free-market capitalism, which is offered as a natural and essential extension of female sexuality. In these narratives the violence and coercion associated with primitive accumulation are completely obscured by images of female accumulation and consumption. The natural female desire for personal adornment, rather than the brutal and forcible separation of peasants from the independent means of survival, was thus offered as the explanation for how capitalist social relations come to take root.

Just as female bodies played an important role in symbolically representing the social ills of the past, so too did their bodies figure in discussions about and representation of an amended future. Images of female sexual adornment have a very specific referent in these texts—the products associated with the imperialism of free trade. The creation of female beauty is always attributed to a woman's desire for commodities that were available only through colonial trading networks. Thomas Pennant, for example, declared that the women of Scotland were "very fond of finery," would "load their fingers with trumpery rings" and wanted "both shoes and stockings" (1776: 126). Samuel Johnson declared that "the appearance of life began to alter" in the Highlands after he had "seen a few women with plaids at Aberdeen" (1775: 41). Mary-Anne Hanaway observed that although the greatest punishment one could inflict on Highlanders was to make them put on a pair of shoes, the women were "tolerably reconciled to them" (1776: 10). "The Hottentot woman," Barrow similarly asserted, "is fond of finery like those of most nations." They had, in his estimation, "an immoderate rage for dress" ([1801] 1968: 154). At a meeting held by the Bethelsdorp missionaries, participants discussed the great difficulty they experienced making the Khoikhoi desire and value purchased clothing. They came to the collective decision that if progress were to be made, it would be made among the women, who could more easily be "prevailed upon to dress better" (Campbell [1815] 1974: 88). John Philip agreed:

> In the manufacturing districts of North Britain, the labourers and artisans look forward to the possession of a house and garden as the summit of their ambition. . . . Taking all the circumstances into consideration, every reflecting mind will admit that the exertions of the [Khoikhoi] people, compared to their means, have been great. And as they have acquired a taste for good houses, particularly the *females*, the improvement of the people in this as well as in many other respects will, I have no doubt, keep pace with our expectations. ([1828] 1969: 218, emphasis in original)

The ultimate effect of these narratives is not only to obscure the active intervention of the state in creating the conditions whereby capitalist social relations supplanted the subsistence economy, but also to make invisible the extent to which the transition to capitalism was specifically predicated on a total transformation and devaluation of women's work. When the authors of these texts wrote female labor out of the history of capital accumulation, they simultaneously authorized a particular view of capitalist society that still remains hegemonic—that the economic and the political are "qualitatively different, more or less enclosed and 'regionally' separated spheres" (Wood 1995: 21).

Gender, the Production Process, and the Construction of Class Power

Practically speaking, the goals of the incipient capitalist class were as follows: (1) to have production in society as a whole come under the control of the capitalist appropriator; (2) to have the organization of production fully integrated with the organization of appropriation; and (3) to have virtually all production made subordinate to the demands of capitalist exploitation. Thus, the whole lives of individuals would be drawn ever more firmly into the orbit of production processes. As was discussed above, free-market ideology held it that the economic order was subject to impersonal laws or forces that determined the transition from one mode of production to another as well as the continual reproduction of the system. In actual fact, capitalists must exercise an unprecedented degree of control over production in order to ensure profitability. This translates into more rigid control over the labor process, which is not accomplished via disembodied economic forces, but through the introduction of political power into the production process. These goals were partially accomplished through concerted attempts to transform both the ways in which women labored and how women's labor was thought about and viewed in popular society.

The starting point of capitalist production was "nothing else than the historical process of divorcing the producer from the means of production" (Marx [1867] 1967: 668). Primitive accumulation, the name that Marx gave to this phenomenon, was a process of class struggle and coercive intervention by the state on behalf of the capitalist class that put women's labor and women's bodies at the center of both its ideological and its practical assault. Production in society as a whole could not come under the control of the capitalists as long as people had the means of producing for themselves and thus avoiding wage labor. Since women's labor was critical to the survival of the subsistence economy, it was represented in the classical texts as the greatest impediment to the "extension of the indirect and direct sway of the capitalist" (Marx [1867] 1967: 739). Hence, women's bodies were literally at the center of the struggle between classes. Successful capitalist production required that productive activity be socially organized in specific, gendered ways. Women had to be actively restricted from participating in the subsistence economy—gathering and preparing foodstuffs, manufacturing key household implements, engaging in petty commodity production, and so on—and forced into a situation of dependence on male wage workers employed outside of the home. These male wage workers, in turn, would be forced into the labor market by virtue of the fact that self-provisioning was no longer a viable option due to the ways in which women's labor had been transformed.

The fact that the gendered aspects of production relations came under scrutiny in the texts of classical political economy and were attacked by the state, under the aegis of the incipient capitalist class, indicates the extent to which relations of production were conditioned by political factors and political struggles. Indeed, rather than seeing the gendered modes of domination and coercion and gendered forms of social organization as simply external supports of a particular productive system, we can now see that they are actually constituents of production relations. In other words, the disposition of power that obtained between individual capitalists and workers had as its condition the gendered configuration of society as a whole. This gendered configuration of society thus became a site for the staging of class conflict and class struggle as control over women's bodies and women's labor was a central determinant of the political configuration of society as a whole.

Social relations between appropriators and producers rested on the relative strength of the contending classes, which were significantly determined by the ways in which the gendered organization of work structured the classes' internal organization. More simply put, differences in class organization were largely a function of the gendered division of labor. Furthermore, the power relationships that conditioned the nature and extent of exploitation were partly a product of, and were significantly influenced by, gender relations within the contending classes. Thus, whether the end result of a socioeconomic struggle would be a breakdown of the old order and old forms of surplus extraction or a retrenchment of the old forms depended, to a large degree, on how gender relations within a particular class shaped its internal organization and, thus, its relative degree of strength.

The economic historian Robert Brenner (1985) has identified three important factors that account for differences in class organization and strength and are thus important determinants of the outcome of class-based struggles: relative levels of internal solidarity, levels of self consciousness and organization, and political resources. Although Brenner does not make this connection, I believe that the status and position of women crucially influence all of these factors. When we look at food riots as an example of popular politics and plebian culture, the important role that women played in determining levels of internal class solidarity are quite apparent. Food riots were "complex assertions of shared memberships and beliefs and obligations" (Sayer 1993: 6). All members of the household, without regard to gender, defended the household economy. However, "it was those areas with the highest ratio of non-agricultural occupations in which women were most often found cooperating with men in food riots" (Honeyman 2000: 25). Women were more active in protests in areas with a high ratio of nonagricultural occupations because these were areas wherein processes of primitive accumulation had proceeded the farthest. Women, who were primarily responsible for providing families with food through self-provisioning, were the most closely affected. They were still responsible for providing families with food, even after self-provisioning had been undermined. Hence, their more active involvement. The least agricultural areas were also the areas were food riots were most prominent, aggressive, and ultimately successful.

The changes that occurred in the apprenticeship system, which were important determinants of class consciousness and organization, also were strongly conditioned by the gendered division of work. Whereas private indentures still served to provide formal vocational training and feelings of solidarity, employers increasingly used parish indentures, through which pauper children who were the responsibility of the parish were indentured at low cost to private employers. In essence, these parish indentures functioned as a disorganized source of cheap labor. Many more girls were apprenticed by the parish than privately and they were thus less likely to receive formal training in skilled work (Honeyman 2000).

Finally, we can view the power to determine the meaning of work as a political resource. The power to inform perceptions about who would work, to judge how well they performed, and to determine if and how they would be remunerated were all indexes of power. A key method of undermining traditional occupations, many of which were female dominated, was to place an increasing value on productivity, scientific principles, and commercial principles. For example, "changes in commercial dairying, which displaced women from one of their few remaining positions of strength in agriculture, can be related to a general transformation in the nature of work at the end of the eighteenth century" (Honeyman 2000: 29). The emphasis on productivity meant that the traditional methods of farming employed by women were replaced by more scientific ones, which required a larger capital outlay, and this mandated that dairy farmers realize profits. Because women did not have access to capital and could not produce dairy products at a profit, they were replaced by men.

Thus, the outcome of class-based struggles was strongly conditioned by gender. The maintenance of absolute private property for the capitalist, and his control over production and appropriation, were strongly conditioned by the gendered organization of work in peasant households. And furthermore, the disposition of power that obtained between individual capitalists and workers had, as its condition, the gendered configuration of society as a whole. The ways in which the authors of the classical texts and those texts' antecedents made these gender relations invisible authorized a common-sense separation of the political and the economic that remains hegemonic and politically disabling today.

Who's Ruling Whom? The Paradox of
Political Rule in Commercial Society

The conceptual emergence of the economic that is so evident in these texts has as its corollary a highly specified view of power and the political sphere. These texts were obviously not written for the benefit or consumption of the working classes or the colonized—even though they were the texts' focal points. Rather, these texts were written as part of a general effort to assert the hegemony of a new ruling class and to discredit the class formations they were intent on displacing. The economic musings of political economists like Adam Smith can also be read as a "violent denunciation of behavioral patterns that differed from those of the petit bourgeoisie [sic]" (Perelman 2000: 205). Missionaries like John Philip were "vehemently opposed to the military, aristocratic culture through which the Cape was governed" and despaired that the Cape would be made a "depot for the dregs of her [England's] aristocracy" (Lester 2001: 32). Thus, the pronouncements on politics in society contained in these texts should be understood as a polemic directed for and against particular varieties of class rule.

The representatives of this new class were acutely aware that they were facing a serious legitimization problem. Adam Smith, for example, despite his great admiration for the bourgeoisie, "knew these people were not attractive to other sectors of society" (Perelman 2000: 197). The classes from which the evangelicals were drawn were aware that their relationship with the aristocracy was characterized by "suspicion and aggressive antagonism" (Ross 1986: 36). Adam Smith spilled a fair share of ink lamenting the bourgeoisie's lack of legitimacy, as well as devising strategies to overcome it. In the *Theory of Moral Sentiments,* for example, he observed that they were a class of people "whom nobody thinks it is worth while to look at," "the man of rank and distinction, on the contrary, is observed by all the world. . . . Scarce a word, scarce a gesture, can fall from him that is altogether neglected" ([1759] 1976: 51). The aristocracy commanded such obsequious behavior because they could support so many dependents. Smith, therefore, expressed strong condemnation for dependency in his writings. "Nothing tends so much to corrupt and enervate and debase the mind as dependency," he opined (Smith 1978: 333).

Under feudalism, "the direct application of force was the condition for ruling-class surplus extraction" (Brenner 1977: 37). Extra-economic modes of surplus extraction were the tools whereby surplus labor was transferred to the private lord in the shape of labor services, rent, or tax. Under free-market capitalism, however, the autonomous laws of the economy and capital, abstracted from any one individual or class, were held to exercise power. The social allocation of resources and labor did not take place by means of communal deliberation, hereditary duty, custom, obligation, or political direction. The corollary of these developments was that the appropriator relinquished direct political power in the conventional sense and lost many of the traditional forms of personal control over the lives of laborers, which lay outside of the immediate production process. Whereas the aristocracy had legitimated itself and its right to rule by virtue of the fact that they provided military and social protection to the tenants from whom they extracted their surpluses, the bourgeoisie could claim no such legitimacy.

Furthermore, although the defenders of the bourgeoisie condemned dependency as something that corrupted, enervated, and debased the mind, they were forced to acknowledge that dependency was a marked feature of life in commercial society as well—only in commercial society the rich were more obviously dependent upon the poor than vice versa. In his *Lectures on Jurisprudence* Smith stated quite bluntly that

> The labour and time of the poor is in civilized countries sacrificed to the maintaining of the rich in ease and luxury. The landlord is maintained in idleness and luxury by the labour of his tenants. The moneyed man is supported by his exactions from the industrious merchant and the needy who are obliged to support him in ease by a return for the use of his money. . . . The poor labourer . . . who supports the whole fame of society and furnishes the means of the convenience and ease of all the rest is himself possessed of a very small share and is buried in obscurity. (1978: 340)

John Philip likewise acknowledged the "great profit which colonists derive from the labour of the Hottentots" ([1828] 1969: 393).

This dependence posed a legitimization problem, not between the owners of capital and workers, but rather between the rising bourgeoisie and the landed gentry they were intent on ideologically and practically displacing—both at home and in the colonies. For example, the rising bourgeoisie could not even claim the honor and distinction of providing protection to the laboring classes in exchange for their subservience. In fact, when the power to appropriate was separated from the performance of military, judicial, or administrative functions, the appropriating classes were relieved of any obligation to fulfill a larger social purpose (Wood 1995). Indeed, the wealthy not only depended upon the laboring classes to produce the wealth and profits they lived off of, they also were dependent upon them to militarily defend the wealth they had produced, but were not destined to enjoy. Adam Smith devoted considerable space in both *Lectures on Jurisprudence* and *The Wealth of Nations* to discussing issues of national security. In the latter text he observed that "an industrious, and upon that account a wealthy nation, is of all nations the most likely to be attacked" (Smith [1759] 1976: 697). He was acutely aware, however, that the propertied classes were unfit for military service. "An army composed of gentlemen has . . . very little discipline" (Smith 1978: 266). Thus, the army would have to be made up of working men. John Philip observed that the Khoikhoi who lived at mission stations like Theopolis would have to play the key role in protecting colonial possessions that had been forcibly taken from other ethnic groups, like the Xhosa. He noted that the location of Theopolis was chosen precisely because it was "favourable for keeping the Caffers [Xhosa] in check in that quarter." He speculated that, "notwithstanding the losses and inconveniences" to which they were subjected, the Khoikhoi could be expected to contribute "much to the security of the district." Despite the key role they were expected to play in generating and defending colonial wealth Philip prophesied that "no sudden alteration in the landed property of the country is to be apprehended from this source" (Philip [1828] 1969: 255–56, 379).

How, then, could the sort of dependence that the bourgeoisie clearly had on the poor be reconciled with their political superiority? Even Adam Smith, who went to great lengths to defend the bourgeoisie, was led to ask how men of such inferior rank could "ever hope to distinguish themselves" ([1759] 1976: 54). I believe that this problem of legitimacy was ideologically managed through aesthetic judgment of the female body, which was a noticeable feature of these texts. An obsession with aesthetic descriptions in travel, evangelical, and political economy texts can be understood as an attempt to overcome the conundrum of rule in commercial society. A dynamic of exclusion by race and class as well as gender and nation structures these aesthetic discourses, and the aesthetic subject has a distinct set of gender, race, and class characteristics and prerogatives that, ultimately, legitimate his right to rule despite his dependence on his social inferiors.

The Aesthetics of Rule

The ways in which these texts formulated and reformulated the idea of beauty also can tell us something about how power was to be rationalized under this new dispensation. The ideal of beauty in Western culture, which was derived from the Platonic philosophical tradition, posited that real beauty had nothing to do with the body or with the world of material things; nor could it take the form of the body and its parts. In this tradition, only the soul could know real beauty because the body, with its deceptive senses, hindered man in his search for true knowledge. Indeed, according to Plato, man's senses simply riveted him to a world of material things that was far removed from the world of reality. In the Platonic tradition, the division between the soul and the body is closely related to a particular vision of how to set up a state. The ideal Platonic state is one wherein the rule of the rational soul over the unruly body corresponds to the rule of the rational few over the irrational multitude. As Elizabeth Spelman explains:

> What we learn from Plato, then, about knowledge, reality, goodness, beauty, love, and statehood, is phrased in terms of a distinction between soul and body, or alternatively and roughly equivalently, in terms of a distinction between the rational and irrational. And the body, or the irrational part of the soul, is seen as an enormous and annoying obstacle to the possession of these desiderata. If the body gets the upper hand ! over the soul, or if the irrational part of the soul overpowers the rational part, one can't have knowledge, one can't see beauty, one will be far from the highest form of love, and the state will be in utter chaos. (1982: 113)

In the texts explored above, however, beauty had everything to do with the physical body and the world of material things. The body, rather than being an obstacle to the possession of knowledge, beauty, and goodness, was a physical indicator of whether one possessed knowledge, beauty, and goodness. The world of material things was the world of reality, and man's senses, particularly his aesthetic perceptions, were a reliable guide to understanding and interpreting that world. In these texts the test of rationality lay, therefore, in one's ability to appreciate and cultivate beauty—to engage in seemingly disinterested aesthetic contemplation and thus act as an aesthetic subject.

The aesthetic subject was always a gentleman, while racial Others, the poor, and women were always the objects of aesthetic contemplation. Aesthetic observation was thereby implicated in class superiority—appreciating beauty in the ways described above demanded comfortable material circumstances. Furthermore, aesthetic contemplation was always aligned with property ownership. Because aesthetic contemplation was akin to visual appropriation, there was a necessary connection between being an observer and controlling one's own property and space. In the words of Joseph Addison, a man of "polite imagination" was "let into a great many Pleasures that the Vulgar are not capable of receiving." Addison further maintained that the polite imagination bestowed upon its owner "a kind of property in everything he sees," for aesthetic contemplation was "a gentlemanly pursuit, a marker of social status, and a training in the experience of individual ownership" ([1712] 1965: 538).

Aesthetic contemplation became implicated in a distinct politics of class rule by virtue of the fact that the practice of aesthetic contemplation distanced the observer from the observed while simultaneously asserting his dominance. According to Kristina Straub (1987), in Britain the visual became a site for the symbolic enactment of asymmetrical power relations during the eighteenth century. Aesthetic discourse relied on the fiction of a generic perceiver (the condition of possibility for any universal standard), which further allowed the language of aesthetics to combine universal pretensions with exclusionary assumptions. The fiction of a universal standard of taste helped to ground the universality of a wide variety of other ruling class values, such as the rule of the wealthy over the poor and the desirability of capitalist over precapitalist social relations, and market values over nonmarket ones. As Elizabeth Bohls explains:

> The subject or perceiver is constructed in mainstream, male authored eighteenth century aesthetic writing through a process that entails disqualifying the vast majority of subjects and falsely universalizing the judgment of the remaining few. These moves are especially apparent in various versions of one well-known doctrine of eighteenth century aesthetics, the universal standard of taste. Hume, Burke, and Kant all arrive at a universal standard by generalizing the response of a particular perceiver or group of perceivers. Hume's difficult task in his essay, "Of the Standard of Taste," is to uphold such a standard as binding on everyone, while deducing it from the response of a select few. (1995: 7)

Ordinarily, the conventions of aesthetic discourse demanded that aesthetics remain rarefied and aloof from the pressures of everyday, utilitarian concerns. There was an urge to deny any "connection between aesthetic practices and the material, social, and political conditions of human existence" (Bohls 1995: 10). The conventions of aesthetic discourse, which demanded a strict bifurcation between discussions about that which was aesthetic and ornamental and that which was practical and useful, could be contravened, however, through ideological categories like gender and race (Brown 1993). The figure of the "native" woman was the discursive means for connecting colonialism and imperialist accumulation with a theory of aesthetics. Indeed, the alleged autonomy of the aesthetic from practical matters made it a discourse that was well suited for advancing a range of practical agendas—

such as the ones having to do with economic transformation. Aesthetic discourses are quite flexible and are able to coexist in individual texts with other types of discourses, such as economics or natural history. This flexibility further enabled them to be mobilized in support of more practical or utilitarian ends. The alleged disinterested nature of the aesthetic thus contradicts its actual implication in the hierarchies of social power.

The implicit message of "applied aesthetic" texts such as travel narratives and missionary tracts is that the aesthetic subject is the natural ruler of society by virtue of the prerogatives he exercises. To be an aesthetic subject is to be a gentleman, an owner of property, and a controller of space. To be an aesthetic object is to be a member of the working class, a woman, or a racial Other who controls neither space nor access to property. Thus, in these works, just as was the case with those produced by Plato, there is an intimate connection between the nature of beauty and its appreciation and larger views about the best way to set up a state and a system of rule. In these texts, the one who can see and appreciate beauty is the one who can exercise the right to rule over all those who are merely aesthetic objects. It is important to note that the elite class to which the aesthetic subject belonged broadened its membership to include men of commerce in the late eighteenth and early nineteenth centuries. The work of Addison was instrumental in helping to "expand that elite by inviting rising merchants and manufacturers to share in genteel enjoyments like literature, music, painting, architecture, and natural scenery, while maintaining these pleasures' exclusive social cachet" (Bohls 1995: 8).

The connection between aesthetic appreciation, race, gender, and the right to rule are nowhere more clearly expressed than in the writings of Samuel Johnson, who penned the following:

> Ladies have as much beauty here [Scotland] as in other places, but bloom and softness are not to be expected among the lower classes, whose faces are exposed to the rudeness of climate. . . . Supreme beauty is seldom found in cottages or workshops, even when no real hardships are suffered. To expand the human face to its full perfection it seems necessary that the mind should cooperate by placidness of content or consciousness of superiority. . . . *As the mind must govern the hands, so in every society the man of intelligence must direct the man of labour.* If the takman be taken away the Hebrides must in their present state be given up to grossness and ignorance. The tenant, for want of instruction, will be unskillful and for want of admonition, will be negligent. (1775: 132, emphasis added)

The Social Body

John Philip invoked none other than Adam Smith when he described the ideal colonial state as a formation that resembled the human body in its fundamentals—with the mind (the property owning classes) controlling the feet (the laboring classes):

> The different members of a state have been beautifully represented by the members of the human body: it may be truly said, if one member suffers, all the members of the body suffer; and if one member is diseased, all the body is affected by its sympathy with this particular member. In allusion to this figure, the Hottentots may be called the feet; but I may be allowed to ask the question—if the feet are in a state of mortification, what becomes of the health of the body? Can the sons of a farmer be industrious—can his daughters be uncontaminated? ([1828] 1969: 386)

In the human body the heart and mind might depend on the hands and legs for optimal functioning of the whole organism, but ultimately the hand and legs are expendable, and the heart and mind are not. In the ideal class society, the laboring classes produced the wealth of society but had little say in decision making, while the propertied classes lived off the labor of others, yet monopolized the prerogative to rule. Viewing society as functioning in ways analogous to the human body was useful in that it provided a way of thinking about how one portion of an organism could be dependent upon another, yet still superior.

In applied aesthetic texts, images of the female body, which served as synecdoches for modes of production, were very frequently placed in tandem with the metaphor of the social body, which anthropomorphized society. Both metaphors posited a relationship between healthy individual bodies and the healthy social organism: healthy, defined as aesthetically pleasing, female bodies were products of a healthy social system; a healthy social organism, the social body, functioned like a healthy human body. The anthropomorphization of society, like the aestheticization of capitalist ideology, referenced and rationalized the ideal system of governance in a class-stratified society.

The image of society as a human body was an abstraction produced also through and alongside other key abstractions like "the economic" and "the political." The image of the social body played an important conceptual role in that it provided a view of the social order that facilitated the conceptual separation of political, economic, and social problems. The metaphorical depiction of society as akin to the human body—literally a social body— was thus a way of conceptualizing the relationship between private property and political power that reinforced the idea that the political domain was essentially extraneous to capitalist relations of production. The fact that the disposition of power between individual capitalists and workers was conditioned by the political configuration of society as a whole became invisible; the metaphor of the social body denied the fact that political power was an essential condition of capitalist appropriation. Thus, the economy came to be seen as a network of disembodied forces existing alongside the political sphere, which was defined as a set of moral relations between superiors and subordinates. The disposition of power to control production and appropriation and the allocation of social labor and resources were completely cut off from the political domain. In other words, the political face of the economy was obscured. Forms of social interaction between classes were not, therefore, conceptualized as integral parts of the material base of society. Thus, when the mind was said to govern the hands, governance was conceived of primarily in moral terms—in terms of the mental, physical, and spiritual disciplining of bodies. Governance was not discussed, however, in terms of the power to appropriate surplus labor or to control production itself by directing producers to meet the demands of a particular class. Thus, while the true nature of political power was disguised, the economy came to be, in the words of one economic historian, "evacuated of social content and depoliticized" (Wood 1995: 21).

The sharp discontinuity between the economic and political spheres that became so central to commonsense understandings of capitalism over the course of the nineteenth century can be traced back to what Marx called the "starting point of capitalist production . . . the historical process of divorcing the producer from the means of production" ([1867] 1967: 668). Crucial to the process, as we have seen, was the insertion of political power into the production process itself, accomplished largely through the control of women's bodies, which became important sites for the staging of class conflict and class struggle. A set of discursive practices that served to represent laboring female bodies in ways that obscured their horrendous exploitation were the means through which an ideological system emerged that insisted upon the total separation of the economic and the political at the very moment when they were becoming increasingly indistinguishable. At the same time that the use of bodily metaphors in economic discourses allowed for a way of conceptualizing problems so that political, economic, and social problems seemed to belong to different spheres of analysis and social action, they also enabled problems and their solutions to be formulated in bodily terms. This process was obviously nowhere near completed at the start of the nineteenth century (neither, for that matter, was the process of primitive accumulation). Indeed, it would continue throughout the century, albeit in a number of different forms. In the next chapter, therefore, I continue the discussion of the social body as a metaphor, this time concentrating on the ways in which male bodies were positioned in texts that claimed to be objective and scientific studies of the poor.

CHAPTER THREE

Savage Paupers: Race, Nomadism, and the Image of the Urban Poor

In the previous chapter I examined the ways in which the female body was made a locus for the intersection of capitalism and aesthetics, with aesthetic representations of colonized female bodies articulating private propositions about sexuality to the world historical enterprise of colonialism. In this chapter I continue in the general vein of looking at how ideas about embodiment articulate with the evolution of capitalism and colonialism by examining representations of colonized male bodies. Specifically, I look at how images of colonized male bodies provided a stock set of images and metaphors for reconstituting public knowledge about the destitute in England. Whereas travel and evangelical writing—examples of "applied aesthetics"—were the main focus of attention in the last chapter, here I deal primarily with texts whose authors claimed them to be objective and scientific studies of the poor. In the previous chapter I examined the rhetorical means whereby travel writers and evangelicals deployed political economy to rationalize the process of separating the producer from his or her independent means of production; the historical processes that concern us here are political economists' attempt to explain the allocation of labor in a capitalist society.

Although primitive accumulation continued both as a historical process and as an object of intellectual inquiry in the decades bracketing the mid-century mark, the attention of political economists turned increasingly to providing rationales for organizing and supervising the labor process as a means of increasing surplus in production. The texts of these political economists, no less than the ones explored in the previous chapter, contributed to the general process whereby the "economic" and the "political" came to be conceptualized as separate entities in capitalist ideology. The ideological treatment of male bodies contributed to a general societal view of the economic in capitalism as a product of disembodied forces rooted in nature,

thus obscuring the fact that social relations between human agents constitute these "natural" laws. Images of male bodies, at home and in the colonies, contributed to the construction of a view of society whereby the social
relations in which the economic is buried—that is, the social relations that
actively constitute the economic—are treated as wholly external to it.

Here I take a closer look at what Michael Shapiro calls the "imaginative
enactments that produce meaning" that are contained in these texts. By
imaginative enactments, Shapiro means those "historically developed practices that reside in the very style in which statements are made [and] the
grammatical, rhetorical, and narrative structures that compose discourse"
(1988: 8). I thus seek to look at economic texts in a way similar to that of
Kurt Heinzelman, who argues that not only do economic texts have a strong
"imaginative" component, but economic systems are also "structured by
means of the imagination" (1980: 11). In other words, purportedly positive
and nonimaginative texts, like those of economics, are literary in certain fundamental ways (McCloskey 1998). My exploration of the imaginative component of ostensibly positivist discourses about the poor focuses on the
metaphorical associations drawn between the able-bodied poor Englishman and the racialized colonial Other. The premise underwriting this chapter is that "the *what* of any knowledge system is radically entangled with
the *how* of its writing/speaking" (Shapiro 1988: 8). Thus, the images and
metaphors deployed in these texts are important because of the power of
these texts to simultaneously produce and alter public knowledge about the
poor. The texts both inaugurated and indexed important shifts in attitudes
about poor people's humanity and, thus, made certain courses of action
thinkable. Specifically, they produced the poor as knowledge objects in such
a way that it was possible for "textual reality to repressively displace situated
reality as its authentic truth" (Green 1983: 108). A critical part of this process
involved the construction of texts that, despite being overrun with anec-
dotes, stories, and images of the poor, didn't allow the poor any meaningful
space or voice within them. Thus readers were able to "contemplate the poor
even as they turn away" (Sherman 2001: 12).

The representational techniques that allowed readers to simultaneously
contemplate the poor while turning away from them are intimately connected to new forms of narrative associated with the advent of what Bernth
Lindfors calls "ethnological show business—that is, the displaying of foreign peoples for commercial and/or educational purposes" (1999: vii).
Ethnological exhibitions can be understood both as cultural institutions of
modern society and as part of a new regime of signs and texts that fundamentally influenced how "people's measures of the real change." Specifi-

cally, these showcases helped to inaugurate a trend whereby, because images mediated virtually the sum total of social existence, the world could also be grasped as though it were an exhibition. "What resulted from these events was . . . a world rendered up to the individual according to the way in which it could be set up before him or her as an exhibit. The colonial nature of the nineteenth-century world's fairs thus consisted less in their celebration of the global hegemony of Western economic and political power than in their redefinition of the nature of knowledge" (Erlmann 1999: 109, 124). Ethnographic showcases thus played an important role in reshaping the nature of knowledge and the idea of reality in ways that critically affected how the poor were represented and understood in the public sphere.

Ethnographic Showcases and the Making of a Bourgeois Regime of Knowledge

Ethnographic exhibitions, alongside travel and evangelical texts, were key means whereby images of empire became a part of English people's everyday reality (Corbey 1995; Gilman 1985; Sharpley-Whiting 1999). South Africa was a particularly rich source of what the *Athenaeum* issue of May 28, 1853, called the "many varieties of the human race as are constantly to be seen in London." Indeed, a stroll through what *The Illustrated London News* of June 12, 1847, called "the ark of zoological wonders—Egyptian Hall, Piccadilly," yielded a view of "extraordinary Bushpeople brought from South Africa" (p. 381). Visitors to Cosmorama, Regent-Street, could see "a very interesting exhibition of three natives of Southern and Eastern Africa" (*Illustrated London News*, September 14, 1850: 236). The sight of "Bushmen in their trees" and "the preliminaries of Kaffir marriage and bridal festivities" entertained visitors to the St. George's Gallery in Knightsbridge. The latter came courtesy of a Mr. A. T. Caldecott, who had returned from Natal with twelve Zulus in tow (*Illustrated London News*, May 28, 1853: 410).

According to Veit Erlmann, ethnographic showcases incited a sort of "spectatorial lust" through which "empire and unreality [came to] constitute each other in ways rooted in the deepest layers of modern consciousness" (1999: 110). A cursory glance through advertisements for ethnographic exhibitions demonstrates the degree to which these showcases produced meanings in the public sphere that, although exhibitors claimed that they conveyed the real, were far more a repression of the real in favor of verisimilitude. David Livingstone, for example, complained that "the Bushmen specimens brought to Europe have been selected, like costermongers' dogs, on account of their extreme ugliness; consequently English ideas of the whole tribe are formed in the same way as if the ugliest specimens of the English were exhibited in Africa as characteristic of the entire British nation" ([1858] 1971: 49). Thus, it was precisely the privileging of verisimilitude that made many evangelicals, who prided themselves on the authenticity of their representations of Africans, see these showcases as inimical to their aims, despite the fact that the entertainment industry relied upon, and oftentimes praised, the evangelicals' work.

Although ethnographic showcases afforded people of all classes a glimpse at what the *Illustrated London News* of May 28, 1853, called "savages engaged in the pursuits of their everyday life," class politics, not unlike those that operated in the case of aesthetic subjects, provided a set of rules about "looking" (p. 410). For the most part, the wealthy were the privileged subjects who took part in this new synthesis of knowledge and power. The extent to which the upper classes—dowagers, belles, and gentlemen—were the privileged viewing subjects is aptly demonstrated in the following satiric poem, titled "Thoughts on the Savage Lions of London," which appeared in *Punch* magazine on July 23, 1853:

> Kafirs from Borioboola, or somewhere—
>   There are delighting the civilized world
> Belles from Belgravia in afternoons come there;
>   Thither the fairest of May-fair are whirl'd.
> Dowagers craving for something exciting,
>   Gentlemen blasé with Fashion's dull round,
> Those who find novelty always delighting,
>   With those dear Kafirs may daily be found. (p. 38)

The poem can be seen as simultaneously explaining popular attitudes toward these exhibitions and providing a commentary on the attitudes the well-heeled adopted toward the Other. The opening line of the poem immediately establishes the propriety of adopting an attitude of studied indifference to the particulars of what one is viewing. The extensive press coverage of the "Kaffir Wars" in South Africa, the existence of numerous ethnographic exhibitions such as the one described, and the frequent public lectures by returned missionaries made it highly unlikely that the average wealthy and well-educated person would *not* know where the so-called Kaffirs hailed from, but the poem underscores that ultimately the particulars of where these black bodies originated and how they happened to end up in England is unimportant. They could be from South Africa, West Africa, or even the fictitious Borioboola—what really matters is that they have been brought to Europe, incorporated into its theatrical machinery, and offered up as objects to be viewed with "delight" by the "civilized world."

Paradoxically, this studied attitude of indifference to particularity—especially the particularity of individual African lives—had as its concomitant a cultural obsession with ethnographic detail that produced the effect of direct and immediate experience with Africa. Lectures from evangelical itinerants like Robert Moffat and David Livingstone drew extremely large crowds of supporters, particularly from the middle classes, who eagerly assembled at mission halls and public theaters to be entertained by tales of adventure in far-off places from Calcutta to the Cape Coast (Thorne 1999). Upon his return from South Africa, Robert Moffat was so in demand that he "was hurried from town to town with scant opportunity for a moments rest" (Moffatt 1885: 223). When David Livingstone toured England in 1857 there was "anxiety on the part of all classes to see and hear him" (Sedgwick and Monk 1858: 25). When missionaries returned with African or Asian converts, they were even more enthusiastically received. In 1837 missionaries John Philip and John Read toured England accompanied by John Tzatzoe and Andries Stoffles, two "native Christians" from South Africa. "On one occasion the two Africans were invited to spend an evening with the students at Highbury College—vivid recollections of which remain in many minds," the Reverend Thomas Aveling reported (1850: 126).

As Z. S. Strother explains, the exhibitors self-consciously sought to "solicit the attendance of the well-educated, those familiar with travelogues" as part of their publicity strategy (1999: 25). Indeed, even a cursory glance through the publicity literature of the time demonstrates the degree to which ethnographic showcases were intimately linked to travel and evangelical writings. The publicity material that accompanied the advertisement for the "extraordinary Bushpeople brought from South Africa," for example, explained that with "the ethnological characteristics of the Bosjemans, literally, 'Bushmen' the public have been made acquainted through the writings of Lichtenstein, Burchell, Campbell, Thompson, Pringle, and other intelligent travelers in Africa" (*Illustrated London News*, June 12, 1847: 381). An exhibition of five "Bushmen" at Exeter Hall, accompanied by a lecture from Robert Knox, an army surgeon who spent five years on the South African frontier, was advertised as being particularly addressed to those interested in "the all-important questions of Christian mission and human civilization in that quarter of the globe" (*Athenaeum*, March 1853). How do we account for this curious paradox whereby the viewing subjects were expected to be familiar with ethnographic detail yet adopt a studied attitude of indifference about particularity? It turns out that this paradox can tell us quite a lot about what Timothy Mitchell terms "a method of order and truth essential to the peculiar nature of the modern world" (1989: 236).

The ways in which ethnographic showcases ordered and presented the Other demanded that viewing subjects adopt certain attitudes—both toward the world and toward themselves. First, they should be "curious" about the world in such a way as to "contemplate" Africa and Africans even as they turned away; they should immerse themselves and yet stand apart. "The curiosity of the observing subject was something demanded by a diversity of mechanisms for rendering things up as its object." This mode of addressing objects in the world inculcated a particular way of viewing the world and the individual's relationship to it. "Ordinary people were beginning to live as tourists or anthropologists, addressing the object world as the endless representation of some further meaning or reality." Thus, the world itself came to be "conceived and grasped as though it were an exhibition" (Mitchell 1989: 219, 232, 222).

Ethnographic showcases were a means of engineering the real so that everything was organized to prompt the recall of some larger meaning beyond it. This attitude toward the world engendered a particular conception of and about "reality" that had a profound impact on how domestic poverty was understood, represented, and managed. As Mitchell explains, reality came to take on a "citationary nature" whereby what was represented was "not a real place, but a set of references, a congeries of characteristics, that seems to have its origin in a quotation, or a fragment of a text, or a citation from someone's work . . . or some bit of previous imagining or an amalgam of all these . . . it is the chain of references that produces the effect of the place." The world, like the exhibit, came to be nothing more than a collection of objects that recalled a meaning beyond reality. In other words, the "characteristic cognitive move of the modern subject" was to transfer onto objects "the principles of one's relation to [them]" and conceive of them as "totally intended for cognition alone." Thus, individual lives "appear as no more than stage parts . . . or the implementing of plans" (1989: 235, 232).

It is important to note that although the wealthy were the privileged subjects of the exhibitionary gaze, a number of reformers sought to inculcate this distinctive way of seeing into the laboring classes as well. George Godwin argued that exhibits, paintings, and other technologies of entertainment that denied the reciprocal nature of vision were methods of educating the working classes superior to books. Somewhat ironically, he invoked the social experiments of the South African missionary David Livingstone as supporting evidence.

> The peculiar education (if we may call it) of this class requires unusual measures, and it may be observed that, although, under the circumstances, books are useless, yet paintings, music, and exhibitions which place a tale of interest before the eye, meet with ready appreciation, and in the absence of the power of deriving amusement from books, we are inclined to think that the penny theaters, as so managed, do more good than harm, and that they might be very greatly improved, not only with advantages to the owners of them, but also to the visitors. Some of our readers will recollect Dr. Livingstone's observation that the views afforded by the magic lantern were the only kind of knowledge he was asked for twice by the Africans. (Godwin [1859] 1972: 96)

This way of conceiving reality, the world, and one's position within it extended far beyond the immediate realm of the ethnographic exhibition space. Everywhere one looked, one could find the technique and sensations associated with the ethnographic showcase—particularly when we consider the production of reality effects in discourses about the poor.

The Ethnological Gaze and the Production of Reality Effects in Poverty Discourse

Just as ethnographic showcases and travel writing distanced the observer and spectator from actual African peoples, so positivist discourses about poverty distanced readers and spectators from the actual poor. As Sandra Sherman puts it:

> However frightened, resigned, wily, or enraged . . . poor people may have been, their existential realities could be depicted only in the metaphors and stories which their social superiors could invoke. In such texts the poor are opaque, present (as subject matter) but absent as voices generating metaphors and stories. Yet this opacity is itself opaque to readers' apprehension. What appears is seeming descriptiveness, honest transcription of "existential reality" albeit untested by the poor's own views. . . . Elite descriptions of the poor indulge the bourgeois conscience: readers contemplate the poor even as they turn away, imagining the poor as silent, controlled, conforming to the mental patterns of their social superiors. Such discourse imposes an imagined reality,

self-interested "metaphors and stories," that substitute for face to face en-
counters while seeming to instantiate transparency. (2001: 12)

Descriptive treatises about the poor, particularly those that were penned
subsequent to the passing of the New Poor Law in 1834, reveal that the
methods of producing truth and order that were made manifest in the ethnographic showcase precipitated a cognitive shift in English public life. These
processes were not simply parallel. Rather, we can draw connections between
the two, seeing them as mutually constituting events. Texts that purported to
explain poverty, like the ethnographic showcases, employed a set of adjec-
tives, definitions, descriptions, and diagnoses that silenced the poor while
appearing to closely document and acknowledge them. The poor, like the exhibited Africans, were made present as subject matter but absent as voices.
This process was accomplished by the textual means of producing reality effects that employed a ready-made vocabulary of images and metaphors from
the empire.

Writers of social reports that claim to describe an external reality "out
there" must employ a number of different rhetorical strategies to make their
reports believable. Issues of language and style are extremely important. As
Bryan Green explains, "a social report in order to produce reality and knowledge effects must be articulated through an existing stock of knowledge containing codes operative beyond the reading process which the person who
reads can use without question. . . . A text must play upon pre-existing plau-
sibility structures in order to achieve referential realism and this is done
through evoking the familiar grammar and vocabulary, the significatory
rules and semantemes, making up a field of discourse" (1983: 104).

The political economists and social thinkers who sought to analyze
poverty used the public stock of knowledge, particularly that having to do
with empire, as a kind of semantic tool kit. Evangelicals eagerly supported
and put themselves at the center of reform movements directed at both the
untutored heathens abroad and the suffering poor at home. It therefore
comes as no surprise that they bear a large part of the responsibility for the
making of images and metaphors from the colonies a discursive resource for
constructing a narrative about the English poor. The literary outpourings of
religious organizations such as the London City Mission and the British and
Foreign Bible society were aimed at exposing, and thereby ameliorating,
conditions in the urban slums. Their monthly magazines, alongside books
with titles like *London as It Is* (1837), *The Rookeries of London* (1850), *The
Habitations of the Industrial Class* (1851), *Curiosities of London Life* (1854), *The*

Happy Colony (1854), *The Night Side of London* (1858), and *The Danger of Deterioration of Race* (1866), are notable for their rhetorical reliance on idioms and images from colonial travel writing. Propaganda written for the purpose of highlighting the need for domestic reform is liberally sprinkled with words like *heathen, savage,* and *barbarism* (see Chadwick 1843: 45; *City Mission Magazine,* January 1855: 4; Hole 1866: 42; Shaw [1861] 1985: 168; Vaughan [1843] 1971: 246).

Dr. John Hogg, for example, remarked that "it has been said that the lower classes of English people are not sufficiently civilized . . . that they are a barbarous and *mischievous race*" ([1837] 1985: 324, emphasis in original). Robert Pemberton, an urban reformer, agreed that English slums were teeming with "thousands of enfeebled human organisms which only are comparable with the savage" ([1854] 1985: 15). The popularity of travel writing from South Africa, coupled with various exhibitions of the San and the Khoikhoi in 1847 and of the Zulu and Xhosa in 1850 and 1853, led the authors of domestic reform literature to liberally sprinkle their writings with references to the aboriginal people of South Africa. To take just two examples among many, writers for the *City Mission Magazine* of 1853 lamented that the children of the poor had "a worse lot than that of Hottentot children in the wilds of Africa" (quoted in Thompson 1985: 30). In his recounting of his travels with the London City Mission, Dr. James Shaw reported seeing pauper children who were "as ignorant as Hottentots" ([1861] 1985: 270). Colonial images and metaphors thus provided the "familiar grammar and vocabulary" that Green identifies as playing such an important role in producing reality effects.

The reality effect that most concerns us here is that which naturalized a view of the social world as embodying a sharp discontinuity between the economic and political spheres. In this view of the world, production is a function of natural laws that are independent of history, and the economy is a network of disembodied forces in which a spatially separate political power occasionally intervenes. This particular reality effect was partially produced through a very specific narrative about the source and causes of and the proper remedy for poverty. This narrative about poverty, in turn, was produced in and through descriptions of the English poor (particularly those who were male) that drew strong parallels between them and colonized people. Thus, just as the ideological treatment of women's bodies in travel writing was strongly connected to a particular way of viewing the economic, particularly in the transition to capitalism, as a product of disembodied forces, so the rhetorical treatment of male bodies cohered around a common concern with capital's control over the labor process.

The transition to capitalist social relations meant that appropriators relinquished direct political power over producers and lost many of the traditional forms of personal control over the lives of workers that were characteristic of economic systems such as feudalism. As Ellen Meiksins Wood explains, "pre-capitalist societies were characterized by 'extra-economic' forms of surplus extraction, carried out by means of political, juridical, and military power. . . . This is in sharp contrast to capitalism, where surplus extraction is purely 'economic,' achieved through the medium of commodity exchange" (1999: 49). Under this new dispensation, surplus appropriation by dominant classes depended upon improving labor productivity, which meant that capital must gain increased control over the labor process itself. The supervision of the labor process as a means for increasing surplus in production became a substitute for the use of coercive power to extract surpluses. Work, therefore, had to be thoroughly disciplined and organized so that the organization of production was fully integrated with the organization of appropriation. In other words, production in society as a whole must come under the control of the capitalist appropriator, and human life in all its myriad dimensions must be drawn ever more firmly into the orbit of production processes (Wood 1995).

Thus, these purportedly positivist treatises about poverty are essentially narratives about the organization of production and the disciplining of labor so as to improve its productivity and thereby create value in production. As the economic historian Mark O'Brien puts it: "The nature of laws surrounding the question of poverty in society are not *only* particular to each historical circumstance throughout the history of capitalism—although they are partly that. Their *essential* logic stems from the nature of capitalism itself. We can therefore only understand poverty, and responses made to poverty, over the course of modern history by seeing it in terms of the essential form of exploitation which defines capitalism as well as the class structure and forms of class struggle associated with it" (2000: 13, emphasis in original).

Nomads and Vagrants: Images of Poverty and Mobility at Home and Abroad

When looking at the verbal and iconic imagery used to represent the poor, especially poor men, one is immediately struck by the attention devoted to one particular class of poor people—the able-bodied and mobile who were tagged with the epithet *vagrant*. These men, more than any others, were likely to be directly compared with colonized people, precisely because colonized people were strongly associated with nonproductive movement. Vagrants were frequently described as "London Arabs," "Arabs of the metropolis," or "Arabs of the streets" (see *Magdalen's Friend,* 1862: 283; *Quarterly Review,* March 1847: 139; Raynard 1860: 16; Ritchie 1858: 32).

Hunter-gatherers, like the Khoikhoi and San, were particularly strongly associated with nomadic and unproductive movement and, as a result, the mention of any ethnic group indigenous to South Africa eventually came to conjure up images of aimless mobility. Dr. Hector Gavin, a representative of the Health of Towns Association, a group of "philanthropic noblemen and gentlemen," reported that because of the inability of the paterfamilias to commit to a single employment and a settled residence, the houses of the poor "had none of the conveniences of civilized life—no more than are to be found in the earth-holes or kralls of the Caffres" ([1847] 1985: 27). The *Eclectic Review* warned its readers about "the existence of a large class, in our metropolis, more degraded than the savages of New Zealand or the blacks of the Great Karroo" (Jerrold 1851: 424).

Henry Mayhew opened Volume I of *London Labour and the London Poor: A Cyclopaedia of the Condition and Earnings of Those that Will Work, Those that Cannot Work, and Those that Will Not Work* with a lengthy disposition on the intermittently employed "London Street Folk." In order to provide a framework for understanding the deliberately nonproductive yet physically mobile—in other words, able-bodied—person, Mayhew turned to the ethnographic literature about the nomadic peoples of Southern Africa. Mayhew opened his treatise with the observation: "Of the thousand millions of human beings that are said to constitute the population of the entire globe, there are—socially, morally, and physically considered—but two distinct and broadly marked races, viz., the wanderers and the settlers—the vagabond and the citizen—the nomadic and the civilized tribes" ([1851] 1968: 1). Mayhew then turned to the specific example of South Africa, and the work of the ethnologist Dr. Andrew Smith, to illustrate the universality of the existence of vagrants and vagabonds who live in a parasitic relationship to the productive members of society:

> According to Dr. Andrew Smith, who has recently made extensive observations in South Africa, almost every tribe of people who have submitted themselves to social laws, recognizing the rights of property and reciprocal social duties, and thus acquiring wealth and forming themselves into a respectable caste, are surrounded by hordes of vagabonds and outcasts from their own community. Such are the Bushmen and *Sonquas* of the Hottentot race—the term "*sonqua*" literally meaning *pauper.* But a similar condition in society produces similar results in regard to other races; and the Kaffirs have their Bush-

men as well as the Hottentots—these are called *Fingoes*—a word signifying wanderers, beggars, or outcasts. (Mayhew [1851] 1968: 1)

The Colonial Origins of the Nomad Stereotype

The frequency with which South Africans, particularly Khoikhoi and San, were invoked in analyses of the able-bodied poor in England is neither coincidental nor accidental. Rather, it reflects the degree to which the labor disputes that occurred with increasing frequency between British emigrants at the Cape and indigenous peoples were influencing domestic social debates. English people were continually made aware of the strife between emigrants and Africans at the Cape. These reports came to them via a number of different media, including lectures, particularly those delivered on a tour undertaken by John Philip to agitate against settler mistreatment of the Khoikhoi (Ross 1986), and the copious advice literature on emigration (Lester 2001). The most fruitful source, however, was English newspaper reports (which frequently excerpted letters and stories directly from Cape newspapers) about events at the Cape, particularly the agitation over the proposed Cape Vagrancy Ordinance of 1834. The latter was a particularly rich source of images and ideology. Settler descriptions of the Khoikhoi in the context of this debate presented the Khoikhoi and San as a "wandering people" by virtue of their unique ethnological makeup while pointing to the many similarities that could potentially be drawn between the "wandering Hottentot" and the English able-bodied pauper.

In the 1830s, two full decades before these comparisons would make their way into mainstream metropolitan discourses about domestic poverty, colonial newspapers and ideologues were already drawing comparisons between indigenous people and the English poor. Indeed, it was perhaps in the Cape Colony, in the context of the dispute over the 1834 Cape Vagrancy Ordinance, that the battle over the applicability of these comparisons was first fought. The proposed vagrancy ordinance was initiated by English settlers who relied heavily on African labor and was intended to control the movements of Khoikhoi servants and freed slaves. Its practical effect was to outlaw traditional means of obtaining economic subsistence. By dint of the ordinance, any person caught engaged in self-provisioning would be subject to arrest and imprisonment, then would most likely be "apprenticed" to a suitable master. The ordinance would also have reintroduced passes and provided for the arrest of any person as a vagrant who could not account for a means of subsistence over the previous three days.

When the colonial bourgeoisie in the Cape pushed for vagrancy legislation, they did so by invoking images of profligate, dissolute, and feckless workers who were reminiscent of British paupers. It is not accidental that indigenous people were frequently labeled with the epithet *vagrant*. In the English lexicon, according to one historian, "vagrants were regarded by both central and local authorities as the lowest of the un-deserving poor, close to the criminal classes, and carrying disease" (Wood 1991: 117). Hence, an editorial in the May 20, 1834, edition of the *Zuid Afrikaan* complained of the "many idle and dissolute Hottentots who overrun the districts and who are notorious thieves and vagrants." The paper printed editorials in its May 16 and June 19 editions the same year that proclaimed that "vagrancy seems to be an instinctive disposition in the native tribes of this colony." The paper followed those with a letter from "A Farmer" in its October 10 edition that railed against the Khoikhoi as "vagrants who live upon game" and an editorial that suggested vagrancy was "an instinctive disposition in the native tribes of this Colony."

It is important to note that the veracity of these comparisons was not axiomatic. Indeed, what we witness in the battle over the 1834 Vagrancy Ordinance is a conflict not only between supporters and opponents of the ordinance, but also an ideological struggle over whether and on what terms metropolitan poverty discourses, imagery, and policy initiatives would be applied in the colonial context. The New Poor Law of 1834, which was founded on the assumption that poor people preferred indolence to work and thus should be denied any form of charity or welfare outside the workhouse, was a lightening rod in Cape colonial debates. This is so for two reasons; first, the temporal proximity of the passage of the two ordinances, and second, the centrality held by discussions of worker mobility and its impact on capital accumulation in both cases. There was much disagreement between English and Dutch settlers, who largely supported the ordinance. and Africans and evangelicals, who largely opposed it. over the comparability of the two situations and, thus, by implication, the comparability of English vagrants and African peoples.

On one side of the debate stood ideologues like "An Englishman," who wrote a two-page editorial in the *Zuid Afrikaan* of May 30, 1834, that elaborately defended the Cape Vagrancy ordinance by pointing to the example afforded by the English experience.

> What we have within our reach is the actual state of the law in England as respects vagrants, dissolute characters, and labourers. England is uniformly held up, and justly, as that country of Europe where the true principles of liberty are best understood. We cannot suppose ourselves very wrong in any proposal

which shall tend to assimilate our state of society with that of our parent country, a country we know to have the most accurate views of the social system, and from whose code the reformed nations of Europe have largely drawn, in the various ameliorations they have adopted. . . . It cannot be otherwise than praiseworthy to attempt to bring our population to similar habits of industry by similar habits of control.

A writer for the *Zuid Afrikaan* of September 19, 1834, reported with much satisfaction that the Poor Law Amendment Bill of 1834 had passed by a majority of 187 to 50 in the House of Commons. "This we trust will tend in some measure to quiet the warm advocates of licentious liberty in this Colony, as we are of opinion that if the representatives of the people in England consider such a Law beneficial, an energetic Law against Vagrancy in this extensive Colony, where labourers are *wanted* is indispensable."

On the other side of the debate stood Khoikhoi people themselves and a few sympathetic missionaries who disputed both the settlers' interpretations of the English Poor Law and, by implication, the veracity of drawing comparisons between English paupers and African peasants. Hendrik Heyn, a wagon driver, said he believed the law was designed "solely to oppress the Hottentots." He also questioned the legitimacy of applying English poor relief practices in the Cape. "It is stated in the papers they have such a law in England" he explained. "But there the people there are born under the Law and brought up, they all know the laws and how to defend themselves. They have friends there in England to plead their case and because they are all the same colour, they have an attachment to each other. Here it is not so. There is no sympathy for us and we have no friends to come up for us" (*South African Commercial Advertiser*, September 6, 1834). James Read, whose parents were a famous London Missionary Society missionary and a slave who had married despite the London society's fierce opposition, agreed with Heyn: "The Law which may be good in England . . . would never do to be trusted in the hands of the Colonists, who are not only prejudiced against people of color, but also expect to benefit by such laws" (*South African Commercial Advertiser*, September 3, 1834). Converts and the missionaries who allied with them stridently challenged the settlers' interpretation of English poor laws, dismissing their justifications as "a total misapprehension of the state of the Law in England" (*South African Commercial Advertiser*, June 26, 1834). "The peculiarities of the Colony and the habits of the Aboriginals render *European Ideas of Vagrancy* inapplicable to this Colony. We have the example of England to show that Poor Laws and Vagrant Laws have accelerated the evils they were intended to remedy and have induced improvidence among the poor and entailed enormous taxation on the community" a writer for the *South African Commercial Advertiser* of October 1, 1834, opined.

Thus, the 1830s witnessed a vigorous debate within the colony over the use and misuse of metropolitan/colonial comparisons. Ultimately the defenders of the ordinance were unsuccessful in their bid to pass the law. However, they were quite successful ideologically in that the debates concretized and lent validity to the practice of drawing comparisons between Khoikhoi people and English paupers. Such was their impact that two decades later, in the 1850s, these comparisons were accepted as a matter of course in discussions about the English poor. The debates played no small part, I believe, in Henry Mayhew's being able to write at mid-century that the "moral characteristics" of "nomad races of other countries" should be used as "a means of comprehending more readily those of the vagabonds and outcasts of our own" ([1851] 1968: 2).

Of course, tremendously horrible things had been said and written about the English poor for centuries. In the debates over the New Poor Law of 1834, for example, poor people were frequently portrayed as both dangerous and subhuman. Thomas Walker, for example, described them as "an overstock of sorry, ill trained animals . . . who are continually invading private property and committing crimes" (1831: 19). The highly critical *Report from His Majesty's Commissioners for Inquiring into the Administration and Practical Operation of the Poor Laws* concluded that the poor were "a set of fierce and reckless desperadoes: a band of savages, in the midst of civilized community" (Parliament of Great Britain 1834: 114). Direct comparisons between poor people in England and the indigenous people of South Africa, however, became far more ubiquitous in the 1850s and later.

Nomadic Male Bodies against the Social Body

Within the context of discussions about primitive accumulation and the transition to capitalist social relations, female bodies were literal and figurative extensions and manifestations of the system of productive relations. They were popularly viewed as being in a state of negative metamorphosis over time due to the fact that the social body was, itself, in a negative state—that is, it was not making the transition to capitalism fast enough. Thus, popular ideology held it that a homology existed between the individual female body and the larger social organism—a healthy female body represented a healthy social organism.

Within the context of popular discourses about control over the mobility of labor, which at heart were discussions about control over the labor process as a means of increasing surplus in production, we see a decisive discursive shift. In these texts, the social and economic significance of the body was reconfigured and reconceptualized: healthy male bodies were depicted as being in opposition to the social organism. Vigorous—that is, able-bodied and mobile—male bodies were viewed as eventually generating a feeble social organism or social body. The opinions John Edward Morgan expressed in his treatise *The Danger of Deterioration of Race from the Rapid Increase of Great Cities* were typical. Although Morgan acknowledged the important role migratory laborers had played so far in increasing the stock of national wealth, he nonetheless worried that the ultimate impact of these nomadic bodies might be to destroy the social body.

> The desire of raising themselves in the world keeps constantly urging vast numbers of the dwellers in rural districts to emigrate to the nearest town. . . . To this cause more than to any other, is to be attributed that extraordinary development of every branch of our manufacturing industry, which induces even the most distant nations to look to this country as the greatest. . . . Yet at the same time arises a momentous question, "May not nations, like individuals, curtail their day of power in the world's history, by overtaxing the physical and mental energies at their disposal, thus prematurely consuming the national life blood on which permanent greatness mainly depends?" This is among the many important subjects connected with this wide-spread migratory tendency. (1866: 3–4)

When able-bodied male workers without employment—vagrants—were depicted in popular poverty discourses, they were generally portrayed not only as savages, but as savages who were continually preying upon the social body by sucking its productive members dry. For example, Mayhew claimed that not only could all races or peoples be divided into wanderers and settlers, but "each civilized or settled tribe has generally some wandering horde intermingled with, and in a measure preying upon it." He went on to note that the productive members of English society were "surrounded by wandering hordes—the 'Sonquas' and the 'fingoes' of this country—paupers, beggars, and outcasts, possessing nothing but what they acquire by depredation from the industrious, provident, and civilized portion of the community" ([1851] 1968: 1). The vagrant populations were seen as "preying upon" the productive in a number of different ways. They were guilty of collecting welfare and aid and thus draining the productive classes of their tax dollars. They were guilty of committing crimes against property and thus carrying off the wealth produced by others. By virtue of being unemployed or unemployable, noncontributors to the workforce of society, they negated the collective power of the social body to produce wealth. According to these texts, society, imagined as a social body, was menaced by overly physical individual bodies that continually deprived it of its sustenance.

All of the above complaints associated with urban nomads ultimately concern control over the mobility of the laborer. As O'Brien explains, the main concern of most poverty legislation was "the restriction of the mobility of the poor. The new puritan ideology of work for the poor and thrift for the rich could not be imposed effectively if labourers could up and leave as the mood took them. The 'freedom' of the wage labourer had to be gutted of any real content beyond its merely ideological form" (2000: 22). What these texts effectively did, with their rhetorical linking of nomads at home and in the colonies, was to remove any discussion of poverty from discourses about poor people. In these texts vagabonds were nomadic simply because it was their nature to be so—just like the hunters and herders of the veld. In neither case did the ideologues who wrote these texts allow for the fact that changes in landownership, prices, and labor markets had an impact on the behavior of workers. In the words of economic historian Bryan Green, "textual reality repressively displaced situated reality as its authentic truth" (1983: 108).

It was never the case that the situated reality of the English poor or of the African people to whom they were so consistently compared was unknown. Rather, poor people were deliberately denied "a knowing and knowable self, a place within the privileged space of the text" (Sherman 2001: 2). The images of the Khoikhoi that traveled across the sea and made it into popular representations of the English poor, for example, were descriptions and analyses of their "natural propensities to lead a wandering life." What failed to make it to England, however, were the structural reasons behind their nomadism—the rational calculation and circumstantial forces pushing and pulling them to undertake certain behaviors and courses of action. This was in spite of the Khoikhois' frequent reiterations of the fact that their behaviors were the result of careful cost-benefit analyses.

The Economics of Mobility: Capital Accumulation at the Cape

Although the settlers attributed the labor shortage to the innate indolence of the South African aborigine, the Khoikhoi were quite outspoken about their abhorrence of the dismal working conditions that prevailed on the farms and their intense desire to avoid them. Esau Prins, a Kat River Mission resident, complained that working for the settlers meant "hard treatment and bad pay. The most we got was six ewes a year and even now many only get 6d per day. What can we make of six ewes? Or the 6d per day, can we buy clothes with them or a spade? Let the Boer hire the settler for that or the settler hire the Boer and let him see what he will make of it." Sliager Zwartbooi from Theopolis mission agreed that he, too, had "wrought for that sum"; as a result, despite his many years of hard toil he was still "very poor." Andries Stoffels likewise complained about having been in the service of a farmer and being obliged to leave 130 sheep and cattle, which the farmer subsequently refused to return. The cruelty of the settlers persisted despite the fact that "the Boers and settlers have abundance of land and the Hottentots not" (*South African Commercial Advertiser*, October 15, 1834).

Carol Laurance, a former sergeant in the Hottentot Corps who "served his King 24 years and was never absent" complained that the English settlers refused to pay their laborers cash wages.

> With regard to wages, there is only one gentleman—Mr. Norden—but all the others that I have worked for have only given me a 6d or a 1s per day, and that was in goods, at a dear price. After working hard all day, and asking my wages, they would answer me "have I no time?" or "Can I not wait?" And when I would again come, they would ask me if I could not take a soopje [alcohol], or tobacco. If I refused they would ask me what I would make of the money. I had to take goods, otherwise I would have to wait long, and in many cases get nothing. (*South African Commercial Advertiser*, September 6, 1834)

At the March 20, 1834, ceremony marking the second anniversary of the Kat River Temperance Society, several participants reported having been given alcohol in lieu of wages. Piet Bruintjes, for example, explained that the English had "taken advantage of his unhappy state" and "fed and paid him in brandy" (*South African Commercial Advertiser*, April 10, 1834). Daniel Klein Hans, a Philipston resident, told a similar tale. "If we hire ourselves we can get at the most 9d. per day, perhaps only 6d. which cannot clothe us. If I buy victuals it is only for my children and I must look on. . . . I am frequently only offered a glass of liquor for my days wages" (*South African Commercial Advertiser*, September 6, 1834).

For a variety of well-articulated reasons, ranging from employer capriciousness and duplicity to the withholding of wages, the Khoikhoi considered mobility both desirable and necessary for survival. When images of the Khoikhoi were employed in metropolitan poverty discourses, however, their voices and claims to subjectivity were actively repressed in favor of an empty, text-mediated "reality" that denied the extent to which capital accumulation by the eastern Cape settlers, which financed much of the economic development of the region, depended upon their exploitation of Khoikhoi laborers.

The growth of the Cape's woolen industry was a response to the creation of a market for colonial wool in Britain. In the 1840s, just as the amount of domestically produced wool began to decline in Britain, the country's woolen manufacturing industry began a period of expansion that lasted for forty years, significantly enhanced by increased investment in mechanization. During this time the consumption of raw wool more than doubled, and the textile and clothing industries began to rely on imports to make up the shortfall. Cape wool exporters soon secured a place in the British market. Indeed, according to Tony Kirk "the welfare of the industry depended heavily on the British market" (1980: 229). The export of wool brought a great deal of wealth into the colony, with figures steadily increasing every year. In 1830, 45,000 pounds of wool valued at £222 were shipped from the eastern districts. By 1835 the numbers had increased to 79,848 pounds valued at £4,261 (Le Cordeur 1981: 37). One decade later the amount exported had risen to 3,195,000 pounds, and total sales amounted to £175,000. By 1851, 5,447,000 pounds were exported at a cost of £286,000 (Kirk 1980: 230). In the decades after 1840 wealthy immigrants began arriving from far-flung corners of the British Empire with funds to invest in sheep farms, thus introducing a new source of capital investment. The woolen industry soon created immense economic spin-off effects as mortgages on frontier farms and estates began to generate income for investors based in Cape Town.

None of this would have been remotely possible without the exploited labor of the Khoikhoi. The profitability of the woolen industry depended upon improving the productivity of labor so as to create value in production. Improving the productivity of labor meant that worker mobility had to be controlled. The degree to which the power to extract surplus labor and the capacity to organize and intensify production had to be united is clearly demonstrated in the following quote from the editor of the *Grahamstown Journal*, the mouthpiece for the business classes of the colony.

> One of the most pressing wants of the colony is that of a better description of labour. All the operations of the field have hitherto been conducted by coloured labourers, but these are found to be quite inadequate to carry out the improvements of the country. Many of them are too independent to engage in service, and others are too indolent to submit to continuous employment. . . . For want of this, capital is often frittered away in unavailing endeavours. (Godlonton 1842: 110)

Despite the close interpenetration of the English and Cape woolen industries—and the intertwined fates of the English textile workers who spun the wool and the Khoikhoi laborers who sheared and bundled it—few facts about the realities of capital accumulation at home or in the colonies made it into popular analyses of English poverty.

Production, Population, and the Paterfamilias

The subjectivity of the English poor was subjected to similar sorts of rewriting in popular analyses as that of the Khoikhoi. Mainstream economic analyses repeatedly failed to register the degree to which the reorganization of landholding to promote the production of wool and foodstuffs for urban centers contributed to the impoverishment of the working classes. The intensified protection of private property that accompanied this shift in landholding promoted individual interests against those of the larger community. The transition to machine spinning also concentrated the production of textiles within specific regions. In an industry formerly characterized by its universality, this change spelled distress for a large majority of workers. Reliance on a steady stream of money income so they could live from week to week made poor people quite vulnerable. Rising food prices, which were rarely discussed in popular texts, played a key role in creating poverty. In most positivist analyses of poverty these structural explanations were effectively marginalized.

The ways in which the authors of these texts used representational techniques to reconstitute the reality of the African played a profound role in their textual reconstitution of the reality of the English pauper. According to Green, the vagrant played a special role in the overall process whereby textual reality came to displace situated reality: "The figure of the vagrant is especially revealing in connection with our claim that textual-documentary rationality must methodically negate the essential features of situated experience. He symbolizes in pure form its open, fluid, indeterminate, ad hoc features, the negation of which constitutes objective knowledge of the social in writing. The play of legislative and investigative words around this figure provides us with a figurative confirmation of the negation principle" (1983: 150). Although Green himself does not make this connection, I believe that the situation he describes can be at least partially attributed to the ways in which colonial metaphors and imagery were deployed with respect to vagrants. When the behavior of the vagrant became explicable in terms of the "inherent nomadic tendencies" of the Khoikhoi, a whole host of facts relating to the situated reality of both were made invisible. Specifically, these images encouraged and rationalized a cognitive separation between the behavior of the individual and the economic system of which he was a part.

Control over the laborer and its impact on capital accumulation is the subtext to most discussions of vagrancy. If we take the textile industry, for example, it is obvious that making it in the industry required an enormous outlay of capital. The factory baron Richard Akwright, for instance, spent £12,000 between 1769 and 1774 before he made any profit. By 1782 his expenditures were as high as £30,000. Because of the high expense of these kinds of ventures, "the factory owner absolutely depended upon cheap labor" (Valenze 1995: 89). Samuel Courtland, for example, ran a textile company whose average level of profit increased 1,400 percent between 1830 and 1880. During the same period wages rose only 50 percent (Lavalette 1999).

The vagrant was so despised because factory owners viewed high degrees of mobility as unacceptably augmenting poor people's capacity to seek economic advantage. Nomadic movement on the part of the laborer crucially curtailed the ability of appropriators to create value in production because it limited the ability of the factory owner to organize production in such a way as to secure the forfeit of surplus labor that was a necessary condition of that production. Hence, the concept that was most frequently articulated in connection with and analytically associated with the vagrant is irregularity. Edwin Chadwick wrote of the "habits of savage brutality and irregularity of life amongst the labouring population" (1843: 45). Hector Gavin quoted the relieving officer of Dover as having stated that "habitual paupers [were] brought up to no regular employment, grossly ignorant and reckless, their time spent between the union-workhouse and the gaol" (1851: 70). John Garwood agreed that able-bodied paupers were "strangely-organized, or rather disorganized, members of society; who, though they might abhor the cannibal for eating a human being, yet have no objection themselves to prey upon their fellow creatures" ([1853] 1985: 18). In these texts irregularity meant a variety of things—lack of a fixed address, discontinuous employment, irregular hours, or simply a lack of personal discipline. In one way or another, however, all of these characteristics resulted in a revolt against supervision of the labor process and a defiant stance against the appropriators' efforts to exert control over that process.

Industrialists were keen to make sure that the poor would work at whatever rates of pay were offered, which meant that they would have no alternative but to combine seasonal employment with various forms of poor relief. For this reason Malthusian analyses, which made surplus population the basic cause of poverty, were often articulated in tandem with images of savage, nomadic, and socially dangerous male bodies. This danger, according to Malthus, was the monstrous outgrowth of the poor laws, which gave able-bodied men a legal right to claim relief. Thus, in the *Essay on the Principle of Population* (1806), male sexuality took center stage. According to Malthus, since poverty was the result of surplus population, the condition of paupers could not be improved until men were made morally responsible for limiting population growth by delaying marriage. "The poor man who brought into the world more children than he could support was increasingly deprecated as having failed to practice the virtues of prudence and foresight" (Cowherd 1977: 59). Thus, these savage nomadic male bodies further threatened the social body by engaging in indiscriminate sexual liaisons.

Closely related to this argument was the idea that poverty was caused by the refusal of the paterfamilias to maintain regular and stable employment, a refusal that endangered both the health of his own family and the ultimate health of the social body. The concomitant of the image of the nomadic male laborer was thus that of the degraded working wife. Hector Gavin quoted the Reverend Mr. Darwell, curate of St. James, Dover, who claimed that a working mother was inimical to a "well ordered family" and that when a woman worked a man was less likely to "remain in his house." Thus "his wife and family are left to seek relief under such circumstances as they may. The domestic bond is loosened if not severed. He ceases to regard his family and they cease to respect him, and so a generation of reckless and unprincipled persons is by these means turned out upon society" (1851: 69). John Morgan, who likened the weakening of the social body to the "deterioration of race," also saw the employment of married women as dangerous. He argued that such employment led directly to the problem of surplus population, for "under such circumstances, by a well-established physiological law, the births will frequently succeed each other with unnatural rapidity." He thus concluded that to preserve the health of the social body, "the employment of married women, more particularly when they are the mothers of young children, should in every way be discouraged" (1866: 36, 49).

The purpose of these narratives of nomadic male bodies and their fecund female counterparts is to make it seem as though these bodies were the cause of poverty and social dislocation because they refused to submit to regular and stable employment and acknowledge the "natural" gender division of labor. By dint of this logic, then, poverty could be alleviated through the removal of "artificial supports" (welfare and charity) that allowed these unnatural gender arrangements to survive and persist. According to Gavin, poor relief was the "origin of the dissolution of family life and all the miseries that follow." The unnatural gender relations within the household caused "the father to avoid his uninhabitable home and seek in the public-house an asylum from the horror with which it inspires him. The wife perhaps remains alone with her children, though even she is tempted often to fly and abandon them to the care of each other, or of some charitable neighbor" (1851: 72).

In actuality, of course, the gendered allocation of tasks within poor households was purposefully designed to ensure economic survival without a complete surrender to the dictates of the appropriating classes. As Deborah Valenze explains, "women's work obviously offered a true boon to the economic well-being of the laboring family. . . . The single male wage-earner, far from embodying a 'breadwinner' ideal, represented a threat to the well-being of the laboring family" (1995: 17). Seasonal male workers such as bricklayers, masons, and navvies suffered from extended periods of unemployment. Many other men held jobs that were poorly paid and could end at any time. Women's work thus provided crucial support for families, and gender roles were flexible, varying immensely according to the dictates of survival. According to Peter Kriedte, Hans Medick, and Jürgen Schlumbohm,

> The struggle for subsistence at times necessitated a maximum of familial co-operation and could go so far as to erase the traditional division of labour between the sexes and the age groups. . . . Occasionally, this adaptation of the organization of familial work to the conditions of survival went even further. It could lead to the reversal of traditional roles: where the necessities of production compelled women to neglect household "duties," this "loss of function" could be compensated by the men's assuming traditional women's roles. . . . The division of labour within the household showed no uniformity. (1981: 62)

Women not only supplemented the family income through waged work, but also played a critical role in articulating and exercising those customary rights that enabled the poor to avoid relying entirely on wage labor. Women often operated as "entrepreneurs, negotiating with overseers for services and supplements" (Sherman 2001: 7). According to Valenze "women figured prominently as applicants for parish relief" and "poor law overseers saw the claims of a great many women as legitimate" (1995: 19). Thus, the control exercised by the capitalist over production and appropriation was partially constrained by the varied activities of women. The power relationships between classes that conditioned the nature and extent of exploitation were significantly inflected by women's economic agency, which was an important determinant of the balance of class forces.

Because gendered forms of labor allocation are partially constitutive of productive relations, critical attitudes toward gender relations in poor households can be seen as a key component of class struggle on the part of the wealthy against the poor. Thus the gendered configuration of work is a political question: the power relationship that conditioned the extent to which capitalists were able to gain control over the labor process was significantly affected by gender relations within poor households. The internal organization of the contending classes, which played an important role in determining their relative strengths and weaknesses as they entered into struggle, was strongly determined by the gendered division of labor in the poor household. Thus, whether the struggle would result in capitalists gaining complete control over the lives of laborers, and thus the labor process itself, or old forms would be able to survive and persist was critically influenced by that division of labor.

The concerted ideological push to demonize poor households for their "unnatural" gender organization can thus be understood as a means whereby the wealthy sought to introduce new forms of political power into the production process while claiming to be removing any political influence from the economy by allowing natural laws to do their work. These new forms of political power worked to displace older, more paternalistic ones that both cost the wealthy more in taxes and did not operate solely on the behalf of the interests of capital. By deploying a specific set of images these allegedly positivist texts provided critical ideological support for maneuvers on the part of the propertied classes to delegitimize public support for the poor despite long-term growth in national wealth. These texts also helped to rationalize the diversion of societal resources toward war and private investment in a time of increasing economic immiseration. In using the image of the nomadic and savage independent laborer as a crucial support for Malthusian analyses of society, the authors of these texts also implicitly supported the idea that social improvement was largely dependent upon a society's ability to accumulate capital faster than the growth of population. The concomitant of this view was that the only hope for social improvement lay in allowing the appropriating classes the freedom to determine their own rate of saving and investment since greater freedom for capital investment was necessary to supply employment for a "redundant" population. The only appropriate role for the government was to prevent the "invasion" of private property on the part of savage paupers and their profligate progeny. The ultimate impact of these discourses was to use ideological assertions about gender and the family to claim that the economy was dictated by natural laws while actively striving to make the introduction of a particular form of political power into the production process itself a basic condition of production.

The Rewriting of Blackness and the
Making of Working-Class Subjectivity

The fact that the poor were being horribly exploited was not lost on their defenders, who seized upon an entirely different set of racialized images and metaphors to challenge prevailing analyses of the economic system. In this way they sought to displace one central coterie of images that was associated with a particular subset of black bodies with another more suitable to the type of economic analysis they were striving to put forward. Even a cursory glance through radical newspapers and leaflets reveals the extent to which working-class radicals sought to alter the image of the metropolitan poor by replacing the nomadic body of the South African aborigine with the enslaved body of the African in America. *Bronterre's National Reformer,* an unstamped paper devoted to the cause of "promoting radical reformation in GOVERNMENT, LAW, PROPERTY, AND MORALS," asserted that the "working classes are in a state of slavery" (January 7, 1837: 8). A writer for the *Northern Star* of November 3, 1849, opined, "Working men are the slaves of intense competition, which, by its grinding tyranny, goads them ever and anon into that *civilized* state of insurrection, known by the name of *strikes*" (emphasis in original). A letter to the editor of the *Nonconformist* complained that fear of being sent to the workhouse caused the average laborer to "cringe before his master as an abject slave" (May 26, 1841). At a public meeting in support of Sadler's ten-hours bill, workers carried signs proclaiming "No White Slavery," "Am I a Man and a Brother," and "Abolish Slavery at Home and Abroad" (Lorimer 1978). *Reynolds' Newspaper,* a radical weekly with a large circulation, argued that "the workers in factories are as much slaves to the money-power as the negroes are to the lash and the law" (April 10, 1853).

Black male bodies were the cornerstone of English debates about the cultural status of labor. Radicalized members of the working classes asserted their own subjectivity through an alternate set of racial images that stressed the degree to which black bodies, rather than being nomadic and unproductive, were actually both productive and victims of superexploitation. English radicals argued that "the slavery of labour in the aggregate, to capital, is almost as prolific of human misery as the bondage of the negro. The money despotism of England is as unscrupulous, as inexorably selfish, and as utterly heedless of the death and desolation it creates, as the bloodhounds who subjugate and murder blacks" (*Star of Freedom,* September 24, 1852). They were not only making a statement about how badly treated English workers were, but were also launching a critique of the ways in which capitalist ideology conceptualized work and productivity.

In much of the mainstream economic discourse capitalists, not workers, were depicted as being productive. In other words, productive work was identified with the economic activity of the capitalist rather than that of the laborer. According to Wood, this habit of conceptual conflation is a staple of economic discourse in Western capitalist societies and has served as a "cornerstone in the ideological justification of capitalism" (1995: 157). On the other side of the debate, by deploying images and rhetoric like that used by Richard Oastler in his letter to the *Leeds Mercury* titled "Yorkshire Slavery," which argued that workers there were "existing in a state of slavery more horrid than are the victims of that hellish system colonial slavery," radicals sought to dramatize a number of similarities between those two systems (Grant 1866: 19). The analogy stressed the cruelty of factory owners, the inhumanity of wage labor, and the degree to which English workers were being exploited.

By drawing this analogy, radicals were able to highlight the degree to which the appropriating classes in both systems sought to treat the appropriation of labor as the equivalent of the performance of labor itself. Popular opinion (at least in antislavery circles) recognized the injustice of a system wherein slave owners denigrated and demeaned the character of the slave so as to displace the virtues of labor and industry from the activity of laboring black body to that of the employer of that labor. It was not nearly as well recognized that this conceptual conflation also characterized relationships between capitalists and workers. By drawing comparisons between their situation and that of chattel slaves, working-class activists were able to use black bodies as a means of highlighting the inequity of a system that allowed the activity of labor and its attendant virtues to become attributes of the employer or master.

Working-class radicals' attempt to reshape the meanings behind the cultural status of labor coexisted, however, with their strong impulse to denigrate black people. Members of the poor and laboring classes, no less than the propertied and literate, were deeply affected by the racism that was an ordinary part of English society. In the course of completing *London Labour and the London Poor*, which was eventually published in 1851, Henry Mayhew interviewed a twenty-eight-year-old beggar who had been plying his trade since the age of fourteen. The mendicant informed Mayhew that his lowest moment had come when he had to enter a low lodging house and "sleep with a black man." Completely disgusted, he said, he "slept on the floor to get away from the fellow." Mayhew went on to describe the abuse one young black boy had to endure upon entering a room filled with what Mayhew took to be "the lowest class of male juvenile thieves and vagabonds." Despite their low position in society, the assembled did not hesitate to greet the boy with "a hundred fifty cat-calls of the shrillest possible description" and "peals of laughter" (Mayhew 1981: 90, 101).

The preferred leisure activities of working-class people clearly indicate that Africans and blacks were rarely, if ever, positively represented. As the historian Douglas Lorimer explains, attitudes toward Africa and blacks were profoundly shaped by portrayals of blacks in popular literature and on England's theatrical stage, which turned the Negro into a "figure of fun" (1975: 32). Indeed, the most depressed members of the working class—the costermongers whom Mayhew derided as the "Sonquas of England" and the residents of the slum areas said to house the "nomads" and "Hottentots" of England—were the ones who most enjoyed these racist portrayals of African people. According to Douglas Jerrold, performances of "Nigger songs," were a favored form of amusement for the costermongers (1851: 426). In 1867, the *Illustrated London News* reported that the inmates of the Bethnal Green Workhouse had enjoyed an evening of minstrel songs and entertainment from the "Old South." James Greenwood described spending an evening at a pub in Whitechapel, a notorious slum area, where he witnessed the following:

> The performance was commenced by a black man, a brawny ruffian, naked to the waist, and with broad rings of red round his ankles and wrists, illustrative, as presently appeared, of his suffering from the chafing of the manacles he had worn in a state of slavery. . . . After a minute of uproar and cursing and swearing and yelling laughter, the black man scrambled on the stage again with a good deal of the blacking rubbed off his face, and with his wool wig in his hand, exposing his proper short crop of carroty hair. . . . He readjusted his wig and became once more an afflicted African bewailing how "Cruel massa stole him wife and lil' picaninny." ([1874] 1985: 14)

These racist attitudes were further entrenched by the actions of working-class radicals who, although they sought to use the image of the black body as part of their efforts to rehabilitate the cultural status of labor, nevertheless were unwilling to construct "the worker" as anything but white and male. The cleaving of racial identities and interests in the pursuit of class action can be identified in the rhetoric of Chartism, in the campaigns for a ten-hours bill, and in the struggles for factory reform. A reporter for the *Morning Chronicle* of November 5, 1849, for example, reported having heard from a "Ten Hours Bill" man that enjoying "Nigger songs" and dancing girls were the favored leisure-time activities of his compatriots. The popularity of minstrelsy among the rank and file of the working class is also demonstrated in the cultural symbols employed by factory operatives in Preston, one of the principal seats of cotton manufacturing in Lancashire, who were striking for a 10 percent increase in wages. Recognizing that "the masses can only be swayed through the feelings, and these can only be roused by large and well defined symbols," one of the leaders of the strike hit upon the idea of using popular songs to lift the strikers' sagging spirits (Ashworth 1854: 31). Thus, at one of the strikers' meetings "Luke Wood, of Stockport, gave out a verse of a 'ten per cent song,' which was sung by the audience to the nigger melody of 'Uncle Ned.'" The verse went as follows:

> So we've thrown away reed, hook, and comb,
>> And hung up the shuttles on the loom;
> And we'll never be content, till we get the "ten per cent,"
>> In spite of the "let well alone."

Ultimately, radicals failed to destroy one of the cornerstones in the ideological justification of capitalism: that the appropriation of another person's labor can be treated as equivalent to the performance of the activity of labor. Indeed, this conceptual conflation still occurs today as much as, if not more than, it did in the nineteenth century. "In the conventional discourse of modern economics . . . it is the capitalists, not workers, who *produce*" (Wood 1995: 156, emphasis in original). One reason for the radicals' failure can be located, I believe, in their use of the laboring black body, and the cultural symbols and inventions associated therewith, to redeem the cultural status of labor without any attempt to redeem black people, to raise the status of the laboring black body, or to make the acceptance of racial equity part of the development of class consciousness. The desire to reverse the process whereby the virtues of labor and industry were taken from producers and bestowed upon appropriators without allowing for the cultural construction of black bodies—the very bodies most victimized by this conceptual displacement—as having virtues equivalent to those of white bodies ultimately undermined their whole ideological enterprise.

Because of slavery and colonialism, black bodies were intimately associated with laboring bodies. Indeed, popular attitudes toward blackness and popular attitudes toward labor often existed in a symbiotic relationship. In some ways, one's attitude toward labor *was* one's attitude toward blackness, and vice versa. According to Lorimer, in the popular British imagination "blacks became identified with the laboring tasks" (Lorimer 1978: 92). In a cultural milieu such as this, it really wasn't possible to rehabilitate the cultural status of labor without rehabilitating the cultural status of blackness.

Yet this was something that working-class people and their radical allies were unwilling to do. Because they chose to adopt the same negative attitude toward African people that the ruling class did, working-class radicals were ultimately unable to overturn the conceptual apparatus that played such a critical role in ideologically justifying capitalism. As a result, their efforts to reassert their own subjectivity and resist the flattening out of the situated reality that occurred when they were subject to the ethnographic gaze only served to reinforce and reinscribe the identification of productivity with the economic activity of the capitalist. This conceptual separation served also to further reinforce the artificial separation between the economic and the political that occurs when capitalist ideologues define "economic activity [as] market exchange and 'labour' [as] capitalist appropriation and production for profit." The corollary is a view of history whereby "the social contradiction that gives history its momentum is not between producing and appropriation classes, between exploiters and exploited, but between different kinds of appropriating classes" (Wood 1995: 158).

It is clear from the actions of Chartists and other working-class radicals that the ability to manipulate racial discourses and the social meanings attached to blackness was extremely important for advancing one's own position in the domestic political scene. In the next chapter I continue to explore how the ability to finesse racial discourse and meanings came to play a critical role in gendered struggles over care of the social body. The conception of society as a social body suggested that the reformers should formulate problems and their solutions in bodily terms. It also opened up the possibility for women to eclipse men as the primary caretakers of the social body. Thus, a struggle ensued between the sexes over how the problems that besieged the social body should be defined, and it is here that the ability to define the meaning of race came to have paramount importance.

CHAPTER FOUR

The Care of the Social Body: Gender Strife, Class Conflict, and the Changing Definitions of Race

In the previous two chapters I looked at how social thinkers represented the human body as a sign—both a metaphor and a source—of the health or infirmity of the larger social body. Here I turn to a more in-depth discussion of the concept of the social body itself. This concept of a social body, of British society as an organic whole, enabled the defenders of capitalism to further entrench the artificial conceptual separation of the economic and the political. The social body was understood to function, in many ways, like the human body; thus, reformers were called on to formulate problems and their solutions in bodily terms, to think of the management of social conflict as akin to the curing of bodies, the movement of bodies, the disciplining of bodies, and the religious and moral conversion of bodies.

Discussion of the colonies always featured prominently in any analysis that used the concept of the social body. There were two competing strains of thought in the social body discourse. Some thought that the colonies were an extension of the domestic social body and, therefore, that the care and nurturing of one translated into the care and nurturing of the other. Others believed that the domestic social body and the colonial social body stood in a relationship of opposition—that the care and nurturing of one was necessarily done at the expense of the other. This debate over whether the domestic and colonial social bodies stood in a relationship of symbiosis or strife was a profoundly gendered struggle over the meaning and domain of care. At its heart was an argument over whether the ultimate salvation of the domestic social body lay with radical working-class men engaged in class struggle on behalf of working-class women, with middle-class men wearing the mantle of science, or with middle-class women working to inculcate traditional feminine values into their poor and working-class counterparts. Racial discourses played a key role in all of these debates. The ability to manipulate racial discourses and the social meanings attached to different ideas of race determined who would have the power to define what problems threatened the social body and who would be given the authority to fix them.

The Metaphorical Use of Race in the
Making of the Idea of the Social Body

According to the economic historian Mary Poovey, during the middle decades of the nineteenth century, the British political nation was reconceived as a social body. This concept was distinctive because the social body, unlike the body politic, included the working classes—albeit as problematic elements in need of discipline and care. The impulse to represent British society as a social body "allowed social analysts to treat one segment of the population as a special problem at the same time that they could gesture toward the mutual interests that (theoretically) united all parts of the social whole. The phrase *social body* therefore promised full membership in a whole (and held out the image *of* that whole) to a part identified as needing both discipline and care" (1995: 8).

A number of urban reformers, particularly those concerned with documenting and analyzing poverty, used the concept of the social body in their work. The contradictory ends that the formulators of the concept intended it to serve were reconciled through a discourse about "race" and ideas about the improvability of subaltern populations borrowed directly from reformers in the foreign field. The concept gained particular salience and prominence in the work of individuals involved in "home missions," who were devoted to the uplift of the urban poor in the metropolis. Their publications are liberally sprinkled with words like *heathen, savage,* and *barbarism* (see Chadwick 1843: 45; *City Mission Magazine,* January 1855: 4; Hole 1866: 42; Shaw [1861] 1985: 168; Vaughan [1843] 1971: 246). Dr. John Hogg, for example, remarked that "it has been said that the lower classes of English people are not sufficiently civilized . . . that they are a barbarous and *mischievous race*" ([1837] 1985: 324, emphasis in original). Robert Pemberton, an urban reformer, agreed that English slums were teeming with "thousands of enfeebled human organisms which only are comparable with the savage" ([1854] 1985: 15). Evangelical reformers, more than any others, were responsible for making the concept of the social body come alive through the use of metaphors and images borrowed directly from travel writing and missionary tracts from the foreign field.

Discursive gestures toward empire were used to illustrate the wide gulf that divided the wealthy from the poor in Britain, to depict them as two nations with vastly different experiences, opportunities, and chances. The casting of the dichotomy between rich and poor as a question of opposing nations was quickly expanded to suggest two opposing civilizations or "races" (see Beames 1850: 37; Garwood [1853] 1985: 86; Raynard 1860: 14; Miller 1853: 190). The reformers' strategy was to invoke the concept of race in order to single out the poor as a special population in need of discipline at the same time that they made gestures regarding the necessity for their inclusion in the social body. Hector Gavin described the inhabitants of the Bethnal Green slum as exhibiting "primitive barbarism" and "complete disregard of all the characteristics of civilization." His work is typical in that these rhetorical gestures toward empire were made to simultaneously serve a social distancing and a social bridging function. His stated aim was to "lay bare the naked truth as to the state of one part of this vast city" and thus elucidate "the bearings of the sanitary question on the poor *and* on the rich" (1848: 42–43, 3).

The frequency with which the savagery and barbarism of colonized people were invoked in these narratives can be attributed to how heavily the concept of the social body was predicated on not only singling out the morality and behavior of the poor as problems, but also emphasizing that the nation as a whole (including the poor themselves) could unite around solving the problems. To invoke the former without the latter was tantamount to saying that the nation was marred by irreparable fissures and divisions. To unite around the idea that poverty was a problem that reformers could solve, however, required a firm belief in the notion that once these problems were identified, that there were, indeed, people with the capability to solve them.

Metaphors about savages and domestic heathens were critical because they served to assimilate the targets of foreign and domestic missions in the minds of many and encouraged the view that they were essentially interchangeable. That individual behavior and morality were amenable to improvement, particularly as a result of the actions of evangelical reformers, had been demonstrated with far greater efficacy in the foreign field than in the domestic. Because of the ideological merging of the two populations, missionaries who worked among the domestic poor were continually reminded of their failed overtures to the working classes. Thanks to the Religious Census of 1851, which definitively proved the irreligious nature of the urban poor, the home missionaries could do precious little to hide their failings. Statistics of church attendance demonstrated that "the urban laborers, by and large, were estranged from every religious body" (McIlhiney n.d.: 17). Even if the census had never been taken, however, missionaries to the urban poor would have been well aware of their low standing in poor communities. "The missioners call sometimes," an informant told Henry Mayhew during his 1850 survey, "but they're laughed at often" (Mayhew 1981: 99). A missionary to St. John's Parish in Westminster who attempted to bring the gospel to some men in a rooming house was disturbed to hear

> several men energetically denouncing the bishops and all ministers of the gospel as the greatest enemies of the poor. As soon as they saw me they yelled at me to go back, saying, "You are not coming here to cram the Bible down our throats and teach us to submit to religious rascals.". . . He rose and put his clenched fist near my face, to induce me to leave the house, vociferating, "Yours is a system of oppression, and the Bible supports it." (*City Mission Magazine*, February 1855: 33–34)

Dr. James Shaw likewise reported that visiting missionaries "had to proceed with the utmost caution and delicacy for fear of giving offense, as only a few, and not the whole of the people allow them to enter their houses" ([1861] 1985: 159).

Publications from the foreign field, such as *Transactions of the London Missionary Society* and the *Wesleyan Methodist Magazine*, on the other hand, were replete with testimonies from and about savages who had found salvation. The Reverend John Philip, writing in the *Wesleyan Methodist Magazine*, challenged the "calumniators of missions" to "show in any part of the world, a people more capable of being improved than the abused Hottentots of South Africa, or attempts at civilization more complete in their success" (*Wesleyan Methodist Magazine*, 1823, 129). A writer for the *Methodist Magazine* of 1824 agreed: "it is pleasing beyond expression to behold the success of our feeble efforts in the instruction of the rising generation of Hottentots. We have now the unspeakable pleasure to see them desirous of being taught the truths of Christianity" (p. 201). The Reverend Henry Calderwood also concurred: "If we examine with candour the good that has been effected in individual cases—the work done by individual missionaries—the labours pursued at the different mission stations, and within the sphere of these stations . . . besides the numbers of genuine conversions to God, we shall be constrained to rejoice that so much has been accomplished, and that, too, with comparatively small means" (1858: 96).

The defenders of home missions not only sought to assimilate the foreign and domestic recipients of missionary outreach, but also tried to emphasize the similarity between themselves and itinerants working in the foreign field. Indeed, many of the evangelicals involved in domestic reform stressed the fact that they had formerly worked abroad or were eligible to do so. The Reverend R. W. Vanderkiste, for example, left his mission in Clerkenwell to "take co-charge of an extensive missionary establishment in India" (1852: 49). The *City Mission Magazine* of October 1855 reported that one of the four missionaries assigned to the Somerstown district had been reassigned to Calcutta (p. 244). Dr. James Shaw recalled meeting a missionary in the Bath district who had given up his post in the West Indies because, "having made himself acquainted with the poor people of his district, . . . he conscientiously believed that he was more needed at home" ([1861] 1985: 177).

Reformers' enthusiasm for extending the discourses of race, refined in the colonial setting in such a way that they became applicable to domestic subaltern populations, can be understood as being motivated by the fact that these racial analogies both made the idea of a social body possible and gave a specific class of persons the social authority to care for that body. The efforts on the part of domestic reformers to collapse the practitioners and benefactors of home and domestic missions into one category can be seen as a critical step toward legitimizing the idea that British society could and should be conceptualized as a social body. This conceptual conflation of domestic and foreign mission work allowed reformers to assimilate the successes of missionaries in the foreign field and make them their own. By assimilating domestic and foreign purveyors and recipients of evangelical outreach and by emphasizing the success enjoyed by the latter, reformers were able to give further credence to the view that they had the social skills and expertise to solve the problem of poverty and, in so doing, to bring previously estranged populations together and to forge a unified society. Thus, we can surmise that their ability to effectively mobilize and shape the meaning of race played a critical role in helping middle-class reformers carve out a specific sphere of social action for themselves. This sphere, which encompassed voluntary agencies, religious organizations, improvement societies, and other such entities, came to be called civil society.

The widespread acceptance of the social-body metaphor further entrenched the cognitive separation of the economic, the political, and the social/civic spheres because of the way the framers of the discourse, in their actions and their rhetoric, depicted poverty as a social problem that occupied its own conceptual realm distinct from the political or the economic. "This distinction . . . insisted that morality and health were separable from one's economic situation." (Poovey 1995: 11). And therein lies the chief ideological importance of the social-body concept.

The civic realm became an important site for conflicts both between the middle class and the working class and within the middle class as different groups of reformers sought to discredit others' claims to be the exclusive caretakers of the social body. Race and gender became critical elements in these struggles. Middle-class male reformers competed with their working-class radical counterparts: each group focused its struggle on the defense of the family, but they differed in their assessment of what the ultimate threat to the family was. Within the middle class itself, male and female reformers each sought to use the idea of race to assimilate domestic and foreign populations in a way that would highlight their own unique suitability to the task of protecting the social body. In the context of these struggles, the notion of an autonomous civic sphere of social action came to occupy an important ideological place in capitalist culture. The full conceptual differentiation of civil society required the simultaneous emergence of the idea of an autonomous economy.

Middle-Class Reformers versus Working-Class Radicals: The Gendering of Class Struggle in and over the Social Body

In the Victorian popular imagination the notion of a civic sphere came to represent a separate arena of human relations and activity, differentiated from an autonomous economy and devoted to the amelioration of distinctly social problems. The civic sphere was extremely important in the making of the English middle class. As Susan Thorne explains:

> Evangelical institutions played a critical role in providing the institutional structure on which middle-class formation depended. It was largely if never exclusively through the associational opportunities provided by organized religion that middle-class Victorians secured credit and employment, produced marriage partners, cemented political alliances, displayed personal piety, and otherwise established the social ties that bound them to similarly situated individuals. . . . It was a principal institutional site at which a middle class fractured at the point of production managed to combine forces long enough and well enough to promote its interests against the claims of social groupings above as well as below. (1999: 55)

Middle-class reformers, whether male or female, sought to negotiate their divided allegiances with the aim of protecting their position of relative socioeconomic privilege against the destabilizing effects of the conflict between capital and labor. We can better understand the middle-class philosophy of social reform if we see that their actions were produced by their desire to negotiate and ultimately rationalize their complicated social position. Their stance on social problems cannot be separated from the fact that "the high costs of operating in the foreign mission field [rendered] missionary and other Congregational institutions ever more dependent upon the propertied classes" (Thorne 1999: 62). Their dependence on wealthy benefactors set limits on the types of social action that middle-class reformers, particularly evangelicals, were willing to recommend.

When the framers of the social body discourse talked about class differences, they emphasized the mutual dependence of the rich and the poor in such a way as to imply that the poor's inequality ensured their well-being. Hector Gavin, for example, reported with confidence that the well-off could be counted on to "alleviate or remove the misfortunes" or the poor (1848: 3). George Godwin pledged "to make known to one half of [the city's] denizens how the other half live, and to this second half what the first half are doing for them" ([1859] 1972: 5). It would not be an exaggeration to say that Godwin's notion that a knowledge gap was the source of England's profound social distress was the "pre-theoretical commitment" that structured evangelical thought and action (Jinks 1997). The notion that "it was impossible to account for the profound indifference which prevails among a great part of the people generally . . . but by believing that they were ignorant as to the amount and extent of the ills which [the poor] endured" (Gavin 1848: 3) was the unquestioned assumption that set the terms for reformers' engagement with society, established the pragmatic and programmatic foundations for solving social problems, and specified the range of insights and critiques that the framers of the discourse could accept. It is thus possible to locate a wide range of reformist writing that identified the source of England's social distress in the physical separation of classes, which resulted in an inadequate transfer of information and thus in indifference to the fate of the poor on the part of the wealthy.

The author of the Second Annual Report of the Ragged School Union, for example, argued that "few of our upper ranks have much practical knowledge of any class greatly removed from their own . . . and hence we believe arises their indifference" (1847: 127). Hugh Shimmin, an urban reformer, likewise asserted that "the more comfortable portion of the public of Liverpool do not know the town they live in. Probably not one in a hundred of them has ever been in one of these places—much less noted . . . the regular gradation from the lowest depths to lower still . . . the public as are strangers to all this misery" ([1856] 1985: 61). James Hole agreed that England displayed "wide extremes of civilization" which he attributed to the "isolation of class from class" (1866: 4). He thus concluded that "these evils have had so long a life because the middle and upper classes have no personal, concrete, knowledge of them, but only some dim abstract idea, gathered from newspapers and speeches" (1866: 117). Middle-class reformers were quick to appropriate the role of interclass interpreters and deliverers of knowledge. Indeed, it was through this role as interpreter that they not only secured a place in the social hierarchy, and in some cases achieved class mobility, but also carved out an exclusive domain of expertise and action.

Working-class radicals, who were the evangelical's fiercest critics and rivals, were quick to remark on this fact. A contemporary writer for *The Comet*, a radical working-class newspaper, penned a strongly worded condemnation of evangelicals, denouncing them as self-serving false prophets more interested in lining their own pockets and securing prestige than saving souls.

> Missionary societies of this kind are so many Pandora's boxes, from which issue various vices, whilst the only virtue (the money they collect) remains firmly seated at the bottom. Yes sir, these are the men that are sent to foreign countries, with handsome salaries, to preach what? Virtue? Morality? Pure religion? No! Nothing but incomprehensible dogmas, about which they even dispute among themselves at home! . . . Their only aim is temporal influence and power; the extension of chapels and the increase of preachers, and the levying of contributions on the new converts as well as on their devotees at home. They care not whether thousands in this country be ruined . . . provided they have their congregations, whether black or white, levy their contributions. (September 1832: 47)

A contributor to the Chartist weekly, the *Northern Star*, contended that a desire to appease their wealthy benefactors accounted for the reformers' continually ignoring the fact that the "benefits of civilization were monopolized by the useless classes, and that the balance of political liberty was all in favour of the same classes and against the wealth producers" (November 10, 1849).

The ire displayed by these two writers is not at all atypical. In fact, throughout much of the nineteenth century, evangelical reformers and working-class radicals could be found on opposing sides. Labor activists and Christian philanthropists did sometimes work together and see their goals as complementary (Fladeland 1984; Turley 1991), but for the most part they were each other's fiercest critics. The source of their disagreement lay in their competing claims to possess the knowledge and skills necessary to heal or redeem the social body. Hence, in their struggle for hegemony, each depicted the other as a dangerous and corrupt influence on the morals of the working-class family—destined to drive it, and by implication the social body as a whole, to ruin.

A missionary assigned to the Somerset District, for example, rejoiced at having converted a family of sinners "from the system of Robert Owen to the acknowledgment of Christ and his Gospel" (*City Mission Magazine,* October 1855: 246). One month later, a missionary to St. Pancras, "the most populous parish in the great metropolis," christened the Literary and Scientific Institution, a meetinghouse for working-class radicals, "Infidel Hall," and he claimed that from there was "a stream of iniquity constantly flowing." Writing for the mission magazine, he expressed despair that the radicals' sole aim appeared to be to frustrate the efforts of the friends of Christianity.

> These lectures profess to supply the people with sound and useful knowledge, but their real object is to uproot our glorious religion. They are attended chiefly by the working class, who are willing to pay 2*d.* for each admission to listen to that which seeks to destroy their souls rather than listen to the good news of salvation. . . . The persons attending the Infidel Hall, and many whom they influence, will not enter a place of worship. Their minds are so warped by the garbled statements of these lectures, and their passions so excited by the declamatory speeches to which they listen, that they have imbibed a prejudice against our holy religion and its ministers such as it seems impossible to overcome in any way. (*City Mission Magazine,* November 1855: 264)

The writer also despaired that although working-class people could not be prevailed upon to read the Bible, they were enthusiastic consumers of radical books and newspapers.

What the writer found even more troubling, however, was the fact rather than attending Sunday school and being converted to Christianity, that the children of the working class were being converted by their parents' radicalism. He despaired that radicalism would undermine the basis of the working-class family and, through that means, destroy society as a whole.

> A book shop is connected with this Institution for the sale of infidel publications, at which there is scarcely anything else sold. Its front is covered with placards announcing the sale of the works of Thomas Paine, and others of the same class, of which a great variety is kept on hand. I am sorry to add, that it is not only the adult portion of the district who are affected by this Institution, but the rising generation are under its influence. A school is connected with it, called a "Secular School" from which the Bible and every other religious book is entirely excluded, and the minds of the children are poisoned by the blasphemies taught them. (*City Mission Magazine,* November 1855: 264)

Never to be outdone, working-class radicals were quick to appropriate the language of their opponents for the purpose of advancing their own political position. Their radicalism was, however, founded on a gendered representation of participants. To achieve benefits for the working class as a whole, activists emphasized the manner in which gender identities and gender roles were structured. An article in the November 10, 1894, edition of the *Northern Star* exemplifies the tactics they used to depict the evangelicals, rather than themselves, as bearing ultimate responsibility for the demise of the working-class family. Instead of focusing on children, the radicals emphasized the fate of working-class women—the mothers of society. The article emphasized the active role the evangelical lobby played in destroying the working-class family by revealing that the Bibles it distributed as part and parcel of its efforts to uplift the heathen at home and abroad were manufactured using highly exploited female labor. The article's author concluded that "the British and Foreign Bible Society, while compassing earth and sea to convert 'the heathen' are at the same time dooming their own country-women to soul and body-slaying ruin."

The writer pointed to the actions of one Miss Watkins, whose firm was contracted to bind the Bibles sold and distributed by the society. Noting that Miss Watkins's firm was chosen because she was able to underbid her competitors, the author remarked, "Piety loves the partnership of Profit." The paper exposed the fact that the operatives in charge of the printing, pressing, and binding work were paid meager wages, and they were also continually being fined, so their wages were being reduced even more. "If they literally swallowed the Bible, page by page, they would still have but eight shillings, or less, weekly, to find them in bodily nourishment, which I imagine they would still need as much as ever, notwithstanding their spiritual food." Workers were also denied access to proper nourishment during working hours. "The sad pious capitalist," the author explained, "refuses the work-women access to water, except between four and half-past four o'clock, and then only to hot water, for which each has to pay one penny a week." The article concluded with a lengthy condemnation of evangelicals and their wealthy benefactors, who were destroying the health and morals of the working-class family and thereby undermining the basis of the whole social foundation (*Northern Star*, November 10, 1894).

The struggles over factory reform illustrate the importance of gender to the expression of class interests as class identities and gender differences were actively constructed in the rhetoric of the campaigns. In their struggles working-class people, no less than members of the middle classes, focused on the defense of the family and the protection of women as a key element in their overall strategy to safeguard their interests. Though they were clearly influenced by bourgeois notions of family life, radicals adapted these ideologies to suit their particular circumstances. Thus, whereas the evangelical philosophy emphasized that individuals should seek personal improvement and respectable habits in acceptance of the existing system, radicals pursued personal improvement and respectable habits to better enable themselves to challenge the social and economic structure.

Despite their many differences, both movements made masculinity a prerequisite for public political activity, and women were constructed as helpless creatures in need of male protection. This type of rhetoric obscured the increasing presence of female reformers in various spheres of social agitation and reform. Women were becoming increasingly vocal in their attempts to carve out an independent space for themselves in the public sphere. They did so not by constructing arguments around gender equality, but by formulating an alternative discourse around race and social problems to that used by male reformers. Their aim was to redefine the problems threatening the social body and to suggest solutions that drew on uniquely "feminine" talents and virtues. In this way they hoped to challenge male claims for exclusivity and dominance in the civic sphere.

Bodies in Cooperation or Bodies in Conflict? Competing Perspectives on the Colonial-Domestic Divide

Middle-class reformers continually stressed the tremendous advances they were making in bringing uplift to poor communities. Nevertheless, a significant portion of them subscribed to the view that the ultimate health of the social body depended upon the periodic siphoning off of problematic social elements to the colonies. Indeed, some reformers justified their dual allegiance to domestic and foreign missions on the basis of the contention that the colonies were simply an extension of the domestic social body; they characterized the relationship between the two entities as one of symbiosis. On the opposing side stood those reformers who argued that the health of the domestic social body was threatened by the existence of the colonies and by the efforts devoted to the uplift of the colonies' black and brown residents. These struggles quickly took on a gender dimension as female reformers were made into scapegoats by their male counterparts, who accused them of putting the needs of colonial populations ahead of those of their domestic counterparts and thus exposing the domestic social body to unnecessary peril.

It is in the writings of Thomas Malthus that we find the first systematic discussion of the problems that plague the social body, as well as a definitive solution. According to Malthus, the most menacing threat to the social body was that of surplus population, which was the result of indiscriminate char-ity. "The poor laws of England," Malthus wrote, "tend to depress the general condition of the poor. . . . Their first obvious tendency is to increase popu-lation" (1806: 172). This surplus population was, in Malthus's opinion, the principle source of social dislocation and unrest.

> To the general prevalence of indigence, and the extraordinary encouragements which we afford in this country to a total want of foresight and prudence among the common people, is to be attributed the principal part of those con-tinual depredations on property, and other more atrocious crimes, which drive us to the painful resource of such a number of executions. . . . The too great frequency of marriage among the poorest classes is one of the principal causes of the temptations to these crimes. (1806: 353–54)

For Malthus, the only hope for the salvation of the social body lay in the abo-lition of the poor laws and the immediate removal of threatening elements from the domestic social body to the colonies.

> It is clear, therefore, that with any view of making room for an unrestricted in-crease of population, emigration is perfectly inadequate; but as a partial and temporary expedient, and with a view to the more general cultivation of the earth, and the wider spread of civilization, it seems to be both useful and proper; and if it cannot be proved that governments are bound actively to en-courage it, it is not only strikingly unjust, but in the highest degree impolitic in them to prevent it. (1806: 147)

The way in which Malthus framed social problems and their solutions had a tremendous influence on popular thinking. In 1826 Parliament ap-pointed a select committee on emigration. On May 5, 1827, Malthus testi-fied before the committee that emigration was the most expedient policy to relieve pauperism in Ireland, and he urged Parliament to apportion funds to finance the emigration of 500,000 people from Ireland to the British colo-nies. According to Raymond Cowherd, "the Committee on Emigration not only wrote Malthus's testimony into their report, but they also endorsed his recommendation" (1977: 163).

Many devotees of Malthus turned out to be far more enthusiastic pro-moters of emigration than he ever was. A significant number of prominent English social theorists, including Thomas Carlyle, Nassau Senior, Charles Dickens, and E. G. Wakefield saw emigration as the best solution to English poverty and unemployment. The *Times of London* of June 1819, for example, offered "our noble station at the Cape of Good Hope" as the ideal destination for England's poor. The traveler John Barrow penned an article for the July installment of the *Quarterly Review* wherein he captured the essence of popular opinion on emigration. He described the Cape Colony as "a land which may literally be said to flow with milk and honey," a land that was thus ideal for relieving England of its laboring and manufacturing poor (1819: 235):

> It will not be necessary, for our present purpose, to take up the time of our readers in discussing the *cause* of that distress which, for some time past, has been pressing hard on certain classes of the labouring and manufacturing poor. It is enough to know that it exists;—and more than enough to apprehend, from the result of the active and anxious inquiries of men competent to the task, that the country does not, and cannot, under any circumstances, command the means of regular and permanent employment for its increased and increasing population. . . . A large portion of the population . . . being thrown back upon the public, must necessarily remain unemployed, and become a burden to the rest of the community. In referring to past times and to the history of other countries, it will be found that, whenever population begins to press severely against the means of subsistence, the remedy resorted to was emigration. (1819: 203, emphasis in original)

Malthus sketched a scenario in which the colonies became a site where the individual white body, particularly if it was male, could physically and morally regenerate itself. In the casting off of a degenerate population to be renewed elsewhere, the English social body would also be physically and morally regenerated. The idea that the colonies would enable the simultaneous remaking of the individual self and regeneration of the domestic social body came to have a profound influence on the ways in which poor Englishmen were encouraged to imagine themselves in relation to the domestic social body. For example, the *Morning Chronicle* of December 1, 1849, described the efforts of parish school leaders to make geography "much more generally taught than formerly—the guardians having at length discovered the stimulus which a little knowledge of geography gives to emigration." The paper went on to note the importance of maps as both a curricular device and a means for stimulating the further development of this imaginative process.

> At first they [the school guardians] could discover no use whatever in maps. "Maps!" said they, when it was first proposed to introduce them, "you'll be

bringing in the dancing-master next." In illustration of the value of geography as regards emigration, the following was related to me: A gentleman, in want of a boy to accompany him to New Zealand, applied at a union school in which geography had not been taught. "Who'll go to New Zealand?" was asked of the whole school, but not one volunteered. The application was next made at a school where geography was taught. "Who'll go to New Zealand?" was again asked, and almost every boy in the school sprang forward, exclaiming, "I'll go!"—I'll go!" On examining them, it was found that many not only knew its position and other circumstances connected with it, but could also state accurately the different routes by which it could be reached. No sooner was the anecdote known abroad than the guardians of the surrounding unions immediately ordered maps for their respective schools.

Working-class people, particularly men, began to see their self-regeneration as predicated upon their exit from the domestic social body. Henry Mayhew, a reporter for the *Morning Chronicle*, convened a meeting of vagrants at the British Union School for "the express purpose of consulting them generally." One vagabond explained that he had been in London three years and couldn't "get anything honest to do." He thus wished he "could get something at sea or in any foreign land." Mayhew went on to report: "The elder boys were then asked what they thought would be the best mode of effecting their deliverance from their present degraded position. Some thought emigration the best means, for if they started afresh in a new colony they said they would leave behind them their bad characters, which closed every avenue to employment against them at home" (*Morning Chronicle*, January 31, 1850). Thus, rather than making demands on the bourgeoisie or the state at home, proponents of emigration encouraged members of the working classes to seek their salvation elsewhere, in a distant geographical locale that offered them the opportunity to finally become part of the regeneration of the domestic social body—by virtue of having left it.

Malthus's writings were taken up with a considerable amount of enthusiasm by evangelical reformers, primarily because his analysis "restored to the Christian church the primary responsibility for charity. . . . The Evangelical Christians, in particular, found in Malthus's principle of population a justification for the multitude of voluntary agencies which they had designed for the education and the improvement of the working classes" (Cowherd 1977: 32). A significant number of reformers not only supported emigration, but also used it as a pretext for defending their right to devote equal amounts of energy to uplifting domestic and foreign populations:

helping the one was tantamount to helping the other. The Reverend New-man Hall, for example, argued that "the best school for getting sympathy for the Chinaman and the Kaffir is the school of home labour" (*City Mission Magazine*, June 1855: 148).

A significant body of opinion existed, however, that the vast amounts of care and attention being directed at foreign populations necessarily sapped the time and attention of the very people who had been entrusted with the care of depressed populations at home. Thus, the health of the domestic social body was being exposed to unnecessary peril. Closely related to this was the idea that individual domestically located white bodies were being sacrificed in favor of geographically distant black bodies. Charles Dickens published an essay in *Household Words* titled "Cape Sketches," wherein he complained: "Thanks to the energy of Campbell, Latrobe, Moffat, and other energetic members of the Missionary Society, the children of the Hottentots, Griquas, and even of some of the Bechuanas are fast being brought into the pale of civilization by attendance at the schools established by those gentle-men. Pity! The offspring of English parents in the 'interior' of England have no such schools to attend" (1850: 608). To dramatize his point that "sad neglect has prevailed respecting the immense mass of heathenism at home," Reverend Vanderkiste referred to the astute observations of the Ojibbeway Indians, who declined the offer of an English missionary and recommended that "it would be better for you teachers all to stay at home, and go to work right here in your own streets, where all your good work is wanted" (1852: 199). Roger Miller of the London City Mission, a domestic reform organiza-tion, also shared this view. He complained that the "richest empire in the world," which was "glorifying in possessions upon which the sun never sets, renowned for her flourishing and numerous benevolent institutions, her vast missionary operations, and her far-reaching schemes of philanthropy," provided nothing for her own poor but prison schools (1853: 83). Hugh Shimmin despaired at having to listen to a "most eloquent divine describing the deep degradation of the poor African, but not a word of the deeper degra-dation at home" ([1856] 1985: 19).

Subscribers to this view often pointed out that the actions of the sup-porters of foreign missions were undermining the efficacy of emigration. The points made by John Garwood, clerical secretary to the London City Mis-sion, were typical:

> In these eddies of civilized society are gathered all the filth, the crime, the sav-age recklessness, which is subsequently carried to the Antipodes, and causes

the sad and melancholy statement from New Zealand, that the white settlers have more to fear from the white man, their countryman, a member once of a refined state of society, than they have to dread from the savage and the cannibal! But whence came this white savage? From this vast metropolis, the seat of wealth, splendour, and refinement! ([1853] 1985: 17)

George Godwin urged his fellow citizens to look at the practical advantages of domestic charity: "We want good artisans—our colonies want them even more—offer money for them. Would it not be better, wiser, cheaper, for the country to turn the neglected infant population of our cellars and streets into men of this class, instead of allowing them to become, as they unquestionably must become if uncared for, rogues and thieves?" ([1859] 1972: 4).

The assumption underwriting this argument is that the colonial and domestic social bodies could exist in a relation of symbiosis only if the physical regeneration of the individual white body and the spiritual regeneration of the individual white self took precedence over that of the black. Indeed, framers of this idea insisted that the regeneration of one necessarily came at the expense of the other. Hence, efforts at regenerating colonized bodies were read as attacks on the individual white male bodies in need of care, which amounted to attacks on the English social body as a whole.

Although male and female reformers alike were chastised for their neglect of the adage "charity to souls begins at home" (*City Mission Magazine*, January 1855: 19), female reformers were singled out for particularly strong opprobrium. They came under attack in their roles as wives and mothers: they were frequently depicted as neglecting their duty of mothering the English nation in favor of mothering black adults and children. Satirical portraits of female reformers present what Thorne has called "feminist dystopias" (1999: 90). More often than not, caricatures of them traded in subtle and not-so-subtle images of irresponsible white mothers and their teeming hordes of savage black children. Poems like "Thoughts on the Savage Lions of London," which appeared in the July 25, 1853, edition of *Punch*, purported to be humorous sketches, but they presented the unseemly spectacle of white mothers nurturing, loving, and stroking black babies. The poem and the accompanying text used the occasion of A. T. Caldecott's exhibition of "Zulu Kaffirs" to underscore the threat posed to England's white nuclear families, and by extension to the nation as a whole, by the misdirected energies of female reformers. These reformers, the author complained, failed to understand the value of the nation, "the conversion and civilization of whose inhabitants are more particularly important to the British public."

And their dear little baby we smother with kisses,
    And stroke and admire its darling bronze skin,
And think that there ne'er was a baby like this,
    As a lion of London its life to begin.
It is all very proper to say that a baby
    Might be found nearer home, if we sought for a pet,
And that in the back courts of St. Giles, it may be,
    Hordes of young savages there we could get:
But they've no fancy dresses to set off their figures,
    And nothing is thought of an every-day sight;
"UNCLE TOM" has roused such a penchant for niggers;
    That dark skins must now take precedence of white

That little dark baby could never have vices
    Like those which degrade us in civilized life
And though he may pr'raps chop his father in slices
    His country has customs that legalise strife.
But, really—what humbugs call—Civilization
    Seems spreading everywhere under the skies,
That soon, I suppose, we shall not have a nation,
    To furnish a savage to gladden our eyes. (p. 69)

Two full years before Dickens gave full vent to his hatred for missionaries in his misogynistic portrait of Mrs. Jellyby, *Punch* published a brief satirical sketch about the fictitious "English Matron's Hottentot Society" and its founder, Amelia Mouser. Mouser, described as a woman with "tenderest feelings, pity, and compassion for her fellow-creatures, especially the fellow-creatures that are dark and distant," could easily have been a prototype for Jellyby (*Punch*, 1850: 225). The plot of the story turns on the deception of Mouser by her husband, who, disgusted by his wife and her compatriots, "women whose hearts beat on the other side of the ocean," disguises a "white boy, a real native of Whitechapel" as a Hottentot. As expected, Mouser coos and fusses over the boy until he is revealed to be "as white and as clean as a new-washed baby, with brown hair and blue eyes." At that point, Mouser, the so-called humanitarian, coldly turns him out into the street, oblivious to the dangers that await him there. Thus we see in graphic relief the familiar white male body sacrificed to the needs of the unknown black one.

The story, like the poem, turns on the question of which mothers should be nurturing which children, and it paints a repugnant portrait of white women giving themselves, body and soul, to black children. The story is punctuated by unseemly images of white breasts being emptied into greedy black mouths while white children go hungry. "Sucking Bosjesmans" latch on to white breasts, and "black children born of charity" demand to be "wet and dry nursed on their benevolence." Mouser's husband despairs that the women of the Hottentot Society have "one hundred thousand infants to whom [they are] all nursing mothers." And Mouser's first instinct, before discovering the boy is an impostor, is to "dry-nurse and protect him." All of this happens at the expense of English white children, "nurslings of their own hearth," who are depicted as "miserable creatures" who "run alone" with "no home but the gutter and no bread."

Images of the American South permeate both satirical sketches. In the poem they come via the mention of *Uncle Tom's Cabin,* and in the story the boy, who is said to be a member of a fictitious minstrel troupe, the Hottentot Singers, serenades Mouser with "Oh Susannah, don't you cry for me." These images of the plantation, when read alongside those of children being suckled by breasts of the wrong color, reference one of the unintended horrors of slavery, the specter of miscegenation and other forms of illicit amalgamation that were threats to the white nuclear family—and by extension to the perpetuation of an Anglo-Saxon nation. The story hints broadly at the theme of miscegenation in a reference to the English children of the matrons as "the lily-skinned brothers and sisters of their own black Hottentots." Sexual liaisons between black men and white women are not explicitly mentioned, but the text does make reference to white male fears about the loss of "female affections." Mouser, reflecting on the possessiveness with which men guard the affections of their wives, surmises that men would "have a woman's affections, like the fire-irons, never budge from their own hearth."

The other specter that haunts the text is the image of a future society where white women become mothers without white men becoming fathers. The subtext of the story is the horror of a society without white men—a society where they are rendered useless in their social and patriarchal functions. Female reformers like those of the English Matron's Hottentot Society are white mothers of children who have no white paternity. Hence the story is also punctuated with references to "offspring borne of charity," women with "one hundred thousand children," and women delighting in their "family in the middle of Africa" while discounting "their own white children." The narrator even has the impostor boy greet Mouser with the words, "Am I not a little boy and a son?"

The devaluation of men as fathers, of both genetic offspring and of the nation, was explicitly linked to the ways in which women used their capacity to sympathize with and represent the interests of Africans as a platform for visibility and prominence in the civic realm. In the story, for example, before the boy is uncovered as a fake, Mouser eagerly anticipates the public recognition that will accrue to her upon her taking "this little burning brand to the platform of the Hall [Exeter] and examining him in the face of the world, showing how [she has] opened his mind and formed his principles!" Thus, male impotence to regenerate the nation—both spiritually and physically—was figured in the form of the activist woman who asserted her claim to dominance in the civic sphere. Efforts by women to claim a space for themselves in the public sphere were thus painted as transgressions that threatened the proper perpetuation of the national family. This nightmare of a feminist dystopia existed not just on the printed page, but as a real and growing threat in the everyday lives of male reformers who struggled to define the civic space in exclusivist terms that denied women any moral claim to representation.

Race, the Social Body, and the Gendered Ethic of Care

When reformers successfully institutionalized the idea that society was a social body and that, like all bodies, it was in need of care, they inadvertently opened up a host of new opportunities for women to intervene in the public sphere. As Thorne explains:

> The emergence of a unitary or organic conception of society was the basis for the growing domination of women in the implementation as well as the administration of philanthropy. . . . Although the authors of this discourse were men, . . . the terms on which they promoted their professional expertise created, without their having intended to do so, opportunities for women as well. . . . Thus could women justify their interventions in the public spheres of philanthropy and reform in terms of their innate maternal talents. They would be the social mothers of society itself. (1999: 105)

Control over the civic sphere had tremendous implications for gender domination within both the private sphere of the household and the public sphere of politics. According to Leonore Davidoff and Catherine Hall:

> Middle-class men's claims for new forms of manliness found one of their most powerful expressions in formal associations. . . . Men organized themselves in myriad ways, promoting their economic interests, providing soup kitchens for the poor, cultivating the arts, reaching into populated urban areas and rural

outposts. The network of association redefined civil society, . . . increased the confidence of middle-class men and contributed to their claims for political power, as heads of households, representing their wives, children, servants, and other dependents. This public world was consistently organized in gendered ways and had little space for women. Indeed, middle-class feminists in the second half of the nineteenth century focused many of their efforts on attempting to conquer the bastions of this public world. (1987: 416)

Thus, an ethic of masculinity was forged on the basis of care for the social body, which was predicated on the exclusion of female agency. Just as the contradictory ends the formulators of the social body concept intended it to serve were reconciled through a discourse about race, so too were the contradictory impulses toward gender equality that were a component of that concept.

Male reformers, particularly those trained in the fields of science and medicine, justified keeping women out of domestic poverty reform by mobilizing a discourse of race that, while it assimilated domestic and foreign populations, did so in a way that stressed the correspondences between their physical and biological attributes. Male reformers justified their exclusive right to care for and protect the social body by emphasizing the dangerous and menacing attributes of the social classes most in need of discipline and care. Their aim was to make domestic populations seem more threatening by portraying their foreign counterparts as animalistic and subhuman. The desired outcome was that both populations would be made to seem so dangerous that women would be disqualified from participating in their uplift. This rhetorical move flew in the face of the substantive social transformations that were occurring in the world of social reform. Women, as it turned out, were already making significant strides in the management of colonial populations. According to Thorne, "rather than simply serving as fundraising adjuncts within institutions controlled by men, evangelical women began to establish independent linkages to the foreign field" (1999: 93). This fact tended to contradict efforts to exclude women from domestic social action by making analogies suggesting that colonized people were too dangerous and threatening for them to handle.

Male reformers thus tended to place emphasis on their superior diagnostic abilities, which were the result of specialized training and expertise rather than simple religious study, or worse, intuitive "feminine" feelings. According to an article titled "Practical Utility of Phrenology," which appeared in the *Annals of Phrenology,* phrenology's usefulness lay in its unique ability to "give to the public a clear and intelligible standard by which to estimate mental capacity" ("Practical Utility of Phrenology" 1834: 137). Phrenologists, who were trained in the measurement of "organs" or "humps" on the skull, maintained that the human mind could be divided into thirty-seven faculties with distinct locations on the brain. Equipped with the relevant charts, a pair of calipers, a keen eye, and a steady hand, a man of science could divine inner character through manual examination of the outer skull. Because they wanted to explain the behavior of the "submerged tenth" of society, phrenologists were unusually interested in investigating relative degrees of "Combativeness," which they defined as "the love of contention for its own sake." This faculty, according to experts, was particularly pronounced in "persons who have murdered from the impulse of the moment," as well as in "Charibs" (Combe 1834: 46). An article disputing "Recent Attacks on Phrenology" drew associations between Negroes, Caribs, and criminals based on a shared overdevelopment of the organ of destructiveness:

> The organ of Destructiveness is very large, and that of Benevolence small, in the skull of Bellingham, who murdered Mr. Percival. . . . The Society possesses casts of the skulls of five Caribs (Nos. 12, 13, 14, 15, 16), who are well known to have been a ferocious tribe, and in all of them the organ of Destructiveness is decidedly large. . . . In the collection of Dr. Barclay, there is the skull of a Negro, who committed several murders. In it Destructiveness is very large. ("Recent Attacks on Phrenology" 1823–1824: 31–33)

Scientific reformers also tended to stress that their diagnostics had superior reliability because they were based on the examination of empirical evidence—research that was only possible with their privileged access to the necessary materials. Phrenologists jealously maintained their exclusive access to hospitals, morgues, and prisons, from whence they derived the skulls and skeletons that allowed them to base their claims on the observation and comparison of empirical evidence rather than on sentiment, intuition, or biblical teachings. One would be hard pressed to imagine a woman having access to the resources and institutional mechanisms that would allow her to assemble a "phrenological cabinet" like the one described in the *American Phrenological Journal* of 1840.

> National skulls might be arranged 1st to furnish specimens of the crania of the various races, nations, and tribes of men and 2nd to illustrate in a more especial manner phrenological principles. For the first purpose, crania might be grouped in five classes. One for the skulls of Europeans, a second for those of Asiatics, a third for those of Africans, a fourth for those of American nations,

and a fifth for those of the natives of the islands of the Pacific Ocean. Each class having its appropriate subdivisions.

For the second purpose, skulls belonging to nations widely differing in character should be placed side by side, that the correspondence of character and development might be manifest. Thus, the skull of the Englishman might be placed beside that of the Hindoo. That of the timid Peruvian, whose opposition to the Spaniards was the packing of the dove against the kite, might be placed beside that of the Carib, whose indomitable courage and independence nothing but death could overcome. ("Remarks on Phrenological Specimens" 1840: 216–17)

Men of science emphasized that they alone had the expertise and training to determine which of these types of people could be safely assimilated into the social body and by what methods this assimilation would best be accomplished—incarceration, moral rehabilitation, or physical discipline. An article in the *Phrenological Journal and Miscellany* of September 1830, for example, argued for the importance of incarceration over moral or religious conversion, noting the "necessity of restraining the criminal as a savage creature." It also made the claim that criminals and savages both had overdeveloped organs of Combativeness and Destructiveness ("The Late Atrocious Crimes in Scotland" 1830: 538). In 1833, the journal printed an article, "On the Principles of Criminal Legislation," that maintained that "skulls of executed criminals collected from various quarters of the globe exhibit the same general character" ("On the Principles of Criminal Legislation" 1833: 115).

On the basis of their expertise and training, medical experts in fields like penitentiary discipline also began to make inroads into the diagnosis and treatment of pauper women and children. This change was quite significant, because women and children had long been considered the special province of female reformers. Experts in penitentiary discipline, however, claimed to have located the biological roots of female impulses and behavior, thus opening them up to exploration and analysis by men. One of the relevant faculties for investigation in this regard was "Philoprogenitiveness," the main function of which was to produce "the instinctive love of offspring in general." Philoprogenitiveness, which "chiefly supported the mother in her toils," was found to be quite pronounced in "Hindoos, Negroes, Esquimaux, Ceylonese, and Charib skulls." "Adhesiveness," another one of the major faculties, caused those persons in whom it was very strong to "feel an involuntary impulse to embrace and cling to the object of their affections." This faculty, according to prevailing scientific opinion, was "stronger and larger in women than in men" (Combe 1834: 41–42, 44).

Hewett Watson, senior president of the Royal Medical Society, argued that "in the lower animals, and in young children, the lateral lobes of the cerebellum are proportionally smaller than the middle one" (1832: 442). Dr. Caldwell, an expert on penitentiary discipline, likened youthful criminals to savages on the basis of his observation of certain shared physical characteristics. He thus argued that the brain of the "savage" Carib Indian and that of the English criminal shared a number of key attributes, including Combativeness and Destructiveness. He adduced that the only method of reform likely to work was one based on scientific principles, as the emotions of these individuals were too undeveloped for moral or religious instruction. "In youthful offenders, possessing what we have denominated the ruffian temperament—the forehead low, the top of the head flat or depressed, the base of the brain, from the temporal region backward, wide, and a large amount of it behind the ear—reformation is always difficult, and sometimes, we apprehend, impracticable. The brain resembles too much that of the Carib, who is perfectly animal, and never feels a virtuous emotion" (1832: 498).

The actions of female reformers stood in marked contrast to this. When female reformers used the rhetoric of race to assimilate foreign and domestic populations, they tended to draw comparisons between the English working classes and savages in foreign climes that infantalized both, making them seem more pitiable than menacing. For example, a female missionary who started a "self-clothing club" for poor women in the St. Giles district painted a far different, more innocuous portrait of the urban slum dweller when she remarked: "The delight of these poor creatures, at such an opportunity of procuring warm and tidy clothing, was unbounded. Their expression of joy was so childish, I could compare it to nothing but what I fancy a party of New Zealanders would exhibit before they were civilized by Christianity" (Raynard 1860: 70). An 1862 article titled "Infanticide: The Sin of the Age," on the other hand, presented a picture of the urban criminal that, while likening him to "a savage beast," also pointed to the transformative power of love and kindness—uniquely female virtues—which filled him with "the tenderness and gentleness of the parent" ("Infanticide: The Sin of the Age" 1862: 292).

In female reformers' writings there were absolutely no references to the biological characteristics of either the savage or the criminal. Rather, both were depicted wholly in cultural terms. Indeed, female reformers were far more likely to emphasize the cultural over the biological or physical definition of race precisely because the former definition allowed for the formulation of social problems and their solutions in terms that put women and their problem solving skills at an advantage. Female reformers were at pains to demonstrate that they too possessed a set of specialized diagnostic skills and that the methods they used, although not "scientific," were demanding and should not be devalued. E. W. Thomas, the secretary to the London Female Preventative and Reformatory Institution, put it this way:

> There is a notion current among some people in the present day, that the task of reclaiming poor outcast females is both easy and romantic. . . . Most fervently do we wish that such was the case, and that the moral injury they have sustained could be so easily effaced. But it is not so, as all who have any experience in this work will testify. This, like every other work of mercy which the Church of Christ is called upon to engage in, is extremely difficult, and trying alike to faith and patience; so much so, indeed, that during the last few years we have seen many put their hands to this work, and because a few cases of discouragement occurred, their zeal soon waxed cold, and the enterprize upon which they entered with so much ardour was abandoned, because of the trials of faith to which we have referred. (1862: 325)

Thus, male and female reformers carefully modulated their use of the discourse of race in such a way that it referenced the specific set of problems among subaltern populations that they alone had the expertise and training to address: their biological proclivity for crime and other forms of antisocial behavior, or their moral and spiritual laxity. In this way, middle-class English men and women competed for hegemony in the public sphere. The sacred ground upon which each group staked its claim for supremacy was its superior ability to diagnose and treat the problems of social inferiors. Each group recognized that the manner in which it defined which traits were more salient for constituting racial difference—cultural or biological—critically affected its ability to define both poverty and the poor as a social problem. The manner in which social problems were defined, in turn, played a large role in determining which set of gender traits and skills were best suited for managing them. The discourse of race was arguably one of the most efficacious tools for making the idea of a social body possible and for giving the middle class, by virtue of their demonstrated successes among foreign populations, the legitimacy and social authority to care for that social body. By emphasizing an alternative set of parameters within which domestic and foreign populations were linked, reformers effectively shifted the very definition of race to suit their particular purposes. In this way, both male and female reformers were able to continue using a rhetorical move that had a significant amount of ideological purchase and, in this way, assert their claim for a privileged space in the public sphere.

Conceptualizing Away Capitalism: The Ideological
Impact of the Social Body Metaphor

The idea of the social body was arguably one of the most important analytical abstractions produced by middle-class reformers. It was produced alongside and through a number of other key abstractions—the social, or civic, sphere; the economic sphere; and the political sphere. The civic sphere was defined by the nature of the problems that were assembled under its domain. As Poovey explains, "the gradual consolidation of a distinctly 'social' domain was facilitated by efforts to comprehend—to understand, measure, and represent—the poverty that seemed increasingly visible" (1995: 8). An analysis of middle-class reformers' policy statements about and policy prescriptions for the social body reveals the ways in which the production of the concept of an abstract civic sphere is associated with the specific property relations of capitalism. Indeed, the ways in which middle-class reformers defined a sphere of civic action and the nature of the problems that it was meant to encompass demonstrate that the full conceptual differentiation of a civic sphere required the simultaneous emergence of another conceptual abstraction: the economy.

The way in which middle-class reformers framed the idea of the social body allowed them to conceptualize away class conflicts. The most salient and defining feature of the social body as a analytical abstraction was that it denied the fact that society was divided into classes composed of individuals whose economic, political, and social interests conflicted precisely because one class had the power to appropriate the surplus labor of the other. The manner in which reformers defined social problems left no space for analyzing the role that the private control and appropriation of collectively managed wealth played in the reproduction of disease, sexual immorality, crime, or any other of the myriad of problems they deemed social. It is clear from the actions of these reformers that they viewed the relations of production and the control of productive property as issues that belonged in an economic realm that was completely separate from the social sphere.

Reformers drew on various racial discourses as part of their effort to understand, measure, and represent poverty and the poor as social problems that could be solved through a variety of different forms of civic action—incarceration, home visits, sanitary education, and moral uplift. The prior status of race as a concept referring to populations defined as problems amenable to being solved by English middle-class "experts" and the incredible malleability of racial discourses are two key reasons that race was central to the making of the idea of the social body. Closely related to this was the role that the idea of race played in the emergence of the idea of civic action. It was through the manipulation of racial discourses and, more importantly, of the social meanings attached to different ideas of race that reformers defined problem populations, and in defining those populations also delineated how they would be managed. The shape of the space that came to be understood as the civic realm was determined by the outcome of conflicts between working classes and middle classes and between men and women. The axis around which these conflicts turned in the former case was that of gender—specifically, the right to define what constituted the greatest threat to the working-class family. In the latter instance the conflicts turned on the manipulation of racial discourses: the ability to finesse the meaning of race was tantamount to the ability to shape the space that bore the title of the civic, or social, sphere.

No matter what racial discourses reformers used to assimilate domestic and foreign populations, however, the ultimate impact was to root societal problems in the subjective dispositions of individuals. In this way reformers were able to formulate plans of action for improving individual lives that in no way encompassed doing anything to alter the structures of appropriation and production. Civic action, as it was defined, comprised neither changing the balance of class power nor altering the social relations that were the bases of productive labor. Middle-class reformers purported to be able to improve the human condition without in any way expanding democratic authority over planning and production precisely because the latter were considered economic issues that belonged to their own autonomous realm. Hence, the actions of middle-class reformers played a key role in reinforcing a view of society whereby a clear divide separated the economic, the political, and the social as conceptual entities and fields of social investigation and action.

In the next chapter I continue to look at gendered struggles for recognition in the public sphere, examining how middle-class women and elite working-class men used the occasion of the Anglo-Boer War and images of suffering "native" bodies as vehicles for representing their own political marginalization. Thus, chapter 5 documents an important shift whereby images of the Other, instead of being put to service in constructing the domestic poor, were mobilized in the interest of constructing the bourgeois self.

CHAPTER FIVE

"Truncated Citizenship":
African Bodies, the Anglo-Boer War, and
the Imagining of the Bourgeois Self

In the previous chapters I have traced the various ways in which images of native bodies became discursive resources for representing working-class populations and poverty as a social problem. My primary concern was to show how British reformers deployed the experience of a group of geographically distant Others in the service of constructing images of a marginalized people who, although they lived in geographic proximity, were commonly believed to inhabit a world apart. In this chapter I examine how and why the same bourgeois individuals responsible for assimilating the experience of the domestic poor and colonized Others sought to use these same racial Others to represent their own experiences of political disenfranchisement and exclusion from the body politic.

My specific focus in this chapter is the impact of the Anglo-Boer War on images of "native" bodies and their subsequent deployment in metropolitan discourses about citizenship. Different groups of English people used African bodies and the Anglo-Boer War as dual vehicles for representing their own political marginalization. During the war there was an important shift in how the bodies of racialized Others were incorporated into metropolitan social debates. When the native body was put to use in constructing an image of the English poor, its depravity had taken center stage. When the native Other was deployed in the service of highlighting the experiences of the bourgeois self, however, its noble suffering took precedence over its depravity. The suffering of two groups in particular became a lightning rod in these debates—African men and Afrikaner men. Their bodies became critical sites for individuals denied full representation in the metropolitan body politic—working-class men and middle-class women—to construct a narrative about the pain of truncated citizenship while they made a plea for fuller inclusion in that body politic. The ways in which middle-class women constructed

narratives of their own suffering and justified their claims to citizenship varied, and also differed from those of working-class men.

A central theoretical concern of this chapter is to account for what Uday
Mehta calls "liberal strategies of exclusion" or the "inclusionary pretensions
of liberal theory and the exclusionary effects of liberal practices." According
to Mehta, "liberal history projects with greater focus and onto a larger canvas
the theoretically veiled and qualified truth of liberal universalism" (1997:
59, 60). In other words, the history of political exclusion that is the legacy of
liberal politics elaborates the truth of the ambivalence of liberal ideas about
universality. Because the Anglo-Boer War shaped public and parliamentary
discussion of the extension of the franchise, the meaning of citizenship, and
the limits of liberal democracy in much the same way as the 1865 Morant
Bay Rebellion in Jamaica shaped public and parliamentary discussion of the
1867 Reform Act (Hall 1992), it is an ideal location from which to trace
some of the sources of the politically exclusionary impulses that got written
into the universalistic theoretical framework of liberalism.

In the first section, I examine the writings of trade unionists and other
working-class radicals who used the African body to launch a critique of capitalist property relations and denounce the cynicism of a system in which socioeconomic exploitation and inequality coexisted with civic freedom and
equality. The trade unionists offered a radically new conception of democracy
as encompassing the right to expand democratic control over production,
but they did so by deploying a discourse on African suffering that cast out
Jewish men and women from the body politic. Hence, although the model
of democratic participation they offered was ostensibly free of class bias, it
had an exclusivist approach to racial politics written into its very foundation.

In the next section I examine the writings and speeches of suffragists who
supported the war effort, but also used the war as a pretext for legitimizing
their protest against their own marginalization and exclusion from the body
politic. Because these pro-war suffragists used the war as an opportunity to
put forth a model of civic participation that made suffering and service to the
empire the main criteria for citizenship, they were able to use their patriotic
support for the war effort to further buttress their arguments for inclusion.
In the narrative of one pro-war suffragist in particular, Josephine Butler, suffering black male bodies became the objects of what Bernth Lindfors (1999)
terms "spectatorial lust." In Butler's text, the alleviation of black suffering
was made the central motive for British aggression in the Transvaal. Her discussion of black suffering not only provided justification for the war, but also
served as a pretext for concretizing her ideas about the proper scope of liberal democracy: woven throughout her analysis of the war is a discourse on

citizenship in Britain. She was thus able to use the war as a vehicle for putting forth a conception of citizenship that was more inclusive—she sought the enfranchisement of women and Africans, although at a much later date and on a limited basis—but was also more restrictive in the sense that the balance of class power was not to be a criterion of democracy. Thus, the conceptual framework of liberal democracy can, while expanding its parameters of inclusion, nevertheless maintain the invulnerability of the economic sphere to democratic power. Despite the professed equality of all individuals, the owners of capital enjoy a privileged juridical status.

In the final section I examine how the "pro-Boers," or antiwar suffragists, used the war not only to critique the gender exclusivity of the British political system, but also to launch a model of citizenship that stressed consent over service as the main criterion for political inclusion. In their discourse the importance of consent was made manifest through images of Afrikaner men, newly imagined as white, valiantly protesting British overlordship. Consent, the fulcrum on which these suffragists' whole notion of citizenship turned, was not, however, an unbiased concept. Rather, the way in which antiwar suffragists constructed the ideal consent-granting subject effectively naturalized the historical inequality between master and subject races and thus undermined the principle's presumed universality. The civic realm in liberal democracy can thus become simultaneously more gender inclusive and more racially exclusive, and the political exclusion of certain groups can be written into ostensibly inclusive and universal political principles.

Suffering Natives, Greedy Capitalists, and the Meaning of Citizenship: Working-Class Views of the Anglo-Boer War

When Britain granted the Transvaal self-government in 1881, the franchise was limited to white men resident in the republic fourteen years or more. The legislation thus enfranchised Boer men and left most of the British men who had come to South Africa in search of gold and diamonds (the so-called Uitlanders) without the vote. In 1899 Paul Kruger, president of the Transvaal Republic, and Sir Alfred Milner, British High Commissioner to South Africa, debated the terms for the enfranchisement and naturalization of British subjects in the Transvaal. Kruger eventually relented and reduced the residency requirement to seven years, and Milner replied with a call for aggressive action. In a dispatch to the colonial secretary, Joseph Chamberlain, Milner decried the "spectacle of thousands of British subjects kept permanently in the position of helots" (quoted in Farwell 1990: 33). A few short months later, in October 1899, hostilities commenced in South Africa, and a vigorous debate broke out in England over the advantages and disadvantages of the war. Because the war was ostensibly being fought to secure the franchise for disfranchised populations and was being defended in a language of liberal political rights, it precipitated a discussion among organized members of the working class of their own relationship to the body politic.

Democracy versus Capitalism and the Antinomy of Citizenship

The irony that British blood was being shed to enfranchise men "such as we do not give a vote to in England" was not lost on working-class activists (*New Age*, December 7, 1899). As F. Maddison explained:

> What adds to the irony of the situation is the fact that the very statesmen who are so zealous for the enfranchisement of the Uitlanders of a foreign country bitterly opposed the endowment of their own countrymen with the full rights of citizenship. But even now, after a century's agitation, manhood suffrage has yet to be gained and our registration laws are designed to make it difficult for poor men to secure their votes. By the present system, many of those entitled to be on the register cannot get their names inserted, and for a variety of reasons, not applicable to other sections of the community, it is calculated that there are no less than two millions of workmen who are excluded from the franchise. It is in this way that the working class leaders look at the demand of the Uitlanders in the Transvaal. (1900: 522)

The annual proceedings of the Trades Union Congresses (TUC) from 1899 to 1902 demonstrate the degree to which the Anglo-Boer War provided the pretext for organized members of the British working class to reflect on the warped workings of class and democracy in their own country. At the final session of the 1899 congress, for example, "the crisis in the Transvaal was the only subject discussed." W. C. Steadman, M.P., pointed out that the British working classes were "in a similar position to the Uitlanders" and that the British laboring man enjoyed only limited rights in his own country: "With our present electoral system not one half of the million and a quarter of workers whom that Congress represented would have a vote if an election took place on the morrow" (*Annual Report of the Trades Union Congress* 1899: 85). The issue of the war was taken up again at the 1902 congress. At that time, members reaffirmed their "continued hostility to all wars of foreign aggression which tended to enrich the sinister figure of cosmopolitan finance, and whose main object is to hold the workers of all countries in universal social and economic servitude." Mr. C. F. Davies of the London Composters took the occasion to remind his fellows that the marked disjuncture between what the British government promised to its citizens at home and what it promised when they were abroad demonstrated that "wars are more often undertaken by governments to distract their people's attention from home affairs" (*Annual Report of the Trades Union Congress* 1902: 77).

The practical effect of workingmen's criticisms was to collapse the artificial distinction between economic and political questions by insisting that capitalist exploitation made all struggles over domination simultaneously political and economic. The workingmen believed production relations to have been created not by abstract laws, but by the actual social phenomena they were contesting—such as the power to organize and govern, to exert domination, and to hold property in specific ways. Their insistence that "the real consideration was not the franchise but capitalism against capitalism, that capitalists had got hold of some of our Ministers and they worked the oracle beautifully" points to the fact that trade union activists were aware that the disposition of power between the individual capitalist and worker conditioned and was conditioned by the political configuration of society as a whole (*Annual Report of the Trades Union Congress* 1899: 86). Much the same was asserted by a Mr. G. A. Fox, representative of the Boilermakers and Iron Shipbuilders, who noted that the war crisis had been "promoted in the interests of capitalists and wealthy citizens, who had sunk money in the Transvaal." Fox also noted the cynicism of the accumulating classes, who, though they lined their pockets with the proceeds of the war, never sent their sons to fight, but rather let the working classes suffer while they "stood a long way off with field glasses watching the operations from a distance" (*Annual Report of the Trades Union Congress* 1899: 87).

The Anglo-Boer War was an important occasion for working-class activists to reflect on the meaning of citizenship in a country where socioeconomic inequality coexisted with civic freedom and the formal exercise of democracy left class exploitation intact. The activists' writings and speeches on the war indicate their recognition of the fact that the workings of capitalism ultimately made civic status less salient—that civic equality did not significantly modify class inequality. The war provided a pretext for critiquing the fact that the balance of class power in society was not a criterion of democracy and, further, that there was no incompatibility between democracy and rule by the wealthy. It also provided a platform for activists to posit an alternative conception of democracy that acknowledged the necessity of extending the meaning of democracy to include the exercise of democratic authority over production and of reversing the processes whereby the economic sphere was invulnerable to democratic power. As Mr. B. C. Cooper of the Cigar Makers explained: "In the opinion of this Congress, the growth of gigantic capitalistic trusts, with their enormous power of controlling production, is injurious to the advancement of the working class, as by such combination the prices of commodities are raised, the standard of comfort of the people can be reduced, the workman's freedom endangered. This Congress hereby declares that the only permanent solution of the above-mentioned difficulty lies in the national ownership and control of these monopolies" (*Annual Report of the Trades Union Congress* 1902: 77).

The critiques launched by members of the trade union council demonstrate the degree to which the rigid separation of the economic and political spheres in capitalism had not only occurred at the conceptual level but had rapidly become an historical reality. The differentiation of the world into two wholly dichotomous and differentiated spheres was not simply an effect of discourse, but was the practical outcome of a society wherein the forfeit of surplus labor was an immediate condition of production itself. This is not to say that the allocation of social labor and the distribution of resources were determined wholly by the mechanisms of commodity exchange. Rather, the special nature of social power in a capitalist system was such that the coercive power that supported exploitation was wielded not necessarily directly by the proprietor but, rather, by the state, which invested the capitalist property with the authority to organize production. In their insistence that the "rock bottom motive for wars" was "the enriching of cosmopolitan financiers," trade unionists demonstrated their recognition that wars were a method of coercive intervention by the state on behalf of the expropriating classes (*Annual Report of the Trades Union Congress* 1902: 77).

What the Trades Union Congress members and other working-class activists were up against, however, was a system that had a remarkable ability to mask the real human suffering that was the inevitable result of class exploitation precisely because the forfeit of surplus labor was an immediate condition of production. Indeed, Marx devoted a large part of the first volume of *Capital* to exposing the monumental disjunctures between the surface appearance of capitalism and the reality that lurked underneath, demonstrating that the exploitation workers faced under capitalism was perhaps the least transparent form of suffering in the world. For Marx and other working-class radicals, the opacity of the suffering of the exploited worker was one of the most debilitating and frustrating aspects of the system, particularly for individuals seeking to effect its transformation.

In a passage on the extension of the working day, Marx attempted to bring to the surface the manner in which the literal death of the laboring body was rendered invisible by the machinations of the capitalist seeking to increase surplus in production. The death of the worker, Marx explained, was literally woven into the fabric of, and thus hidden in, the interstices of the working day. "The capitalistic mode of production (essentially the production of surplus-value, the absorption of surplus-labour), produces thus, with the extension of the working day, not only the deterioration of human labour-power by robbing it of its normal, moral and physical, conditions of development and function. It produces also, the premature exhaustion and death of this labour-power itself. It extends the labourer's time of production during a given period by shortening his actual life-time" ([1867] 1967: 265). In a subsequent passage, Marx described in vivid detail the many invisible insults and injuries suffered by laboring men and women. They ranged from the ability of capital to "usurp the time for growth, development, and healthy maintenance of the body" to its never-ending quest to "steal the time required for the consumption of both fresh air and sunlight" and "reduce the sound sleep needed for the restoration, reparation, and refreshment of the bodily powers."

Although the tenor of his critique suggests that Marx believed the suffering of the English worker was evident enough to need no embellishment, the rhetorical means whereby he made that suffering palpable and visible are quite telling. To render the suffering of the white body visible, Marx literally had to assimilate the black laboring body into the white laboring body—calling upon the reader to mentally substitute Irish, English, Scottish, and German bodies for the African.

The rice grounds of Georgia or the swamps of the Mississippi may be fatally injurious for the human constitution; but the waste of human life which the cultivation of these districts necessitates is not so great that it cannot be repaired from the teeming preserves of Virginia and Kentucky. . . . It is accordingly a maxim of slave management, in slave-importing countries, that the most effective economy is that which takes out of the human chattel in the shortest space of time the utmost amount of exertion it is capable of putting forth. It is in the tropical culture, where annual profits often equal the whole capital of the plantations, that negro life is most recklessly sacrificed. It is the agriculture of the West Indies, which has been for centuries prolific of fabulous wealth, that has engulfed millions of the African race. *Mutato nomine de te fabula narratur.* For slave trade read labour market, for Kentucky and Virginia, read Ireland and the agricultural districts of England, Scotland, and Wales, for Africa read Germany. We heard how over-work thinned the ranks of the bakers in London. Nevertheless, the London labour-market is always over-stocked with German and other candidates for death in the bakers. ([1867] 1967: 266–67)

It is worthwhile to ask why Marx and trade union members so frequently felt the need to present white and black suffering in tandem—to use the suffering of black bodies to make the suffering of white bodies visible. Most people, after all, considered black bodies utterly dispensable. Whether or not black people were capable of feeling the same emotions as their white counterparts was by no means a settled question, and the general insensibility to black pain and suffering was made manifest in the quotidian nature of the slave market, the Middle Passage, and auction block. Why then would we find any discussion of black bodies in a document designed to arouse sympathy and overcome indifference to white suffering? After all, the standard rhetorical device employed by the writers of abolitionist tracts was to substitute the white body for the black—to ask white readers to imagine themselves in the place of the enslaved, either being sold on the auction block or held captive in the hold of the slave ship. As Saidiya Hartman puts it: "The effort to counteract the commonplace callousness to black suffering required that the white body be positioned in the place of the black body in order to make this suffering visible and intelligible" (1997: 19). The curious reversal we find in texts aimed at rousing the sensibility of those indifferent to the suffering of the exploited white body under capitalism can be better understood through an exploration of the ways in which black bodies and white bodies were juxtaposed in the discourses produced by working-class activists who opposed the Anglo-Boer War.

The Invisibility of Whiteness and the Spectacle of Blackness: Images of Suffering in Antiwar Discourse

It would not be an exaggeration to say that black suffering has a spectacular character. One of its most distinctive characteristics is its incredible visual accessibility, especially to the white gaze. The primal scenes of slavery's brutality, the slave pen and the auction block, highlighted above all else the incredibly public nature of black suffering. Unlike the suffering of most people, which occurred in the private, interior spaces of the home, heart, and mind, black suffering was always on display. One could run one's hands, eyes, and mind over it. No social sanctions existed whereby one was required to steal a furtive glance and then look away; rather, in the face of black suffering one could fully succumb to one's basest voyeuristic inclinations. This suffering could be stared straight in the face, contemplated, touched, tasted, and even enjoyed. Walter Johnson calls this the "shared communion in the rites of the slave market—the looking, stripping, touching, bantering, and evaluating" (1999: 149). In abolitionist tracts the rites and rituals of the slave market were transferred to the written page as the authors painstakingly sought to convey "the minutest detail of macabre acts of violence" (Hartman 1997: 18).

The general indifference to the interiority of black life, however, meant that this suffering could be not only looked at, but also looked *through*. The spectacle of black suffering was marked by the elasticity the viewer was allowed in formulating a response. One could be alternately shocked, disgusted, aroused, amused, or any combination thereof. The only thing stable about the suffering black body, therefore, was the fact of its existence. Indeed, it is possible to read the ubiquity of the image of the satisfied plantation "darky" and the relentless insistence that slaves were happy and contented as responses that were elicited by the inescapable nature of black suffering. In the black body we see the meeting of two contrary impulses — of a suffering that could not be denied but that nevertheless had an incredibly fungible character.

The ideological malleability of the suffering of black bodies — bodies that occupied the status of commodities, "social things whose qualities are at the same time perceptible and imperceptible by the senses" — is a natural outgrowth of the commodity form itself (Marx [1867] 1967: 72). The uniqueness of the commodity, which gave it what Marx termed a "mystical character," was its interchangeable and substitutable nature. And so too the nature of black suffering. Indeed, Marx's description of the commodity is fully applicable to the suffering black body: "A commodity appears, at first sight, a very trivial thing, and easily understood. Its analysis shows that it is, in reality, a very queer thing, abounding in metaphysical subtleties and theological niceties" ([1867] 1967: 71). Thus, the physical darkness of the black body, and the lack that that darkness seemed to signify — of human feeling, of sentience, of sensitivity — was the foundation of its figurative, metaphorical, and ideological transparency. The blackness of the slave was the highest form of invisible visibility, and since the status of enslaved blacks shaped and compromised the existence of all blacks, the invisible visibility of the slave became the condition of all blacks, including those in the colonies.

In chapter 4 I described the ways in which the ubiquity and centrality of the ethnographic showcase in British culture engendered a way of seeing whereby life itself came to be experienced and comprehended like an exhibition. I argued that one of the effects of the modern politics of visuality was that it enabled observers to contemplate the Other even as they turned away. It is possible to see lingering traces of this in a variety of disparate phenomena, including the spectacular descriptions of black suffering in contemporary newspaper accounts of the Anglo-Boer War. Working-class and trade union activists' antiwar discourses that appeared in publications such as the

New Age demonstrate the degree to which wounded, damaged, and exploited black bodies were constantly put on display not to enhance public knowledge about blacks, but to give visibility and tangibility to the suffering of the white worker—particularly as it related to injuries that resulted from capitalist exploitation and the limits capitalism posed to the exercise of democratic citizenship.

The suffering of black bodies (especially laboring black bodies) was continually brought to the forefront in antiwar discourses produced by working-class activists—presumably to forge ties of sentiment and to raise consciousness. The actual effect of the discourses, however, was to make a spectacle of black suffering and, in the process, reduce its salience. Readers were urged to contemplate the suffering of the black body but to ultimately turn their attention elsewhere. The manner in which the suffering of black and white bodies was juxtaposed in these texts served to redirect toward white bodies—specifically the bodies of white working-class men—the empathy and outrage that presumably should have been directed toward and expressed on behalf of the suffering black bodies. What began as meditations on black bodies, lives, and suffering ended up being extended reflections on the meanings and limits of democracy in class society. In other words, the fungible nature of blackness—the ways in which black bodies were made to function less as flesh and blood entities than as fertile discursive sites to be mined for images and metaphors—meant that the sympathy aroused by mutilated and exploited black bodies was easily rechanneled into sympathy and outrage for politically and economically marginalized white men.

The *New Age* of August 24, 1899, for example, asked readers to contemplate "the wholesale butchering of natives" that was likely to be the outcome of any military campaign in the Transvaal. The horror of the spectacle of the mutilated black body in the colonies was a pretext, however, for a meditation on the meaning of democracy in the metropole. The author of the article charged that "the state of public affairs, especially in the Transvaal, suggests we should do well to consider the scope of democracy at home." While he reaffirmed his support of the exercise of "civil rights by all reasonably competent permanent inhabitants, regardless of colour," the author's main purpose was to protest the paucity of democratic rights enjoyed by working-class people in England itself, where socioeconomic inequality and exploitation coexisted with civic "freedom."

> Within our own particular borders, within these British Isles, there are matters
> that come within the scope of Democracy, but as to which Democracy is lam-

entably indifferent. The condition of the people in what we call the lower ranks of society is shameful. It is, as a matter of fact, much worse than savagery. The savages have at least fresh air and pure water and good food, and they are not overcrowded as our workers are. A walk along Fleet Street, in the hub of the universe, in the early hour of the morning will discover wretchedly clad people hungrily sorting out the contents of the dustbins and waste paper baskets. . . . This is but one indication of the blasphemy going on in our midst every day and every hour. True Democracy embraces within its scope the feeding of the hungry and the clothing of the naked.

"A British Workman" penned a letter for the *New Age*'s October 29, 1899, edition that opened with a condemnation of the "the practical slavery involved in the English treatment of the defeated Bechuanas." The author went on to note that despite the British government's castigation of the Boers for their inhumane treatment of Africans, the plain truth was that "both Britishers and Boers have sinned against the native races in their thirst for land and gold." The main point of the letter, however, was to expose the bitter irony of the fact that a war fought to preserve democracy and the franchise abroad would have the practical effect of increasing class inequality and exploitation at home. "And the poor, the workmen of these islands, are bound to suffer and to pay for it all. War is ever against the poor. It may further enrich the wealthy but it intensifies the suffering of the poor. It was during the American Civil War that the general growth of millionaires first began and the phenomenon 'tramp' first appeared in the States." The June 28, 1900, edition of the *New Age* carried an article titled "What Doth It Profit?" which raised the specter of "thousands of natives of whom no record has been kept who have perished." The author speculated as to whether the dead were better off than the living, who were destined to become wage slaves. "Mining capitalists have announced their intention of reducing wages and employing native labour under much more stringent terms than have hitherto prevailed in the Transvaal." The article quickly turned, however, to a lengthy discourse arguing that the end result of the defense of "democracy" would be that England's "great industrial populations will cry for bread and work. . . . At home poverty and drunkenness and overcrowding will not be removed." F. Maddison also pointed to the suffering of the "overworked and low-paid black laborer in a state of semi-slavery" who belonged "to his employer during the whole of his contract period" to make the point that capitalists "have as little respect for white labour as black" (1900: 524).

The uses to which the black body was put in discourses produced by trade unionists demonstrate the precarious nature of empathy. In using the suffering African body to make a point about their own suffering—in some ways making the suffering of the African worker their own—they ended up largely eclipsing the suffering of the African. The British male worker and his concerns came to displace those of the African as the very act of showing empathy ultimately elided any sustained engagement with the African worker's pain. Although on the surface level these texts appear to be about black pain, suffering, and economic marginalization, the general indifference to black suffering in British culture meant that the suffering of the white male body would ultimately replace that of the black.

After the war concluded and the 1904 Congress took up the issue of Chinese labor in the gold mines, concern with the British worker and his pain and suffering at the hands of capital at home and abroad rendered the suffering of the African almost completely invisible. Noting that the British capitalists "must have had the employment of Chinese in view when they went to war with the Transvaal in 1899," the Congress decried the precipitous drop in wages that occurred on the Rand. A report on labor conditions there protested the fact that mining capital had seized on the opportunity to "offer white men the wages they previously paid to the Kaffirs." There was neither concern for nor even mention of the so-called Kaffirs who presumably were now receiving even less. One senses a keen awareness among the trade union activists that the logic of capital was such that their geographical location in the West in no way protected them from the suffering in Africa. Indeed, their concern was that the processes of capitalist accumulation had the potential to make the suffering of the African their own. As the author of the motion on Chinese labor concluded: "The government and their supporters would bring the same state of things into the industrial affairs of this country if they dared" (*Annual Report of the Trades Union Congress* 1904: 18).

When the trade unionists made the suffering of the African their own, they did not ameliorate indifference. Instead, they exacerbated the difficulty of making the suffering of the Other visible and ultimately elided a true understanding and acknowledgment of the condition of the African worker. The paradox of empathy was that the processes of identifying with the African were the very processes that made the African disappear. Thus a delegate to the 1904 Congress maintained that "one of the chief reasons for employing Chinese labour was the dislike of the mineowners to the British working man in this country with his Trade Union and his determination to see things fairly adjusted." The Parliamentary Committee of the Trades Union Congress resolved that every Trades Union and Trades Council should "cooperate in making a great national and effective protest against this return to slavery and insulting injustice of capitalism." Despite the copious ink that had previously been spilled lamenting the suffering of the African worker, members were encouraged to protest the importation of Chinese labor into South Africa not because of its impact on the African, but because it "was a question vitally affecting the workers of this country" (*Annual Report of the Trades Union Congress* 1904: 54).

When trade union activists and other working-class radicals used images of physically maimed and economically exploited black bodies to communicate their critique of capitalist social relations, it did little to increase empathy for Africans, but it did, paradoxically, link the experiences of the two groups as workers. Radicals' emphasis on the common experiences of all workers subject to systems wherein production was under the control of the accumulating classes did not erase the blackness of the African worker, but did tend to upset the traditional dichotomy of Africa as a locale of suffering and England as the site of privilege from which that suffering was observed and ultimately alleviated. Their analyses produced Africa and the West as sites of suffering that were both analogous and connected. Hence, at the same time radical discourses were making the suffering of the African invisible, the notion of Africans as fellow laborers tended to raise their esteem in the eyes of the British workingman. They were less visible in their particularity as Africans, but somewhat more visible as abstract individual workers. There was a tacit acknowledgment of coevalness that came via a discursive system wherein the pain of class exploitation provided a common language of humanity.

The paradoxical effect of radical discourse was to bring some Africans, primarily men working in the centers of industrial capitalism, back into the main body of the human race, from which they had been expelled by scientific racism and associated movements, while ousting another body of racial Others. When capital, the source of African suffering—and thus, by extension, that of European suffering as well—was transformed from an abstract entity into a living, breathing, human form, that form was inevitably raced as Jewish. Hence, although the model of democratic citizenship proposed by working-class activists who strove to make the balance of power between rich and poor the central criterion of democracy was a radical departure from the governing model of liberal democracy, it was actualized through a discourse of racial exclusivity. The urge to anthropomorphize capital by making it Jewish was inextricably related to the inherent difficulty of representing class power. The corollary of the invisibility of the suffering worker was the invisibility of the perpetrating agent. According to Marx. capital was "not a thing but a social relation between persons" ([1867] 1967: 766). The question remained, however, of representing the social relations between persons in an

era when images "mediated all social existence . . . [and] the world [was] not
so much put on exhibit as grasped as though it were an exhibition" (Erlmann
1999: 124). The answer was found in the Jewish body, which came to represent in human form the social relations that permitted the expropriation of
direct producers, the maintenance of absolute private property for the capitalist, and the control by capital of production and appropriation. Just as the
invisibility of white suffering had the black body as its antidote, so the invisibility of class power had the Jewish body as its antidote.

Anti-Semitism and related articulations of national belonging, which
made substantive membership in the national community an exclusive racial privilege, provided the unacknowledged yet critical framework through
which this new conception of democracy was articulated. Thus, even though
working-class radicals conceived of an expanded form of democratic citizenship—one that reached into the domains sealed off by capitalism and
thus refused the conceptual and practical bifurcation of the political and the
economic—they did so in a way that reified the fusing of race and national
identity. Ethnic absolutism not only was made compatible with this expanded notion of citizenship, but was written into its very foundation.

The exclusion of Jewish people from the body politic, which formed the
critical backdrop to the assimilation of capital and the Jewish body, was
part of a general trend to construct Englishness in ways that linked nationalism, patriotism, militarism, and racism. The attempts by Jewish people to
refuse the ideological conflation of Jewishness and capitalist exploitation
and the manner in which they used the occasion of the Anglo-Boer War to
make suffering and service, rather than race, the primary criteria for national
inclusion had important implications for the ways in which feminists,
particularly those who supported the war, framed their own campaign for
enfranchisement.

Suffering and Citizenship: Jewish Bodies in War Discourse

By yoking empathy for suffering Africans with the expression of anti-
Semitism, the authors of radical discourses frequently made the scapegoat-
ing of Jews the precondition for the rehabilitation of the African. This tendency became particularly marked during and after the Anglo-Boer War. As
a correspondent to the *Jewish Chronicle* of August 10, 1900, put it: "In Russia
we are suffering from the intelligent classes, while we are respected by the
peasants. In England we suffer from the working classes. . . . The British
working man hates the Jew." The author went on to note that the Boers, contrary to how they were portrayed in the press, harbored less racial animosity,

at least as far as Jewish people were concerned, than the British. "Never will we hear from them what we hear from Englishmen: 'Go back home, we did not ask you to come here' and etc" (p. 6).

Discussions of black exploitation and suffering at the hands of mining capital quite often provided a platform for assimilating Jewishness, as a "racial" identity, with the excesses of capital accumulation. J. C. Ward of the London Navvies Union, for example, declared that:

> Practically £100,000,000 of the taxpayers' money had been spent in trying to secure the goldfields of South Africa for cosmopolitan Jews, most of whom had no patriotism and no country. . . . Did they imagine that the wages of the Rand under Rhodes, Beit, and Eckstein would be as high as those which prevailed under the old farmers? It was clearly a question of wages, and it was the duty of those who represented the working men of Great Britain to raise their voice in defence of those people who were rightly struggling to be free. (*Annual Report of the Trades Union Congress* 1900: 55)

John Burns expressed a similar sentiment in a speech delivered shortly after the relief of Mafeking. He amalgamated the categories of "Jew" and "alien capitalist" through his assertion that Jewish people had "no bowels of compassion" for the African and that their greed as capitalists had only been "kept in check" by Kruger (1900: 4). Sidney Shippard agreed that the British workman "does not like to think that the veldt has been dyed red to make it easier for a small clique of capitalists, in which the German Jew is conspicuous, to grow rich at the expense of the wretched Kaffirs" (1900: 522).

Closely linked to this impulse to make the Jewish body stand in for capital was the propensity to define the categories of Englishness and Jewishness in such a way as to stress the impossibility of inhabiting them both simultaneously. This tendency became particularly marked during the period of the Anglo-Boer War, when the connections between patriotism, race, and imperialism became even more tightly established. Thus, although working-class radicals and defenders of imperialism like Sir Alfred Milner disagreed fundamentally on the question of British expansion and in their stance on capitalism, they shared a racially exclusive conception of Englishness that necessarily excluded Jewish people.

The *Jewish Chronicle*, which took a great deal of interest in the question of whether Jews could be Englishmen, printed a letter from J. A. J. de Villiers of the British Museum, who answered the question with a definitive no. The letter captures the prevailing sentiment on the question of Jewish racial identity and its relationship to English national identity. In de Villiers's estimation, the likelihood of a Jew becoming an Englishman was about the same as the likelihood of a Zulu becoming one. His letter encapsulates the degree to which racial characteristics of any kind other than "white" were judged as incompatible with authentic forms of Englishness.

> I have always been amused by the intensely eager desire of the majority of British Jews to masquerade as Englishmen and by the most aggressive attitude (generally indicative of a weak cause) they invariably take up. . . . There can be no such thing as an English Jew. . . . When we speak of a man as an Englishman we do not mean that he is a Protestant or a mere dweller by chance or choice in England but that he belongs to the Anglo-Saxon race, and when we speak of a man as a Jew we mean that he belongs to the Semitic race, and the two are not and cannot be synonymous. . . . We would really never think of calling a Zulu, born of Zulus married with a Zulu, and having Zulu children, an Englishman, lived he either in Natal or London, and as fine as his race undoubtedly is. (November 2, 1990: 8)

The idea that Englishness and Anglo-Saxon racial purity were indissoluble became much more deeply entrenched with the advent of settler colonialism and imperialism. As Benedict Anderson demonstrates in *Imagined Communities*, the idea of a nation cannot cohere without a mode of apprehending the world that makes it possible, in his words, to "think the nation" (1991: 22). What unified the British Empire as an imagined community and gave it coherence was the notion of Anglo-Saxon racial purity.

J. A. Froude wrote *Oceana* as a paean to this ideal of Anglo-Saxon unity. The British Empire, according to Froude, was founded on an ideal of Anglo-Saxondom as a unity among people who, despite living in far-flung colonies, were linked by common descent, common origin, and a common language. Froude's guiding principal was that because the English had founded the colonies, "the people at home and the people in the colonies are one people" (1886: 14). He hoped to one day see English families in all the white dominions—Australia, New Zealand, Canada, South Africa—thriving and multiplying "without ceasing to be Englishmen" (Bennett 1870: 245). In an essay titled "England and Her Colonies" Froude further expanded on his idea of the British nation as an imagined community.

> Let it once be established that an Englishman emigrating to Canada or the Cape or Australia or New Zealand did not forfeit his nationality, that he was still on English soil as much as if he was in Devonshire or Yorkshire, and would remain an Englishman while the English Empire lasted. . . . Once settled they

would multiply and draw their relations after them, and at great stations around the globe there would grow up, under conditions the most favorable which the human constitution can desire, fresh nations of Englishmen. . . . With our roots thus struck so deeply into the earth, it is hard to see what dangers, internal and external, we should have cause to fear, or what impediment could then check the indefinite and magnificent expansion of the English Empire. (1895: 173)

According to Froude, it was because of their superior blood that the British were able to accomplish great feats in arts and letters, emerge victorious from battles and wars, and be the leaders of nations and great men. Here lay the root of Froude's insistence that nations must only comprise one race—that they must be racially pure—and that the limits of the nation should coincide not with geographic boundaries, but with the lines of race.

This fundamental link between blood, achievement, and national belonging was also articulated by Sir Alfred Milner, British High Commissioner to South Africa during the Anglo-Boer War. "I have emphasized the importance of the racial bond," he wrote. "It is the British race which built the Empire, and it is the undivided British race which can alone uphold it. . . . Deeper, stronger, more primordial than these material ties is the bond of common blood, a common language, common history and traditions." Milner, like Froude, believed the "racial bond" of the English transcended national boundaries. He maintained that the British race included "all the peoples of the United Kingdom and their descendants in other countries under the British flag" (1913: 35). The combined effect of these discourses was to cast Jewish people in England as permanent aliens and, in the words of one writer to the *Jewish Chronicle*, to "cast doubt on [their] being an integral part of the body politic" (November 2, 1900: 6).

Despite, or perhaps because of, the ways in which they were maligned and made out to be the exclusive purveyors of working-class suffering, English Jews saw the occasion of the Anglo-Boer War as an opportunity to assert their fitness for inclusion in the English nation by emphasizing the services Jewish men and women had performed for empire. As the *Chronicle's* August 17, 1900, edition put it: "The distinction between Jews as such and Jewish Englishmen should be drawn in the thinking over South African matters" (p. 12). An example of this reasoning can be found in one writer's assertion that "among the imperial troops serving in the Transvaal were a due proportion of English Jews, who, side by side with English Christians, have been battling against Boer Christians and Jews." The writer asked: "If these things don't bring conviction, what will?" (*Jewish Chronicle*, November 2,

1900: 6). Jewish men and women were even more committed to the Uit-lander cause and the war because "the Jews, who have sad experience else-where of how soon the exclusion from political rights leads to contempt, and contempt to plunder and outrage, have perceived the danger of allow-ing the dignity and rights of Uitlanders to be assailed with impunity in the Transvaal" (*Jewish Chronicle,* January 19, 1990: 15).

The *Chronicle* also carried a series of letters from readers that stressed the fact that Jewish people should be counted among those who had suffered during the war. They were thus able to assert their attachment to the body politic by insisting that not only were they not the exclusive purveyors of suf-fering, but they also had endured suffering. Every edition of the *Chronicle* that appeared during the war carried lists of Jewish casualties and profiles of Jew-ish soldiers who had fallen in battle. Further, articles like one entitled "Jew-ish Patriotism" were careful to emphasize that not only were Jews enrolled among the regular forces who at that moment were defending the Empire, or on their way to join the defense, but during the previous week some hundreds had "enthusiastically responded to the call of duty as volunteers" (Decem-ber 24, 1899: 16). The previous month's edition had reminded readers that there were "800 Jewish soldiers and volunteers" at the front, and a corre-spondent had complained in a letter that: "When we are told that Jews never fight it is forgotten that in the late Langeberg campaign the only officer who fell in action was a Jew, Lieutenant Harris" (November 17, 1899: 21–22).

The *Chronicle* also carried a number of articles that emphasized that Jew-ish men and women were among those who suffered under the yoke of class exploitation. The *Chronicle's* December 15, 1899, edition noted that the "few Jewish capitalists who are interested in the Transvaal—and the many who are not—have already given their full quota to the patriotic funds." The real focus of the article, however, was on the "poor Jews of the East End who were also called upon to pay their share and who responded heartily" (p. 11). The writer of an article titled "Some Mistakes about the Jew" complained that the English "spoke of the usurer as Shylock, as though Christian money lenders never existed." The article went on to note that "it was sometimes urged that the Jew deprived the British working man of his bread. He never deprived the British working man of his beer. Jews are poorer in London than any other men to be found in this vast metropolis" (November 9, 1990: 12).

To combat their exclusion from the body politic, Jews sought to make suf-fering and service, rather than race, the necessary criteria for being included in the universal category of citizen. Bodies were thus made into evocative signs of social and political injustice and could be used as a basis for claims for inclusion in the body politic. Simply to have suffered, however, was not sufficient to establish a claim for inclusion; injured parties also had to demonstrate that they had performed a service—that the suffering had occurred in the course of service to the body politic. In the case of the Anglo-Boer War, the emphasis was on the services the suffering bodies had rendered to the empire. The problem with basing claims for inclusion on the twin criteria of service and suffering, however, was the peculiar invisibility of the latter. Neither suffering nor service was self-evident. Rather, both had to be continually produced and reproduced in various media of representation—books, newspapers, personal narratives, plays, or stories.

It is thus possible to draw a link between the importance of print capitalism to the rise of nationalism, which Benedict Anderson identifies, and the importance of suffering and service—or more specifically, of the representation of them—for inclusion in the body politic. Anderson argues that the convergence of capitalism and print technology created the possibility of a "new form of imagined community" that "set the stage for the modern nation" (1991: 46). If Anderson is indeed correct that the formation of a nation was contingent on the entering of particular experiences into the "accumulating memory of print" so they became national experiences and memories, then it would stand to reason that individual experiences would also have had to be entered into the "accumulating memory of print" in order for individuals to assert their claims to national belonging (1991: 80). If a group's claims to national belonging were contested, the importance of having their story of suffering entered in print would have been particularly great.

This strategy also became a marked feature of feminist discourse. The Anglo-Boer War provided suffragists the ideal pretext for protesting their own political marginalization, just as it had for trade union members. It also provided a context for advancing the new model of civic inclusion that stressed service and suffering over biological inheritance as the most salient criteria for national belonging. This emphasis on suffering relied on an "Africanist presence" (Morrison 1990) to make the claimants' suffering visible and discernible.

Suffering Natives, Woman's Suffrage, and the War: Pro-War Activism and the Struggle for Female Enfranchisement

The year 1869 was a signal year in British feminist politics. This was the year John Stuart Mill began to seriously search for an outlet to publish *The Subjection of Women*, now popularly known as the "bible of equal rights feminism" (Mill 1989: xvii). Mill was an important figure in the suffrage movement. As Edward Turner explained, the idea that women should be granted the right to vote was a "novelty which encountered ridicule more than re-spect until Mill became its champion" (1913: 593). During the debate on the 1867 Reform Act, Mill distinguished himself by calling for the equalization of national franchise qualifications for men and women, and in 1869 men first granted women local government voting rights that were the same as those they enjoyed.

The year 1869 was not one of unqualified success, however, for it was also the year that Parliament constructed a legally enforceable gender identity for women in the form of the Contagious Diseases Acts and the Infant Life Protection Bill. The former gave state agents the power and authority to de-tain and forcibly examine women believed to be prostitutes. The latter made it a criminal offense to give birth without notifying a public authority. This bill amounted to an attempt to control infant mortality by means of state surveillance of women and police regulation of female sexual behavior, particularly as they related to childbirth and child rearing. Both of these measures sought to regulate and criminalize the actions of women while turning a blind eye to those of men. The measures angered Victorian femi-nists, who began to view the state as an instrument of male oppression. Thus was inaugurated a new era in feminist politics wherein gender activ-ists sought to bring the issue of women's rights into the general debate on lib-eral individualism.

Activist women began to organize themselves into national networks of volunteers who took it upon themselves to act as "permanent watchdog[s] against state encroachment on civil liberties and as articulators of the under-lying principles of political and social ethics on which all individual citizen claims to liberty rested" (Roberts 1995: 87). Women's suffrage societies were founded in London, Edinburgh, Manchester, Birmingham, and Bristol in the late 1860s. They soon united to form the National Union of Women's Suffrage Societies, whose constitution stated that its aim was to "promote the claim of Women to the Parliamentary vote on the same terms as it is or may be granted to men" (quoted in Turner 1913: 602). At its high point the union had forty thousand members enrolled in more than four hundred branches and was publishing a paper entitled *The Common Cause*.

Although suffragists could differ quite strongly from one another in their emphases and tactics (see Rosen 1979), a large majority agreed that the for-mulation of a gender-specific definition of individual liberty was an impor-tant step on the journey toward full enfranchisement. It was thus that lead-ing feminists were able to closely align themselves with thinkers, like John Stuart Mill, who were widely known advocates of libertarian principles. Josephine Butler, a well-known suffragist whose ideas will be explored more fully below, wrote one of her earliest treatises not on feminism, but on the history of citizen-state relations. The text, entitled *Government by Police,* used arguments first developed by Mill to make the point that laws like the Contagious Diseases Acts, which told people how to conduct themselves in their personal lives, led to "despotic tendencies" in government and "enfeeble[d] the sense of responsibility in the citizenry" (Butler 1880: 64). If we substitute *women* for *people,* it is easy to see how Butler was able to bring together arguments about civil liberties and arguments about gender. She, like other feminists of her time, was attracted to the abstract individualism of liberal theory because it provided a basis for challenging the idea that because of their sexuality women could safely be subjected to controls by the state that would be considered an egregious affront to the ideals of liberty if they were applied to any group of men.

In 1912, Sir Almroth Wright penned a letter to the London *Times* wherein he chastised suffragists as "incomplete and sexually embittered" and proposed as a remedy that they should "join their men in newer lands beyond the sea" (quoted in Turner 1913: 592). Wright thus advocated emigration to the colonies as a means for relieving England of the distressing problem of women demanding sexual and social equality. Wright's impulse to introduce a discussion of the colonies into the suffrage debate was not unique. Suffragists themselves were among the first to see the value of drawing metropole and colony into a single discursive field. Their position differed quite strongly from Wright's, however, in that for them the colonies provided an important point of reference, rather than a means of escape.

Advocates for extension of the franchise to women used similar tactics to those employed by working-class activists. They too noted the hypocrisy of a British government that sent people to fight for rights that were not yet fully enjoyed by all British citizens at home. As one feminist wrote in *The English-woman's Review of Social and Industrial Questions:*

> Great Britain is on the brink of war with the Transvaal, and the grievance which focuses all other grievances, and is the point on which the whole question of war depends is the denial of the franchise to the Outlanders. . . . Englishmen understand the hardship for the Outlander, who is placed on an unequal footing with the Boer. But they do not realize that the self-same exclusion can press hardly on their sisters at home. They are conscious they wish well to their sisters, and are blinded to the fact that they are not doing them as they would be done by. Perchance, out of this turmoil and strife of arms to gain a peaceful right, our brothers will learn to appreciate better the right reasonableness of the claim of their sisters at home. (October 16, 1899: 246)

The *Review*'s April 17, 1900, edition also noted the ways in which the war made the inconsistencies of the British government with regard to enfranchisement glaringly obvious.

> The House of Commons has shown anxious care to secure that Reservists and Volunteers who have gone to the war in South Africa shall not, in consequence, forfeit their votes. This is quite right: since absence on the battle-field neutralises their qualifications for voting. But to what a *reducto ad absurdum* the Electoral Disabilities (Military Service) Bill brings that favourite objection to Women's Suffrage, that women must not vote because they do not go fight, when the men who do go to fight thereby lose their votes! (p. 91)

Suffragists who defended the war not only pointed to the parallels between their situation and that of the Uitlanders, they also made a case for their fitness for citizenship on the basis of the unique services they, as women, performed for the empire during the war. The following poem, which first appeared in a publication entitled *Poems on the War* and was later reprinted in the July 16, 1900, edition of the *Englishwoman's Review*, succinctly presented the case for linking suffrage and service:

> Owing but the ballot's power,
> Best to serve thee in thine hour
> Never then shall brain or heart
> Fail to do their worthiest part,
> When their sons and daughters stand
> Equal workers for their land. (p. 297)

The author of an article in the *Englishwoman's Review* of April 17, 1900, also noted that although men had undeniably "responded nobly to their country's call," it was equally important to recognize that "women have also had their share of work" and to acknowledge the "serious and varied . . . parts they found themselves called on to take in the strain of a nation's endeavour" (p. 7). Another writer for the *Review* agreed that "it is not only those who bear arms that can do valiant service in defence of their country" (January 15, 1900: 46). Yet another noted that the war had shown British women how important it was for them to

> honour their own nature and use their own distinctive power, aptitude, and character for the service of society. The call to fulfill the duties of citizenship was not a summons to an entirely different order of duties from those which

women fulfilled as daughters, sisters, and mothers. Rather was it a call to do in the community what they did in the home, a call to public service that was in the direct line of their own distinctive capacity and character. It was as women they were called to serve society and relate themselves directly to public life and activity. . . . The truth is men have hardly learned the rudiments of the work which competent and cultivated women can do in society. In all their Agencies for relieving, rescuing, uplifting, and training the dependent classes they needed just the elements which only women can supply. (October 16, 1899: 283)

Middle-class women were thus making a conscious effort to simultaneously recapture control over the home and family from male experts and plead for civic inclusion. As one contributor to the *Review* put it, the "one-sided economy that has shut the mother element out" was also the reason that women were being "denied their status as citizens" (October 15, 1990: 225).

Over the course of the previous three decades male reformers had used the "incapacity" of working-class women as a wedge by means of which they slowly usurped the domain of the household from all women. When middle-class women stressed the important services they rendered to the empire, they were also attempting to distance themselves from working-class women, at whose feet many male reformers laid the responsibility for the nation's dismal performance during the war.

Mothers, Sons, and Empire

The sentiments expressed by General Frederick Maurice in an influential article that appeared in the *Contemporary Review* were typical. According to Maurice: "the young man of 16–18 years of age is what he is because of the training through which he has passed during his infancy and adulthood" (*Contemporary Review*, 1903: 432). Therefore, if he failed to show promise, the root cause lay in "ignorance on the part of the mothers of the necessary conditions for the bringing up of healthy children." Maurice was not alone in his belief that "maternal ignorance" was the principal cause of the poor quality of recruits and Britain's less than stellar performance in the war. Even prior to the outbreak of the war, middle-class male reformers were already expressing alarm at what they perceived as a precipitous decline in the morals of females of the "submerged tenth" or "vicious" class. As William Booth explained, "The bastard of a harlot, born in a brothel, suckled on gin, and familiar from earliest infancy with all the bestialities of debauch, violated before she is twelve, and driven out into the streets by her mother a year

or two later, what chance is there for a such a girl in this world—I say nothing about the next? Yet such a case is not exceptional" (1890: 47).

Middle-class reformers considered the degeneration of poor women particularly dangerous because of the possibility that they would populate the
world with the dysgenic offspring of their depraved unions. There were, according to Booth, thousands upon thousands of people who were "begotten
when both parents were besotted with drink, whose mothers saturated themselves with alcohol every day of their pregnancy, who may be said to have
sucked the taste for strong drink with their mothers' milk." Male reformers
exclusively blamed poor women for the prolific nature of the degenerate
classes as compared to the more enterprising. It appeared to many reformers
that the procreative irresponsibility of poor women was making conditions
in England such that the mentally and physically weaker were set to outstrip
their betters. Speaking before the Literary and Philosophical Society in 1905,
Karl Pearson, author of *National Life from the Standpoint of Science*, used the
occasion of the Anglo-Boer War to reflect on the dangers this trend posed for
the future of the British nation.

> The average net size of our families has been falling for perhaps fifty years.
> Who will venture to assert that this decreased fertility has occurred in the in-
> ferior stocks? On the contrary, is it not the feckless and improvident who have
> the largest families? The professional classes, the trading classes, the substan-
> tial and provident working classes—shortly, the capable elements of the com-
> munity with a certain standard of life—have been marrying late and having
> small families . . . all at the expense of the nation's future. We cannot suspend
> the struggle for existence in any class of the community without stopping its
> progress. We cannot recruit the nation from its inferior stocks without deteri-
> orating our national character. (1905: 29)

Pearson argued that it was the duty of the state to impress on women the
gravity of their responsibility to the nation and to "inculcate a feeling of
shame in the parents of a weakling, whether it be mentally or physically unfit" (1905: 28). Like many other middle-class male reformers, he thought
that because poor women could not be trusted, it was reformers' special
province to restore health and vitality to the English family and through that
family to the nation. Since the rearing of boys in particular was seen as an
imperial as well as a national question, reformers sought to remove the responsibility for raising sons from poor and working-class women and de-
volve it to the state and voluntary agencies run by men. Francis Galton, for
example, believed not only that the state should take responsibility for en-

couraging eugenic unions, but that once they were forged, they should provide a safe, stable, and secure environment for the conception and rearing of children. He thought that a state-supported housing or "cottage" scheme could best accomplish this.

> There is yet another existing form of princely benevolence, which might be so extended as to exercise a large effect on race improvement. I mean the provision to exceptionally promising young couples of healthy and convenient houses at low rentals. A continually renewed settlement of this kind can be easily imagined, free from the taint of patronage, and analogous to colleges with their self-elected fellowships and rooms for residence, that should become an exceedingly desirable residence for a specified time. It would be so in the same way that a good club by its own social advantages attracts desirable candidates. The tone of the place would be higher than elsewhere, on account of the high quality of the inmates, and it would be distinguished by an air of energy, intelligence, health and self-respect and by mutual helpfulness. (1909: 32)

Male reformers thus focused on women's procreative capacity, while female suffragists emphasized every type of service to the nation but procreation. The *Englishwoman's Review*, for example, noted that women had contributed money, had assembled publications "endeavoring to place before some of the foreign critics of England more exact information," and had sewn uniforms (April 17, 1900: 81). According to the *Englishwoman's Review* of July 16, 1900: "Every soldier out in South Africa carries in the lining of each garment a linen label containing the name of the girl who made it" (p. 198). The Anglo-Boer War thus provided a pretext for middle-class women to emphasize the positive contribution they were making to the future of the nation and the British Empire while reversing the negative stereotypes that made all women the source of the nation's degeneration. It is important to note that these suffragists for the most part focused their energies on seeking the enfranchisement of British property-owning women. Rather than trying to undermine the negative stereotypes about working-class mothers and about the negative impact of their actions on the body politic, middle-class women distanced themselves from them and in the process advocated for a class-stratified though gender-inclusive system of representation.

Female suffragists also emphasized the degree to which British women had suffered, once again bringing to the fore suffering and service in the construction of claims for national belonging. The *New Age* of June 28, 1900, for example, lamented that many women's "souls are heavy with sorrow." A poem entitled *"The List of Casualties; Or, Who Has Given Most?"* which appeared in the April 17, 1900, edition of the *Englishwoman's Review,* explored a similar set of themes:

> She who rests secure to-night, remote from shot or shell,
> Sore grieving in an English home, while learning how he fell,
> Has given—not her life, indeed—but very light of life.
>
> Ay, who in truth has given most, since loving hearts must bleed,
> While brothers, sons, and husbands rush to die for England's need?
> The one who faithful stood till death against the Transvaal host?
> Or she who living gave her life? Say, who has given most? (p. 83)

Suffragists wrote passionately not only of their own suffering, but of the suffering of others as well. As Antoinette Burton explained: "Western feminists seeking entrance into the public sphere relied upon a fundamentally gendered identification with suffering others to legitimate their quest to be counted as political subjects" (2000: 19). Feminists who supported the Anglo-Boer War, like working-class radicals, frequently invoked images of suffering African bodies in their discourses. Because black bodies were marked by the same interchangeable nature that was a characteristic feature of the commodity, it is not surprising that they could be put to almost any ideological use. Indeed, feminist supporters of the war used images of black bodies and black suffering with as much agility and aplomb as their antiwar counterparts. The critical difference between the two groups lay not only in their respective stances on the justness of the war, but also in the uses to which they put the image of the suffering black body. While working-class radicals invoked the black body in order to make class exploitation visible and, in the process, to challenge the artificial separation between economic and political matters, the pro-war suffragists used the black body to obscure class exploitation and to emphasize the necessity of separating economic from political and, above all, moral concerns.

Pro-War Suffragists and the Discourse of Black Suffering

Although they were far outnumbered by their antiwar counterparts, there was a significant number of pro-war suffragists, most of whom were active in the production and dissemination of literature for both the war and suffrage. Among them, for example, was Millicent Fawcett, who recalled in her memoirs that "the origin and cause of the war were on lines that very strongly emphasized the reasonable and irrefutable nature of the claim of British women to a share in the government of their country" (1925: 149). During the war, Fawcett was quoted in *New Age*, as having said that "if women were to be able to hold their own in the matter of retaining privileges already possessed by them they must first of all possess themselves of the suffrage." She went on to note that "some of the value that an Englishman sets upon this mark of citizenship may be gathered by considering the cause of the present War" (November 30, 1899: 207). She was supported by an unnamed contributor to the *Englishwoman's Review* who argued that the "cooperation of women in wartime" demonstrated the urgent necessity of "increased fellowship in work and in privileges between the sexes" (October 15, 1900: 231).

The work of pro-war suffragist Josephine Butler, who was a close associate of Fawcett and one of the most prominent suffragists speaking out in favor of the British campaign in South Africa, exemplifies many of the trends that featured prominently in the work of pro-war suffragists. In 1900 Butler published her treatise, *Native Races and the War*, in which, like many suffragists before her, she remarked on the irony of a war fought to extend the franchise abroad when "for fifty years English women have petitioned for it, and have not yet obtained it" (1900: 134). Following in the well-trod footprints of a generation of reformers, Butler mobilized images of suffering African bodies, culled mostly from secondhand accounts. Her stated aim was to "bring witnesses together who will testify to the past and present condition of the native races . . . among whom there shall be representatives of the native peoples themselves." Butler used these witnesses and their accounts to document the suffering inflicted on African bodies by the Boers and, in the process, to dispute those who would "attribute this war to a sudden impulse [of] Imperial ambition and greed" (1900: 21).

In the opening chapter of her text Butler commented on whites' general inability to fully appreciate that blacks were capable of suffering in the same ways that they did. She used the occasion of the war to ask the question: "Do not Natives suffer, love, hate, fear, and hope as others?" Then Butler went on to stress that her work would be devoted to reversing this peculiar trend.

> So far as my own experience of natives has gone, I have found that in all the essential qualities of mind and body they very much resemble white men. Of them might be aptly quoted the speech Shakespeare puts into Shylock's mouth: "Hath not a Jew eyes? Hath not a Jew hands, organs, dimensions, senses, affections, passions?" In the same way, I ask, has a native no feelings or affections? Does he not suffer when his parents are shot, or his children stolen, or when he is driven a wanderer from his home? Does he not know fear, feel pain, affection, hate, and gratitude? Most certainly he does. (1900: 17)

Unlike the narratives produced by the trade union members, which placed the blame for the African's suffering squarely at the feet of "Jewish capital," Butler located the source of that suffering in the moral turpitude and arrested development of the Boers. Hence, in the secondhand accounts she reproduced, all of her "native informants" stressed their attachment to the British metropolitan body politic while recounting the injuries they experienced at the hands of the Boers. In a typical account an informant stated:

> I wish to hear upon what conditions Her Majesty will receive me, and my country and my people, under her protection. I am weary with fighting. I do not like war, and I ask her Majesty to give me peace. I am very much distressed that my people are being destroyed by war and I wish them to obtain peace. I ask Her Majesty to defend me, as she defends all her people. There are three things which distress me very much—war, selling people, and drink. All these things I find in the Boers, and it is these things which destroy people, to make an end of them in the country. (1900: 14)

In painting the war as an exercise in imperialistic chivalry designed to save suffering Africans from the Boers' depredations, Butler reified the separation of the economic from the political and the social by insisting upon seeing the war as a moral crusade devoid of economic influence.

> In regard to the assertion that "England coveted the gold of the Transvaal," what is here meant by "England"? Ours is a representative Government. Are the entire people, with their representatives in Parliament and the Government included in the assertion, or is it meant that certain individuals, desiring gold, went to the Transvaal in search of it? The expression "England" in this relation is vague and misleading. The search for gold is not in itself a legal or moral offense. But the inordinate desire and pursuit of wealth, becoming the absorbing motive to the exclusion of all nobler aims, is a moral offence and a source of corruption. (p. 108)

In Butler's text there is no economic system with overarching laws of accumulation. There are only greedy, uncivilized, or amoral individuals whose actions threaten to derail an otherwise healthy and well-functioning system. For Butler the political system was not an entity that constituted relations of production and exploitation; rather, that system stood wholly apart and was "inherently just . . . eternally firm and unchangeable . . . and founded on the highest ethics—the ethics of Christ" (1900: 108).

Butler further reified the separation between the economic and political realms when she used the question of the extension of the franchise in South Africa to insist that civic equality should have no bearing on class inequality and that formal democracy could—indeed should—coexist with class exploitation. In response to those who suggested that relations between classes should be affected by civic status, Butler had this to say: "Even in these enlightened days there seems to be in some minds a strange confusion as to the understanding of the principle of Equality for which we plead, and which is one of the first principles laid down in the Charter of our Liberties. What is meant in that charter is *Equality of All Before the Law;* not by any means social equality, which belongs to another region of political ideas altogether" (1900: 133). Butler used African suffering as a means not only of reifying the economic and political aspects of the conflict but also of calling for the prolongation of a system of rule at home that embodied the relationship between capital and labor in a political division between appropriating rulers and laboring subjects. She urged that that undesirability of Africans "too early becoming full fledged voters" was akin to the undesirability of too rapidly expanding the franchise to the laboring multitude in Britain. She urged that in both cases "some sort of Education test, some proof of a certain amount of civilization and instruction attained, might be applied with advantage" (1900: 134). She noted approvingly that "to have to wait a little while for it does not seem, from the Englishwoman's point of view at least, a great hardship, when it is remembered how long our agricultural labourers had to wait for that privilege" (1900: 152).

Butler thus used the situation in the Transvaal as a tool for arguing for a mode of citizenship that was more inclusive because it gave women the vote, but ultimately was less empowering, particularly for the working classes. She advocated for a democratic system that despite its gender inclusiveness did not in any way make the balance of class power a criterion of democracy. Butler opposed extending the franchise at home and abroad if it threatened to interfere with property relations. In essence, she argued for civic equality only when the power of the capitalists to appropriate the surplus labor of workers was dependent not upon the appropriators' privileged civic status, but upon the workers' propertylessness. In a situation where purely economic status replaced political privilege as the source of economic power, civic status was less economically salient because the economy became confined to a formally separate sphere, totally invulnerable to interference by civic action. Butler was clearly in favor of a system of universal suffrage wherein class inequality was able to survive—and perhaps even thrive. Her ideal of democracy, and that articulated by most pro-war suffragists, thus stood in polar opposition to that articulated by the trade union activists.

The suffering black body played a pivotal role in Butler's treatise precisely because it provided the ideal pretext for presenting the war as a moral crusade above all else. Her deployment of the suffering black body was strategic in that she used amelioration of black suffering to deny the fact that war was a coercive intervention by the state on behalf of the expropriating classes. Indeed, Butler denied any connection between capitalists and the men responsible for the spread of the British Empire. In her words, "capitalists, left to themselves, would mercilessly exploit the labour of the coloured man. That is precisely the reason why they should not be left to themselves, but should be under the control of the British Empire" (1900: 138). Butler thus denied the essentially political nature of the disposition of power between capital and labor, and to deny that was to deny the possibility that property relations could be vulnerable to democratic influence. In other words, the formal equality of political rights would have minimal impact on class inequality.

In the writings of Butler and her fellow pro-war suffragists it is possible to discern the processes whereby the democratization and extension of civic and political rights coexists with, and can perhaps even exacerbate, the limitation of the scope for the exercise of political power. Liberal democracy permits the extension of citizenship by restricting its powers. In looking at the Anglo-Boer War as a moment in the struggle for women's parliamentary enfranchisement that presaged the development of "new strategies, idioms, and organizations" around the expansion of liberal notions of democracy and citizenship, it is possible to see it as a pivotal moment in the historical trajectory that culminated in "the devaluation of citizenship entailed by capitalist social relations [becoming] an essential attribute of modern democracy" (Wood 1995: 211).

The suffering black body was thus an extremely malleable ideological construct that could used to provide either a justification for the coexistence of democracy and rule by the rich or a critique of a system that allowed the coexistence of political equality and class inequality. There was, however, another group of suffragists who did not mobilize images of black bodies as part of their argumentation about the war. They called for a different conception of citizenship that placed neither suffering nor service, but rather consent, at the center.

Antiwar Suffragists, the Anglo-Boer War, and a New Model of Citizenship

The writings and speeches produced by female suffragists who opposed the war are striking on two accounts. First, they lack images of suffering native bodies. Rather, they contain repeated references to the suffering of the Boers that had as their corollary a conscious attempt to reverse the stigmatization of the Dutch as racial Others and to assimilate the Boers into the white race. Second, the model of citizenship they proposed did not focus on the services performed by the citizen in exchange for rights, but on the actions of the government, which determined whether citizens were likely to give their consent to be governed. The whitening of the Boers was by no means incidental to this new model of citizenship. In fact, antiwar suffragists deployed the Anglo-Boer War in the evolution of a model of citizenship that, although it attempted to shift the conception of the state onto a more completely democratic basis, had class and racial domination written into its very foundation.

The antiwar suffragists were in agreement with both working-class radicals and pro-war suffragists that there were "other Uitlanders than those in the Transvaal" and that women in Britain suffered no less from the injustice of being denied the vote than the Uitlanders did (*New Age*, July 6, 1899). A writer for the *New Age* of September 14, 1899, agreed:

> There is one aspect of this "Outlander" difficulty in the Transvaal which is peculiarly interesting to British women and which, end how it may, should cause them to rise in mass and claim their own rights! Our statesmen are showing us that they consider the question of political enfranchisement of the Outlander a matter of extreme importance. They tell us that the unenfranchised must inevitably be the wronged and stultified. Then let the women of Britain invite them to look at home and redress the wrongs that are easily within their own reach! The unenfranchised women of Great Britain are "inlanders," born on the soil. . . . Most of the arguments in favour of enfranchising the Outlander of the Transvaal, tell in favour of the enfranchisement of British women! Such an opportunity to bring forward and assert their rights may scarcely occur again. (p. 30)

The antiwar suffragists tended to focus their attention on two issues: the legitimacy of the state's use of force and the question of whether citizens were obliged to obey a state that acted in their name but without their consent. Most of those who defended the Boers did so on the grounds that the British government's use of force against them was not legitimate. It is in these discussions of the British government's lack of legitimacy that the fact came most strongly to the fore that England was "in the midst of a war with two small Dutch States in South Africa" whose populations were less than that of Nottingham and not half the size of Derbyshire (*New Age*, June 21, 1900: 397). It was also in these discussions that the Boers' racial kinship with the

English—or as a writer for the *New Age* put it, the fact that the inhabitants of the Boer republics were "allied to us in blood and religion"—was emphasized (June 21, 1900: 396).

Hence, at a demonstration held in the Queen's Hall to protest the war, speaker after speaker condemned the illegitimacy of the British government's use of force against a weaker state. A Mrs. C. P. Scott decried the "great crime that had been committed by the British government" and lamented that it was causing "the natural forces tending to unite the two white races" to be wrenched asunder. A Miss I. O. Ford reminded her audience that although she had spoken "as though the Dutch in South Africa were a foreign race, this resolution reminds us that we come of the same stock. It is not difficult for us to recognize the likeness in a people." She also admitted to being envious of the Boer women because "they had none of that sting behind them of feeling that their country had not acted as it ought to have done."

The fact that the South African republics, "little States where liberty and independence are so dear," were engaged in what a writer for the *New Age* of June 28, 1900, called a "heroic defence of their independence" also took center stage in suffragist discourse. The antiwar suffragists seized on the fact that the Boer republics were nations whose subjects had the right to resist the encroachment of a foreign power that threatened to govern them without their consent. They were in further agreement that as disfranchised citizens women had never granted their consent for this illegitimate war to be waged in their names, and they were thus led to question whether they were obliged to abide by the laws of a state to whose illegitimate actions they had not consented. The author of a column in the *New Age* titled "Woman Inlanders," for example, argued that women should not be obliged to pay taxes to support a war being waged without their consent as citizens.

> Such an opportunity to bring forward and assert our rights may scarcely occur again. As the Government still turns a stubbornly deaf ear to the orderly pleas of British women for some share in control of the national expenditure, which they bear their part, might not an organised protest on the part of British women against paying taxes, concerning whose enactment they are allowed no voice be expedient? . . . British women would not be fighting for their rights merely. . . . They would be making a stand for justice and truth all over the world! (September 14, 1899)

An article in the *New Age* of June 21, 1900, also pointed to the argument that women were not obliged to consent to be governed by a state that denied them their right of free speech. A Mrs. Tomkinson was quoted as having said: "Not the least of the many paradoxes in which this war abounded lay in the fact that the war was ostensibly undertaken to give political rights to a certain portion of the population of a Dutch Republic. It had ended in practically muzzling for many months a goodly proportion of the population of Great Britain." A Mrs. Amie Hicks said that the war had "taken the right of free speech from the people of the country." She maintained that, like the Boers, the antiwar suffragists would fight for their right of free expression "even if it cost them their lives."

Consent, then, played a central role in the antiwar suffragists' political discourse, replacing service as the central criterion for citizenship. The pro-Boers drew on a Lockean conception of government, according to which the legitimacy of any political authority is grounded in the consent of the governed. The Anglo-Boer War was ideal for their purposes because it was the preeminent contemporary example of an independence struggle waged on the principle of the right of individuals to refuse to give their consent to an encroaching power that threatened to refuse to acknowledge them as citizens. As Laura Mayhall explains, the antiwar suffragists made the independence struggle of the Boers, alongside those of the American colonists, Greeks, and Italians, "analogous with their own cause" (2000: 12). Indeed, the "embattled farmers" of the Transvaal were considered the "worthy sons of their fathers who, facing in Holland the overwhelming power of Spain, maintained the liberties of Europe, and the world, and shielded and schooled the Pilgrim fathers for the planting of New England" (*New Age*, June 28, 1900). Mrs. C. P. Scott, who had proclaimed her belief in "nationalities working out their own salvation," asked her fellow suffragists whether they had "forgotten our sympathy for Poland, for Greece, and for Italy" (*New Age*, June 21, 1900).

No African polity, in the antiwar suffragists' estimation, could claim such a legacy for itself. Nor could any African nation claim to have "acquired the patriotism that came from making a country their home" (*New Age*, June 21, 1900). Indeed, in the pro-Boer discourses, Africans, when they appeared, were portrayed solely as wronged individuals, never as citizens of legitimate governments or states who had the right to resist British or Boer aggression on the grounds that they were being governed without their consent.

Thus consent, the concept on which the antiwar suffragists' whole notion of citizenship turned, had exclusive effects despite its inclusive pretensions. As they deployed it, the concept of consent harbored a politically exclusionary impulse precisely because it implicitly sanctioned the historical subjugation of so-called subject races by Europeans. The belief in "anthropological capacities" (Mehta 1997) upon which their notion of consent was predicated can be discerned in both the nationalist histories they invoked and their insistence upon the Boers' essential whiteness. The fact that the Pilgrims displaced and oppressed the Native Americans without regard for their consent when they planted New England in no way figured into the antiwar suffragists' discourse. Nor did the Boers'—or English settlers', for that matter— displacement and oppression of indigenous Africans, who never gave their consent either.

What we see in the antiwar suffragists' discourse, then, are examples of resistance past and present, near and far, invoked to configure the boundary between the politically included and politically excluded. Behind the supposedly universal capacity to grant consent was what Mehta calls "a thicker set of social credentials that constitute the real basis of political inclusion" (1997: 61). In pro-Boer discourse these social credentials amounted to specific cultural and psychological conditions that were made synonymous with whiteness and formed the preconditions for the actualization of the capacity to grant consent.

The antiwar suffragists did not challenge the anthropological basis on which their notion of consent was founded. They simply sought inclusion. But that inclusion necessitated that they distance themselves from any association with indigenous peoples. They had to distance themselves because scientific racism and sexism frequently classed Englishwomen as belonging with savages and children—subgroups that shared inferior mental characteristics, the most important being the incapacity to exercise reason, the necessary requisite for the expression of consent.

Thus, although consent as the criterion by which responsible citizenship was reckoned had both inclusionary elements and the potential to move the relationship between the citizen and the state in a more democratic direction, in practice exclusionary effects were written into its foundational logic. The presumed universality of the principle of consent was undermined by the manner in which the framers of the concept implicitly naturalized the historical inequality among different races. When this anthropologically and ideologically loaded notion of consent was transferred into and transposed onto feminists' struggles to alter the basis of civic inclusion, their ostensibly inclusionary political projects also came to bear the indelible stamp of exclusivity. If we take the Anglo-Boer War as a "significant turning point in the struggle for women's parliamentary enfranchisement in Britain" (Mayhall 2000: 3), and, further, if we treat the extension of the franchise to women as a signal moment in the history of the expansion of liberal democracy, then it becomes possible to understand how a liberal democratic system can make some forms of exclusion more deeply entrenched at the same time as it adopts more inclusive principles.

CHAPTER SIX

White Skins, White Masks: Unmasking and Unveiling the Meanings of Whiteness

Colonized black bodies were "absent presences" in metropolitan texts in the period roughly spanning 1800–1900. During that same period, Africans struggled to forge and articulate a sense of selfhood within social systems that sought at every turn to render them invisible, totally lacking in agency, and subhuman. Of course, the ways in which African people refused to remain simply objects, instead demanding recognition as subjects, deserves book-length treatment. Such a text would have to consider the myriad of ways, ranging from undertaking military campaigns to making music, through which African people asserted their agency. In this chapter and the one that follows, I offer an analysis of those aspects of resistance most closely related to the themes of imagery and representation. Hence, in this chapter I explore representations of whiteness in the African imagination, and in the next I consider representations of blackness.

We have heard and continue to hear a great deal about the black image in the white mind. No doubt this is because that image played such a critical role in the making of the European self. Indeed, its importance is such that Frantz Fanon could argue that "the presence of the Negroes beside the whites is an insurance policy on humanness" (1967: 129). We hear much less, however, about the white image in the black mind. Indeed, what David Roediger says about white and black Americans holds equally true for Europeans and Africans and for colonizers and the colonized: "Few Americans have ever considered the idea that African-Americans are extremely knowledgeable about whites and whiteness. . . . Lost in this destructive shuffle is the fact that from folktales onward African-Americans have been among the nation's keenest students of white consciousness and white behavior" (1998: 4). Given the nature of colonialism, it is far easier to assemble a picture of what the oppressor thought of the oppressed than vice versa. Nevertheless, it is possible to gather suggestive fragments and piece together a rudimentary picture of the reverse.

In a colonial situation, especially one as brutal as the South African one, Africans had to at least try to penetrate the psychology of their oppressors. Particularly striking in Africans' accounts is the consistent attention paid to unveiling whiteness—their relentless insistence that they could not only see whites, but see *through* them. The complex power dynamics that surrounded the phenomena of looking, observing, and critically evaluating are aptly expressed by bell hooks: "To be fully an object then was to lack the capacity to see or recognize reality. These looking relations were reinforced as whites cultivated the practice of denying the subjectivity of blacks (the better to dehumanize and oppress), of relegating them to the realm of the invisible. . . . To look directly was an assertion of subjectivity, equality" (1992: 168). For obvious reasons, very few of the undoubtedly complex and discerning observations of Europeans by Africans appear in the written historical record. Nevertheless, in the records that do exist one can clearly discern a critical attitude toward whiteness and a strong desire among African people to unmask, unveil, and expose its pretensions, its hypocrisy, and its hegemonic ambitions. Reading between the lines of missionary texts, travel writings, and government documents, one is particularly struck by the consistent inversion of the myth of the civilizing mission. Whereas texts produced by European explorers, travelers, and missionaries linked whiteness with goodness, light, elevation, and salvation, responses produced by Africans frequently connected whiteness with cruelty, terror, and harm. Thus, the civilizing mission was rendered its opposite—a mission of unmitigated savagery and barbarism. I have identified three mechanisms through which Africans unmasked and unveiled whiteness: the politics of refusal, the politics of bearing witness, and the demythologizing and desacralizing of whiteness.

The Politics of Refusal: African Responses to Christianity

Missionary accounts and other religious writings are literally overrun with Africans professing their love and respect for Europeans, particularly the English, and gratitude for the blessings of the gospel. For example, David Jantjes, a Khoikhoi resident of the Kat River Mission, was quoted in the *South African Commercial Advertiser* of November 19, 1834, as having professed his "indebtedness to the Gospel." Martinus van Bulen, another Khoikhoi convert, praised "Dr. Philip and the missionaries for what they have done for us" in the *Advertiser* of September 6, 1834. The Reverend Stephen Kay quoted Chief

Congo as having said that God had made the English "great men" (1833: 57), and Robert Moffatt proudly referred to an unnamed African chief who pointed to the Gospel of Luke and proclaimed: "That has made you what you are and taught the white people such wisdom" (1844: 502).

There was an equally powerful, although much more muted, strain within indigenous thought, however, which questioned both the efficacy and the utility of Christianity. This questioning sometimes took the form of outright refusal to accept the gospel. The Reverend Allen Gardiner explained that Chief Tambooza had told him that his people "did not wish for teaching; that they could never learn; that such words as these they were sure they could not understand. If I would instruct them in the use of the *issibum* (musket) I could stay, but these were things they did not care about" (1836: 68). Chief Soga "told the missionaries to their faces that they were villains and impostors, men who pretended they had the word of God which was all lies" (Brown 1855: 158). And the Reverend Alan Gibson averred that he could "not say with truth that, as a nation or as tribes, the Kaffirs care about Christianity. . . . The tribal feeling is briefly this: the man gained to Christianity is lost to the tribe—a sentiment that has been evoked against Christianity with all the force of patriotism" ([1891] 1969: 16).

For the most part, however, refusal took much more subtle forms, like avoidance, deferral, or laughter. Chief Maqomo employed avoidance: the Reverend Henry Calderwood said he "skillfully prevented me from discovering his real sentiments." Calderwood admitted that Maqomo's evasive tactics "filled me with anxiety" (1858: 40). One unnamed African's refusal took the form of deferral when he told Reverend Kay that he would pray if it weren't for the fact that "God requires men to pray all their lives, even to death—now that is too hard. If the Almighty would be satisfied with two or three days praying, that might be done. But to pray all our lives is too hard" (1833: 36). Other Africans responded with either bemused silence, or, more frequently, outright laughter. Reverend Kay said he found the task of "arresting the Kaffirs' attention or making them keep silence during the time of service" to be nearly "impossible" (1833: 39). David Livingstone described how his efforts to teach the Tswana to sing and pray were greeted with "fits of uncontrollable laughter" (Sedgwick and Monk 1858: 156). The Reverend William Shaw agreed that it was "very difficult" to get Africans to listen as they were "so fond of argument and disputation." He recalled trying to instruct a group of Xhosa on how to "kneel on the grass and speak to God." His pupils collapsed into such fits of laughter that "worship was rendered impracticable" (1874: 30, 112).

Refusal sometimes also took the form of skepticism. Potential converts frequently expressed their doubts about the English missionaries' true motives in bringing them the gospel. Their disbelief was such that Kay commented that on the whole Africans possessed a "much greater degree of acuteness and skepticism" than he expected to find among a "wild and untutored race" (1833: 37). A number of Africans were skeptical, for example, about why the gospel, unlike beads or money or cattle, was dispensed with such ease by the English—indeed, the English seemed more willing to share the gospel with Africans than with their own people. Dyani Tshatshu, a Xhosa chief, was quoted in the proceedings of the Select Committee on Aborigines as having asked the missionaries: "How do you come and teach the Kaffirs? Why do you not go and teach your own people who shoot us every day and take our cattle?" (Parliament of Great Britain [1836] 1966: 572). Chief Maqomo also wondered "what brings white men over the sea" and asked if they had "no people of their own at home" (Calderwood 1858: 211).

It was precisely because of the English missionaries' willingness to dispense the gospel so freely that many Africans surmised that evangelism was a cover for more crass material motives. As one "Kaffir evangelist" explained to Kay, "the English are slaves of money" (Kay 1833: 122). The Reverend William Taylor recalled a Xhosa convert telling him that his people's objections to the gospel stemmed from their belief that the missionaries wanted to convert them "so as to get lots of money" (1895: 53). The Africans' explicit challenge to the English rendering of the nature of the connection between Christianity and commerce—seeing the former as merely a ruse to attain the latter, whereas the English maintained that the latter was an accidental (although beneficial) outgrowth of the former—was inextricably linked to the conflation of Englishness with duplicity and hypocrisy.

Ironically, the opacity of black skin was correlated with an ideological stance that suggested that black people could be looked through—that their physiological darkness made them more morally transparent to the penetrating white gaze. It was not uncommon for settlers, particularly if they were English, to declare themselves as having superior abilities to see through the innocuous performances of Africans to the depraved core lurking inside. As one missionary put it: "The chiefs, instead of being as some travelers have represented them, 'of an open and generous character, disdaining in their wars and negotiations any sort of chicanery or deceit,' are in truth men whose depraved minds and schemes generally evince the very opposite of 'natural rectitude'" (Kay 1833: 214). Those fortunate enough to have been born white, especially the English, saw white skin as conferring moral and mental impenetrability—particularly to the gaze of the Other. Thus, the translucent nature of whiteness was correlated with an opacity that made them morally indecipherable, at least, supposedly, to the African.

Bell hooks aptly captures the arrogance of the white subject confronted with the "return of the look": "Racist thinking perpetuates the fantasy that the Other who is subjugated, who is subhuman, lacks the ability to comprehend, to understand, to see the working of the powerful. . . . In white supremacist society, white people can 'safely' imagine that they are invisible to black people since the power they have historically asserted, and even now collectively assert over black people, accorded them the right to control the black gaze." The consistency with which African people, when given a chance to speak, chose unveiling as their preferred method of critique demonstrates their profound awareness of how invested the English were in the idea of "whiteness as mystery," as well as the Africans' determination to name what they saw (1992: 168). Indeed, the Reverend William Renton testified before the Select Committee on the Kaffir Tribes that Africans were "very acute in marking the inconsistencies and bad conduct of Englishmen" (Parliament of Great Britain 1851: 463). Hence, looking became oppositional, a means of contestation and confrontation and a critical part of the politics of refusal. Africans were refusing the prerogative of Europeans to dictate to them how the Europeans' actions would be seen and interpreted. Although the politics of refusal had little immediate impact on the material conditions of existence and the gross inequalities of power, resources, and privilege that obtained between blacks and whites, it did have a tremendous amount of psychological importance. For, as Fanon explained, the colonizer needs the colonized to "corroborate him in his search for self-validation" (1967: 212). The colonized African exercised psychologically valuable agency by denying the colonizer that validation.

When the British settlers began to press heavily for vagrancy legislation in the Cape Colony, for example, the Khoikhoi, who were the intended targets of the law, spoke out publicly at a series of meetings convened at various mission stations in the fall of 1834. At these meetings they named Englishness as inextricably connected with hypocrisy. In other words, they refused to see the English as they wished to be seen. The immediate impact of this refusal on the trajectory of the legislation was, without question, minimal. The real impact of the refusal lay elsewhere, in the tortuous intersubjective space between oppressor and oppressed, wherein the former demands nothing less from the latter than his own self-consciousness. As Fanon explained, the colonizer wanted only "to read admiration in the eyes of the other" (1967: 212).

Admiration would not be forthcoming in this instance. Andries Botha, for example, asked this question about the English: "How is it the same people who had sent the Hottentots the Gospel now wish to throw them back into the hands of the Boers from whom they had already suffered so much?" (*South African Commercial Advertiser,* September 6, 1834). Andries Stoffels, also struck by the hypocrisy of the British, ruefully remarked: "We went to the English government for protection in the first place because we expected that these people would have done us good. Now you often see a Hottentot who has spent his days in the service of the Government with only a skin on his back, walking about the streets, oppressed in every way" (Parliament of Great Britain [1836] 1966: 588). Maqomo agreed that although the English claimed their objective to be "coming among us to teach the word of God," they were quick to "give over teaching that word . . . and go to the military posts where there is war." He thus expressed his doubt about "whether any of [them were] true men of peace" (Brown 1855: 76).

Maqomo, Botha, and Stoffels thus asserted their subjectivity by turning a critical eye toward English people and casting judgment on their behavior. The reclamation of subjectivity, which involved both looking and retelling, amounted to a form of truth telling that included renarrating historical events in such a way that the duplicity and underhandedness of the English would be exposed. Another strategy for unmasking whiteness, therefore, might loosely be classified as bearing witness to an alternative history. The politics of bearing witness was immensely important to the process of unveiling the mystery of whiteness as well as to that of documenting the historical and contemporary agency of black people.

Unmasking Whiteness through Renarrating History: The Politics of Bearing Witness

Most historians and sociologists agree that the process of writing and telling (or in most cases rewriting and retelling) history is a crucial site for identity formation, both for groups and for individuals. The process of writing themselves into history was particularly important for the British who settled in South Africa. As Alan Lester explains, the British settlers' sense of affinity and shared identity "could have been an ephemeral phenomenon were it not for considerable, continuing investment in the construction of a collective, legitimating past. . . . These notions allowed not just settlers themselves, but also many of their subsequent historians to create and nourish the idea of a united and 'natural' settler community" (2001: 67). Settler historiography, which included such seminal texts as Robert Godlonton's *A Narrative of the Irruption of the Kaffir Hordes* (1836), the *Grahamstown Journal* (which was published by Godlonton), and John Bowker's *Speeches, Letters, and Selections from Important Papers* (1862), simultaneously analyzed the present and future predicaments of the settler class while constructing a shared history. Texts such as these focused on portraying settlers as heroes who had brought civilization to a benighted continent and people. Their authors were particularly careful to emphasize certain core values—strength, independence, drive, ingenuity—which the settlers were depicted as sharing to a uniquely great degree. A coherent settler history was thus able to serve not simply as a documentation of fact, but also as a template for the construction and reconstruction of the self. Regarding the texts of this history, Lester explains that individual settlers' "personal recollections were often drawn straight from their pages" (2001: 69).

African people, particularly those of Khoikhoi descent, were clearly aware of the importance of this history to the settlers' sense of personal identity, and therefore they challenged the settlers' assertions of dominance by telling an alternative history of white settlement. One of the elements that is most striking about this alternative history is the manner in which it undermined English claims to self-sufficiency and self-mastery through its recounting of the myriad of ways that the settlers were helpless and dependent on the generosity of the government and Africans when they arrived.

A translated letter signed "Piet Knapsack, A Hottentot" appeared in the *South African Commercial Advertiser* of August 24, 1834. The original writer, a resident of the Kat River Mission Settlement, reflected on the relations that obtained between hungry settlers and aboriginal people before the settlers completely embraced invidious notions of white supremacy: "I have seen that my companions were very friendly to them. They were then as poor as we were. My friends gave them food to eat, and some lent them their cows to milk, and have ploughed for some." Andries Stoffels, a Khoikhoi resident of the Philipston Mission, echoed Piet in his description of desperate English settlers throwing themselves on the mercy of the Khoikhoi: "When the settlers came out they asked where the Hottentots were that they heard of in England. The old English settlers pointed them to the Hottentots of Theopolis. The settlers were then without horse or cow or sheep or hen—but the Hottentots there lowered the prices of their horses, their cows to 12s., the oxen to 22s. out of compassion for them, for they were very poor" (*South African Commercial Advertiser*, September 3, 1834). Martinus van Bulen expressed his desire to remind the British emigrants that he had "assisted some of the greatly. I plowed for them. I used to shoot game for them. I used to lend them my old horse."

Rewriting the history of British settlement encompassed exposing not only British reliance on African generosity, but their reliance on the largesse of the state as well. Thus, an outraged Kat River resident protested that the Khoikhoi, unlike the settlers, were never given rations, spades, or picks from the government. The "Piet Knapsack" letter also made the point that the government had given land to the settlers, "which they may sell or use as they like," as well as "daily food . . . every kind of tool and enormous sums of money." Cobus Junger agreed that the colonial government never deigned to give the Kat River residents "a pick or a spade, whilst the English settlers received rice, sugar, tea, and spirits in abundance." Andries Stoffels maintained that although the settlers feigned to put on airs, he knew for a fact that "the government supported them" (*South African Commercial Advertiser*, September 6, 1834).

Pointing out that African generosity and state-supported charity, rather than English initiative, had played a significant role in the eventual success of the settlers in South Africa was a way of suggesting that the English, far from being self-made, were to a significant extent the creation of others. The discomfort such a revelation posed is evident in the remarks of one writer to the *Grahamstown Journal* of September 18, 1834:

> Some of them remind the Settlers of acts of kindness performed to them on their first arrival in the colony. In particular Martinus van Bulen says he plowed for them and gave them other assistance, but he omits to add that he was well paid for such services. He boasts of his brotherly kindness, but we believe from what we have heard that the whole settlement can testify that he is the last man who can be charged with an excess of zeal in this respect.

The writer's anxiousness to note that van Bulen was "well paid for his services" demonstrates the settlers' profound discomfort with the idea of being the recipients of charity. This discomfort is not difficult to fathom when we consider that in the English worldview the ability to grant charity was invariably associated with superior social status. Receiving charity was increasingly coming to be associated with membership in a separate and degraded caste—with being a little less English than one's friends and neighbors.

Many of the English settlers who emigrated to South Africa did so precisely to escape the shame and humiliation that accompanied a loss of social status. John Centlivers Chase described the majority of settlers as having left England with the intent of "fleeing with their offspring from actual penury, or its gradual yet certain approach" ([1823] 1967: 82). David Hockly, for example, explained to the colonial secretary on emigration that he had been "reduced under Providence by misfortune and losses" (Hockly 1964: 2).

Miles Bowker likewise admitted to having left England because he was "unable to provide for a family of eight sons and one daughter without reducing them to the lowest ranks in society" (Theal 1902: 253). Once settled in their new land, however, the settlers sought to deemphasize the poverty that had characterized their past and to emphasize the ingenuity and initiative that would bring them success in the future. There was no place in these revised narratives of the self for acknowledgment of social intimacy with or dependence on Africans. Indeed, silencing this aspect of their history was critical to the emergence of a white colonial subjectivity.

The process of unmasking whiteness not only entailed reversing the received wisdom on who were likely to be the beneficiaries and benefactors of charity. It also encompassed a careful reconstruction of the circumstances in which notions of inferiority and superiority emerged. A crucial part of bearing witness was the reconstructing of history to show that the settlers had to *learn* that "it was not the fashion for white people to associate with black men, that white men must be masters and black men servants." "Piet Knapsack" reminded his fellows that he could name many English who were now "great gentlemen" who had "eaten at the tables of [his] friends" (*South African Commercial Advertiser*, August 24, 1834). This form of bearing witness used history to undermine the naturalness of white supremacy. The process of renarrating the history of white-black interchanges was thus a way to challenge the idea that Africans were a naturally servile race whose inferior capacities doomed them to forever be in a subservient position.

Although it was impossible for African people to precisely date the moment when the settlers' attitudes shifted, it was important for them to document that a shift had, indeed, occurred—that "race" had not always been the primary determinant of the form of relations between indigenous Africans and emigrant Europeans. In recounting the friendly, even intimate, character of "interracial" relations that had existed when the settlers first arrived, they demonstrated a keen awareness that the urge to discriminate did not emanate from innate and automatic feelings of repulsion aroused by the Africans' different appearance. The fact that they relied so heavily on African people and lived and worked side by side with them initially demonstrates this. Rather, it was an act of discrimination that constructed the categories of black and white themselves and attached to them the labels of superior and inferior. The practical effect of this rerendering of history, therefore, was to expose race as a phenomenon that was in significant respects a human invention, an invention that humans, if they wished to, could also unmake.

Although the ideological wall erected between whiteness and blackness was made so thick and so high as to prevent any crossing, within the category of whiteness there remained a certain fluidity. Individuals who were basically accepted as white, in this case the Dutch, could be and were cast out at the whim of the English, who kept for themselves the exclusive right to decide who counted as white and when. The Dutch were selectively accorded the privilege and status of whiteness when the English sought to augment their power against Africans. As Michael Streak explains, when the English desired the "cooperation of the Afrikaners," opinion makers could be counted on to "awaken an awareness of the similarities existing amongst the two white population groups while minimizing or overlooking differences" (1974: 84).

The 1830s marked a critical turning point in relations between Boers and Britons. It was during this time that racial enmity between the two groups was submerged in their common pursuit of a more rigidly controlled African labor market. John Fawcett concluded that whatever animosities separated the Dutch and English farmers, mere mention of frontier policy or labor laws caused the farmers to cast differences aside and "bring up their combined forces" (1836: 87). The *Zuid Afrikaan,* one of the colony's leading newspapers, which published articles in English and in Dutch, played an important role in encouraging Dutch and English farmers to see themselves as a common race besieged by hostile Africans on one side and meddling British philanthropists on the other. The October 17, 1834, edition of the paper, for example, accused the *South African Commercial Advertiser* and its supporters of taking "every opportunity to make a division between English and Dutch." The paper called on its readers to "beware of the snare being laid for them" and to seek to "foster, support, and cement that cordiality, unanimity, and friendly feeling which so happily exists between the English and Dutch population." The October 24, 1834, edition of the *Zuid Afrikaan* carried an editorial that alleged that the *South African Commercial Advertiser* "endeavored to excite and promote separation, discord, dissension, and an acrimonious feeling of animosity between the English and the Dutch Colonists." The *Zuid Afrikaan* encouraged the two communities to come together and thus "shipwreck the plan upon its own shores. . . . Let us live in harmony and peace, and be like brethren of one family. Let not the Dutch insult the English, or the English throw odium upon the Dutch, and thus we will promote the happiness and welfare of our dear country!"

When it came time to apportion the blame for the brutality and sins of colonialism, however, the English could be counted on to distance themselves from the Dutch in a vain attempt to make them carry the sins of colonialism for both groups. They frequently accomplished this distance by "blackening" the Boers' inner character, thus throwing their white racial status into question. When the English accounted for the cruelty of the Dutch, they most often did so in explicitly racial terms, making their churlishness an index of their innate cultural barbarism and racial savagery. James Boon's castigation of the Dutch was typical: "The Dutchman's home we had arrived at was one of the most miserable mud or raw-bricked buildings, and turned out to be nothing but a human propagating establishment. . . . On our arrival there came into view a motley number of white and black young ones of all sizes and ages, and in the home were to be found lazy fat Dutch women squatting on their settees or on their beds. . . . The Dutch farmers beg shamelessly" (1885: 59). Hence, the English reserved the right to render the Dutch more white or less white, depending upon the circumstances. When the Dutch were kind, progressive, or enterprising they were "white"; when they were mean, backward, or retrograde they were "black." Paradoxically, if the ideological purity of whiteness was to be retained, the boundaries around the category had to be made fluid and permeable—the polar opposite of what was required to maintain biological or physiological "purity."

Indigenous people took the prerogative to decide for themselves what constituted the boundaries of whiteness at any given moment. Khoikhoi people, particularly those who resided on mission stations, were well aware of the settlers' growing sense of racial solidarity. The Kat River missionary James Read Jr. testified before the Select Committee on the Granting of Lands in Freehold to Hottentots that "several of the Coloured people subscribe to the colonial newspapers: *Greensblad, South African Commercial Advertiser, Grahamstown Journal, Port Elizabeth Herald, The Mercury,* and the *Cape Frontier Times*" (Parliament of Great Britain [1854] 1972: 45). He also confirmed that the Kat River Mission had a reading room and a circulating library. African people, then, were aware of how the settlers defined the boundaries of race, but they declined to accept those ever-shifting racial boundaries as their own. At times they refused to allow the English to maintain the ideological purity of whiteness; instead they claimed, as Maqomo did, that "all white men are alike" (Calderwood 1858: 211). Thus Boer and Briton were made to bear the sins of colonialism equally. One Xhosa informant told George Brown that his people were "despised and oppressed by the white man" (Brown 1855: 28). The informant made no distinction between the Dutch and the English. Andries Stoffels, likewise, insisted that all white men were cruel and that the only difference was that oppression by the English was "not murder, but like a newspaper that you put in and press down" (Parliament of Great Britain [1836] 1966: 588).

The conflation of whiteness and terror that is such an integral part of African representations of Europeans must be understood as having been generated by the callous indifference to black life that was perhaps the defining characteristic of colonialism, rather than as a reversal of the dominant images of Africans as frightening, evil, dangerous, and so on. It would be incorrect to characterize black representations of whiteness as simple exercises in reversal. Rather, these images and representations should be understood as having emerged "as a response to the traumatic pain and anguish . . . of white racist domination" (hooks 1992: 169). It was their utter refusal to see black people as human that allowed the same people who pioneered the "civilizing mission" to be at the forefront of efforts to "civilize" certain populations off the face of the earth. It was this attitude that led one Xhosa leader to ask the Reverend Charles Brownlee, "Is it only the white people that are people? Are we not people?" ([1896] 1977: 67).

At one time or another, every group of indigenous people in South Africa who encountered British rapacity asked some version of that same question. Earlier in the century vocal members of Khoikhoi communities had asked similar questions of the English. Andries Stoffels used the occasion of the second anniversary of the Kat River Temperance Society to lay the blame for the fact that "every nation on earth still exists but the Hottentot nation" squarely at the feet of the British. "Before the white man came and introduced brandy amongst Hottentots, they were a healthy, brave, and honourable nation, but the Hottentot nation is now good for nothing" (*Grahamstown Journal*, April 10, 1834). Several months later, at a demonstration against the proposed vagrancy ordinance of 1834, he again identified himself as speaking "on behalf of his nation," and he again asked the question "Where is there now a Hottentot's kraal on their own ground?" (*South African Commercial Advertiser*, September 3, 1834).

Africans' fears that Europeans harbored genocidal ambitions were by no means unfounded. The settlers and the British colonial state had both at one time or another taken the extinction of the aboriginal South African as a foregone conclusion. As early as 1801, John Barrow predicted that because of colonial wars, diseases, miscegenation, and dispossession, "the name of a Hottentot will soon be forgotten or remembered only as that of a deceased person of little note" ([1801] 1968: 144). A Mr. Roebuck argued before the House of Commons on April 15, 1851, that the eventual triumph of civilized over primitive peoples was a certainty. The English colonists, he argued, "cannot be placed in South Africa without the inevitable consequence of annihilating the aborigines. That is what has been done in New Zealand, in

Australia, in North America, in all our colonies. And this is what will be done in South Africa" (Great Britain Parliament 1851: 275).

Although it might appear that the English articulated their genocidal ambitions with candor, in actuality they were always careful to sidestep the issue of white agency in the matter. Indeed, it is in discussions of the disappearance of indigenous peoples that we see perhaps the whites' strongest denials of their own volition. In all other spheres of life, whiteness was associated with purposeful action—conversion, exploration, and conquest. As an identity, whiteness was predicated upon no less than the subduing of nature, on making it submit to whites' hegemonic ambitions. When the elimination of indigenous populations was discussed, however, white men were, for the first time, depicted as completely helpless in the face of nature's divine workings.

The English portrayed war, conquest, and dispossession as being less about the scramble for territory and profit than about natural and inevitable biological processes. Hence the ubiquity of passive statements such as the following, which appeared in the *Grahamstown Journal* of October 19, 1850: "The black man is melting away before the white man. . . . The force of arms is not necessary to do this. A law of nature appears to be sufficient—civilization is enough to accomplish the task." The Reverend Thornley Smith agreed that the Khoikhoi were once "a numerous and powerful people" but had mysteriously "disappeared" (1850: 8). The *Grahamstown Journal* of July 3, 1852, quoted a speaker in the British House of Commons who predicted that "the black man [would] disappear before the white man" but refrained from explaining why. John Bowker adopted a similar stance of innocence through ignorance when he wrote that "the extinction of races even among men is a palpable fact which we have everyday experience of, and over which we have no control" (1862: 249). Unlike the unnamed speaker in the House of Commons, Bowker placed the blame for the demise of the South African aborigine squarely on the workings of divine providence, proclaiming that "scripture shows that God at times wills it that one race should *summarily* make room for the other" (1862: 249, emphasis in original).

A critical component of confronting whiteness thus entailed unveiling the agentic nature of English violence. When Africans discussed English terror, they were adamant in their refusal to allow the white man and woman their innocence. Chief Maqomo, for example, declared that the English "belong to a race that wishes to destroy the Kaffir" (Green 1853: 46). Chief Kreli agreed with Maqomo that the English were purposefully "destroying his people" (Parliament of Great Britain [1851] 1971a, 225).

A poem titled "The Black Side of Things," which appeared in the August 1, 1895, edition of the *Christian Express*, exemplifies the extent to which Africans were coming to locate the crucial site of white sociality in the perpetration of violence against Africans.

> Englishman come
> He preachee God . . .
> Englishman beat
> Englishman kill
> He preachee God—
> Tum, Tum!

In poems and songs such as this one, Africans both depicted and expressed their resentment toward white power and privilege. This song is typical in that it simply describes the power that English people exercised over Africans and criticizes the veil of religious hypocrisy that hung over and threatened to obscure the brute face of colonial genocide. The song does not, however, make any claims about the inherent proclivity of English people for violence. It thus exemplifies the relative absence in indigenous thought of a concern with delimiting any special qualities or personal characteristics distinctive to the white race that could be invoked to explain individual behavior.

Demythologizing and Desacralizing Whiteness

African attitudes toward white people changed significantly over time. This change was largely precipitated by the capitulation of missionaries and other "humanitarians" to the racism of the settlers and colonial state officials. The fact that a number of missionaries became government agents in the 1840s and 1850s did not go unnoticed; it led the Xhosa and Khoikhoi people to question the claim that missionaries were morally superior to the settlers. As Timothy Keegan explains, "in the end, liberal humanitarianism turned out to be a shallow, tawdry, deceptive thing. The LMS [London Missionary Society], the very seedbed of humanitarian thought in the 1820s and 1830s, was by the 1840s and 1850s becoming infected with racial sentiment" (1996: 127).

Long experience was teaching black people that white people privileged color above all else in drawing distinctions and making alliances. Physician Andrew Smith testified before the Select Committee on the Kaffir Tribes that his sixteen years as a go-between, mediating between African communities and the colonial government, had shown him that blacks "do not consider the governor to have an interest in them. They fancy that as the governor is white and the colonists are white that therefore the governor must have a special affection for white people. . . . They themselves would not befriend the white man in preference to the black man" (Parliament of Great Britain 1851: 51). Africans became less convinced of the utility of judging white men and women individually and came to believe that the interests of whites as a group were inimical to theirs. Such was clear to a man like Maqomo, who told the Reverend Brown that the "teachers" would inevitably become magistrates: "one of those who make war" (1855: 76). Less than a decade before, Maqomo had defended the missionaries, calling them "a different race of men, men of peace. They did not ask for war. The settlers belong to the race that wishes to destroy the Kaffir" (Green 1853: 46). Likewise, Antonie Peterward, one of the Kat River rebels, accused the missionary James Read Jr. of being, "like all other ministers, on the side of the settlers" (Read 1852: 22).

At other times, however, Africans allowed for more flexibility in the category "white" by distinguishing between the Dutch and the English, reversing the hierarchy whereby Englishness stood for salvation and civilization and Dutchness represented cruelty and barbarism. In these instances, the Dutch were imagined as being better "friends of the natives" (a title the English had bestowed upon themselves) than the English—casting doubt on yet another of the central tenets of the civilizing mission. As early as 1838, the *Grahamstown Journal* reported the following:

> The Hottentots are attempting to incite in the minds of the Kaffirs a hatred for the English name and character. . . . They say that the English are the usurpers of their country and the British settlers are at this moment endeavouring to reduce them to a state of abject slavery. So strong are these impressions on the mind of the Hottentot that, notwithstanding all the English government has done for them, . . . the Dutch are held in far higher estimation than the English. (April 26, 1838)

John Fairbairn testified before the Select Committee on the Kaffir Tribes that "the natives consider the Dutch natives like themselves and they consider the English as intruders who have come to take their country from them" (Parliament of Great Britain 1851: 85). Governor Sir Peregrine Maitland testified before the same select committee that "the Kaffirs have repeatedly sent messages to the Dutch Boers to ask them why they do not stand aside so that they may drive the English into the sea" (Parliament of Great Britain 1851: 85). The Reverend Renton confirmed that the Xhosa had "feelings of injury from the aggression of the white men that [were] concentrated more towards the Englishmen than towards others" (Parliament of Great Britain 1851: 431).

Another English settler, John Green, likewise averred that "the natives hold the Dutch in far higher estimation than the English" (1853: 67). Meanwhile, the Khoikhoi leaders of the Kat River Rebellion were expressing their desires for "an independent government in the country, which was only to be inhabited by Hottentots, Boers, and Kaffirs" (Godlonton [1852] 1965: 176).

Africans refused to abide by one of the cardinal rules of a "racist culture" (Goldberg 1993): that only whites are afforded the privilege of determining what whiteness means. In these oppositional narratives, whiteness expands and contracts to encompass different meanings other than the ones the English created. Thus, "all white men are alike" not because of their intelligence, their valor, their Christianity, or even their color—but because of their cruelty. When the Dutch are deemed to be behaving in a civilized manner—in other words, when they are not behaving cruelly toward Africans—they are depicted as being farthest from and least like the English in culture, character, and race. At this point the Africans are said to consider them "natives like themselves." Thus blackness stands for civilized and humane treatment of other people, while whiteness represents the reverse. This reversal of the English mapping of race and civilization was also the basis for the emergence of an alternative means of configuring the essential set of characteristics that broadly defined whiteness. Whereas for the English the characteristics that defined the internal boundaries of whiteness were those of civilization, for Africans the will and capacity to commit acts of unspeakable and unjustified terror defined the boundaries.

It was through the process of bearing witness and rendering an alternative history of English settlement that Africans were able to create alternative configurations of whiteness and blackness. The act of renarrating history made it possible for Africans to assume for themselves the prerogative of defining what constituted the boundaries of race. Those boundaries were wholly socially defined: culture and character rather than biology and genetics determined the confines of whiteness. Whiteness is defined above all by the superior economic and social power that it commands, rather than by any particular physical characteristics.

Another striking feature of indigenous thought is the relative lack of concern with establishing the physical or biological limits to any particular racial category. Unlike the racial ideologies produced by whites, which tended to point to biological and physical characteristics like skin color to explain black behavior, the racial ideologies produced by blacks made no such claims about whiteness. Take, for example, the rueful observation of Andries Botha, who contrasted the ethics and behavior of the British with those of the people of his own nation. He explained that he had "never heard that the

Hottentot nation possessed or had taken another people's land, or had oppressed them" (*South African Commercial Advertiser*, September 6, 1834).

Many Khoikhoi people, while acknowledging their "mixed" racial ancestry, adhered strongly to the view that race is socially, rather than biologically,
produced. Esau Prins, for example, observed that although he was a "Boer's
child," he was made to "sit behind the chairs and stools as my mother was a
Hottentot woman" (*South African Commercial Advertiser*, October 15, 1834).
Prins's remark anticipates those of W. E. B. Du Bois, who wrote that he could
always tell a black man because "the black man is a person who must ride
Jim Crow in Georgia" (1991: 153). Recognizing the futility of reading race
off of the body, Africans were most likely to connect whiteness with the will
and capacity to exercise brute force, rather than with biology or phenotype.
Thus, anyone who had committed acts of illegitimate or reckless violence
could be considered English or white. The amaFengu "tribe," who were actually dispossessed and displaced Gcaleka Xhosa who had agreed to serve
under governor Benjamin D'Urban in exchange for grants of land during the
Sixth Frontier War (1834–1835), were castigated by other Xhosa for being
"like the white men" (Brownlee [1896] 1977: 140). The so-called Bastaards,
who despite their Khoikhoi ancestry enjoyed some of the rights of citizens
and had signed petitions in support of the 1834 vagrancy ordinance, were
also deemed by the Xhosa to be "true Englishmen" (Green 1853: 67). Indigenous thinkers' move to connect whiteness with the exercise of power
anticipates the comments of Amiri Baraka, who once observed that the
white man is not a person but "a system and an ideology" (1991: xiii). The
amaFengu and Bastaards were rendered white not by their appearance, but
by virtue of the ethical choices they had made.

In naming whiteness as a signifier of terror, Africans were not only expressing the feelings of fear and helplessness it was capable of arousing, but
were also engaged in an active process of demythologizing white supremacy
by questioning the "illusion of permanence" that was a critical component
of the English will to power (Hutchins 1967). Even as the Xhosa were, in the
words of one settler, "being taught to feel the hopelessness of a contest with
the Government," they were engaging in a process of challenging English
claims to power and stripping the English of their seeming omnipotence
(*Cape Frontier Times*, February 23, 1847). Chief Sandile, shortly before the
outbreak of the Seventh Frontier War, expressed this quite strongly when he
remarked that the Xhosa had formerly "thought white men could not be
killed but we see they are only like us, they can also be killed" (Parliament
of Great Britain [1857] 1972: 585). John Maclean, Commissioner to the
T'Slambie, reported that it was widely believed among the Xhosa people that

Chief Umlanjeni had "the power to resist the English and that he [would] cause all the white population, and the coloured adherents to die" (Parliament of Great Britain [1851] 1971b, 34). These pronouncements were declarations that despite British attempts to prove the contrary, the inevitability of their triumph and the permanence of their victory were by no means foregone conclusions.

Therefore, an important aspect of the demythologizing of whiteness involved searching for and finding inspiration from instances where the English had suffered military defeat. Indeed, this is why the Indian Mutiny of 1857 was widely discussed among the Xhosa. The mutiny was an example of a dark-skinned people having risen up against their lighter skinned oppressors. The excitement that followed in the wake of the mutiny was such that Governor George Grey (1854–1861) expressed concern that the chiefs were using news of the mutiny to revive a desire for war against the colony (Weldon 1984: 67).

When the Russians killed Sir George Cathcart, former governor of the Cape (1852–1854), during the Crimean War, the word quickly spread among the Xhosa. Many Xhosa people believed that Lynx, Ngqika, and Mlanjeni (three deceased Xhosa leaders) were across the sea fighting against the English in the Crimean War. As one informant told Governor Grey: "They say it is a lie, which has been told about the Russians being a White nation. The opinion is that they are all blacks, and were formerly Kaffir warriors who have died or have been killed in the various wars against the colony" (Parliament of Great Britain [1857] 1972: 592). In 1856 the Xhosa people acted on the prophesies of a young girl, Nongqawuse, slaughtering their cattle and ceasing the planting of crops in the belief that these deeds would lead to the resurrection of their ancestors, the expulsion of the British, and a return to a precolonial idyll (Peires 1989). Mhlakaza, one of the principal interpreters of the cattle-killing prophesies, reported that he had been visited by Russian spirits and figures who had come from fighting against the English and were now able to help the Xhosa (Brownlee [1896] 1977: 129).

Implicit in the above statements are several important challenges to the hegemony of the British worldview, the most obvious being the refusal to accept the English metaphysics of life and death. Beyond that, proposing that the Russians were African rather than European was a powerful reversal of the hierarchy whereby the more power a nation possessed, the more it was said to approximate the European standard. The British had long ascribed "European" traits to indigenous groups whose abilities did not conform to the stereotype of the hapless native. Indeed, the Xhosa were once themselves so described (see Barrow [1801] 1968: 205; Calderwood 1858: 32; Lichtenstein [1812] 1928: 301; Pringle [1835] 1966: 413; Smith 1850: 74). For example, the naturalist J. G. Wood insisted that because the Xhosa were "lofty" and "intellectual" they should be "marked out from all other groups of the dark-skinned natives of Africa" (1878: 12). George Combe subjected the Xhosa to phrenological investigation and found that they were "ingenious in several arts." He concluded that they bore "no trace of the Negro features" and "differ little from the most perfect Europeans" (1851: 578). When the Xhosa insisted that the Russians were an African nation, they demonstrated that they did not accept the idea that white skinned people were destined to rule the world. In the words of Chief Maqomo's son Kona, who had studied for seven years in England: "England has no more right to our country than we have to take England. It is merely a question of might against right" (Adams [1884] 1941: 275).

Africans recognized the urgency of not only demythologizing white supremacy but desacralizing it as well. One of the distinguishing characteristics of white supremacy as an ideology was (and remains) the manner in which it continually invoked religion—basing the will to dominate on the transcendental authority of God. The notion that the destiny of human beings was controlled by a God to whom the English had privileged access, and of whom they had privileged knowledge, reinforced the view that the English were gods themselves—operating everywhere at once, dictating the conditions of life for the multitude, accountable to no one. Many African people who accepted Christianity, and even some who did not, used it as a means for launching a critique of white supremacy. They posited that the distribution of the peoples and the resources of the world was an expression of God's will, for example, and suggested that any forcible alteration of these relationships was a form of heresy. Indeed, any person or group that undertook to transform these relations was guilty of nothing less than blasphemy.

It is for this reason that Xhosa leaders frequently likened the settlers' aspirations to global dominance to attempts to assume even greater powers than those of God—the same God whose word the English were purportedly bringing to the heathen. The Reverend Renton testified before the Select Committee on the Kaffir Tribes that a Xhosa chief had asked him: "Why did the English come across the sea to invade him? He did not send any of his people across the sea-water to England to invade their country. The Queen did not make him a chief. She could make great men. She could even make a governor, but God had made him a chief. God had given the white man England and he had given the Coloured men Kaffirland. Why then do the English wish to undo what God has done?" (Parliament of Great Britain 1851: 437). George Brown likewise related how Sandile had compared his fate to that of

Jesus: "The white men put the Son of God to death although he had no sin. I am like the Son of God, without sin, and the white men seek to put me to death also. God made me the chief. The white men now say that I cannot be a chief. How do these men think to undo the word of God?" (1855: 155).

The English no doubt interpreted these protestations as a form of blasphemy. Much more profound than simple sacrilege, these were attempts to translate social and political problems into theological language in order to make them ideological weapons in the struggle against white supremacy. The manner in which African people used Christianity can be understood as having arisen in response to the diverse forms of brutality visited upon them by white people. For the English saw their mission as not only robbing the Xhosa of their country, but also making them accept the myth of their own inferiority. In this way they would dismantle African society from within as they attacked it from without. As a writer to the *Cape Frontier Times* of January 19, 1847, explained: "The native communities must be made to feel that they are *subjects* and not masters. . . . And thus by degrees out of wild and savage races will be formed communities of men . . . who will be British subjects not only in name, but also in practice—in their sentiments and thoughts, their wants and wishes" (emphasis in original).

This strategy was not unique. Making the colonized see themselves as the colonizers saw them so they would aspire to be more like the oppressors rather than opposing them has always been integral to the exercise of colonial rule. As Fanon explained: "I begin to suffer from not being a white man to the degree that the white man imposes discrimination on me, makes me a colonized native, robs me of all worth, all individuality, tells me that I am a parasite on the world, that I must bring myself as quickly as possible into step with the white world" (1967: 98). The British were failing in their project of making the Xhosa see themselves as the English saw them, of making the Xhosa aspire to become like them. The politics of refusal, the practice of bearing witness by narrating an alternative history of British settlement and "interracial" contact, and the sustained effort to demythologize and desacralize whiteness can all be read as forms of resistance to the ideological hegemony of British rule.

Conclusion: The Legacy of Indigenous Racial Thought

Historian Mia Bay has observed that "few categories have been established, other than reverse racism, for the interpretation of the racial thought of non-dominant groups" (2000: 224). Racial ideologies produced by blacks about whites encompass a variety of elements. Although it is not difficult to locate instances where the response to white racial chauvinism was black racial chauvinism, the complexities of indigenously produced racial ideologies are in no way captured by the simple descriptor *reverse racism*. The varied associations Africans drew between whiteness and unique forms of power, whiteness and terror, and whiteness and authorial voice in history are just a few among the many different elements that went into the making of indigenous racial ideologies. These indigenous ideologies, while they emerged in response to existing white ideologies and the social behaviors those white ideologies justified, are much more than simple reversals.

Unlike white racial ideologies about blackness, which sought to definitively prove that a link existed between a person's color and capabilities, black ideologies about whiteness did no such thing. This is a highly important, yet rarely remarked-upon distinction. Indigenous racial ideologies began early on to formulate alternative conceptions of race that did not allow dominant discourses and dominant assumptions to determine the contours of or set the parameters for discussions about human difference. Contemporary scholars have noted the importance of positing "a radically different worldview, with different perceptions of reality, goals, and points of reference" for mounting a challenge to racist ways of thinking (Stepan and Gilman 1991: 101). Barbara Fields rightly observes that when scholars—even anti-racist ones—take up positions "within the terrain of racialist ideology," they become its "unknowing and therefore uncontesting victims" (1982: 144). That being said, we might look at the ideologies about race produced by indigenous people in the past as important precursors to the most innovate and insightful work being done on race in the present.

David Theo Goldberg has identified two important and divergent strands in white nineteenth-century racial ideology: historicism and naturalism. The naturalist strand posited that blacks were inferior not by political design, but by God's design. Thus their subordination was both immutable and permanent. "For the naturalists, whites and colonizers are considered agents of biological or inherent destiny. . . . Europeans are living out the superiority of their biology or inherent nature" (2002: 94). The historicist strand, which displaced the naturalist one in the latter half of the nineteenth century, maintained that biology was not destiny. With the benefit of tutelage, colonized people were capable of improvement. The historicists did not argue that nonwhites were "inherently inferior," but that they were "developmentally immature, historically not yet capable of self-governance and so requiring the guidance of European colonial benevolence" (2002: 82). Representatives of the historicist tradition in racial thought emphasized the determinative potential of external and mutable factors such as climate and social customs over biological ones like blood or race. Historicist thinking provided the ideological backdrop for racial reengineering schemes like those of General Richard Pratt, whose motto was to "kill the Indian and save the man" by removing Native American children from their parents, placing them in boarding schools, and teaching them to be socially and culturally white (Lindsey 1995). Although historicism underwrote a theory of white supremacy, whiteness was a far more mutable and potentially expansive social category for the historicists than it was for the naturalists.

The notion that racial characteristics could potentially be done and undone and that whiteness was less a biological than a political phenomenon was important also in the constitution of oppositional racial ideologies. Blacks, for example, always maintained that white superiority was political, not natural; designed by people, not by God. Thus, whites' hegemony was both temporary and mutable. Unlike those of the historicists, blacks' arguments refused to give the doctrine of white supremacy any legitimacy.

It is possible to see in the racial thought of nineteenth-century black South Africans one of the earliest examples of a social constructionist view on race. Long before the first postmodernist put pen to paper, a self-consciously antiessentialist position on whiteness and blackness was emerging in the racial ideologies of indigenous people. In attaching the attributes of whiteness selectively and without regard to physical appearance, this first generation of critics demonstrated their awareness that whiteness and blackness were a set of variable social relations between persons, rather than a matter of physical and biological attributes.

Indeed, the reflections blacks made about white people are notable for the degree to which color distinctions were given relatively short shrift and physical features (hair texture, eye color, lip and nose size) were not discussed at all. Africans never crafted a unified set of ideas about the physical characteristics of white people to explain their power and status in society. Not only was the physical appearance of individuals never made an index of their innate qualities as human beings, it was rarely even discussed. This marks an important moment in the history of racial reasoning because it is one of the few examples of a nineteenth-century racial ideology that was not tied to, rooted in, or grounded upon the materiality of the body in any significant way. In indigenous thought, whiteness was produced wholly by social relations between persons; it was not produced by biological fiat. In folk observations on whiteness and blackness, race was understood as a wholly ideological entity.

Contemporary theorists have demonstrated the importance of refocusing attention away from the materiality of the body if the power dynamics that govern the actions and choices of individuals and groups are to become visible and analyzable rather than remaining hidden behind the ideological smoke screen of race. As Fields explains, a preoccupation with a physical notion of race "becomes an obstacle to clearer understanding if it obscures the fact that race is a complicated and far from obvious concept, even when—perhaps especially when—it appears most physically precise" (1982: 150). Only a racial ideology that refuses to fetishize the materiality of the body, as we find in indigenous thought, is capable of maintaining such a view.

The refusal to become preoccupied with the physical attributes of bodies allowed African people to better comprehend and explain why the so-called Bastaards supported the vagrancy law even though it went against the larger interests of their "racial" community. The settlers who supported the ordinance pointed to the blacks who also supported it as proof that the ordinance could not possibly be racist, either in its conception or its implementation. Those indigenous thinkers who did not adhere to any notion of racial identity being fixed on particular bodies, however, had no difficulty in understanding that "men, whether Hottentot or Bushmen, as soon as they get forward in the world are immediately inclined, like other men, to oppress the poor man instead of assisting him" (*South African Commercial Advertiser*, October 4, 1834). Racial ideologies that fetishize the body are notable for the degree to which their adherents cannot comprehend or explain these types of supposed contradictions.

One of the main pitfalls of bodily centered racial ideologies is that they can neither accommodate nor account for the variability of individuals. When individual persons occasionally overcome their inferior bodies, they are considered exceptional—or better yet, they are exceptions that prove the rule. Only a racial ideology grounded in the body can produce the idea "black yet comely" or "intelligent despite being black." This type of thinking was far less prominent in the ideologies blacks produced about whites than the reverse.

Indigenous ideologies were thus able to avoid becoming entangled in the skein of racial essentialism. Consider, for example, the testimony of Dyani Tshatshu before the Select Committee on Aborigines on crime in the colony. At a time when racial scientists were increasingly coming to see crime as an innate racial propensity, Tshatshu aptly observed that "they have white thieves in the colony and they have gallows and prisons. I do not say there are no thieves among the Kaffirs but I say the nation is not a nation of thieves" (Parliament of Great Britain [1836] 1966: 571). By directing his attention away from the bodies of particular criminals, Tshatshu shifts the discussion of crime back to the terrain of the social. Thus, the manner in which social structures and social forces (including racism) work to shape and determine individual behavioral choices becomes the starting point for making judgments and formulating analyses. This analysis anticipates that of a scholar like Diana Fuss, who writes that "the body image of the black subject is not constituted by biological determinations from within but rather by cultural overdeterminations from without" (1989: 75).

The forms, relations, and institutions of power wielded by whites quite naturally conditioned the forms of resistance employed by blacks. Nevertheless, that resistance was not wholly produced and controlled by the ideological apparatuses of colonial power. Blacks' efforts to challenge racial stereotypes went far beyond engaging in a simple politics of reversal and thus were the genesis of an ideology about race that proceeded from a wholly different set of assumptions about the nature of human difference and that allowed for the construction of a very different worldview. This worldview emerged as a result of its engagement with white racism, but its contours were not determined by white racism. Although these practices of resistance and ideologies about whiteness give us glimpses into who African people were, ultimately they give us only that—glimpses and guesses. Despite the sometimes overwhelmingly oppressive nature of white rule, Africans adopted a stance toward the English that is similar to the one adopted by African Americans toward their oppressors: according to the historian Mia Bay, African Americans "never inscribed white images across their culture and imaginative life" (2000: 5). As a result, although it may be the case that "by means of what the white man imagines the black man to be . . . the black man is enabled to know what the white man is" (Baldwin [1955] 1998: 123), the obverse is simply not true. It is possible to get a slightly better idea of what the black man is, however, through an exploration of how he represented and imagined blackness. I turn to a discussion of this subject in the next chapter.

CHAPTER SEVEN

What Is (African) America to Me? Africans, African Americans, and the Rearticulation of Blackness

Several decades before Countee Cullen asked the question "What is Africa to me?" black South Africans were already grappling with the question "What is African America to me?" The diamond mines of Kimberley, South Africa, were a key site where images of African Americans became instrumental in providing African people, whether they were miners or not, with a means for thinking about and thinking through the diverse meanings of blackness. Due to the world-historical nature of plantation slavery and the precocious transnationalization of minstrelsy, one of the earliest components of what was to become the American "cultural industry," African Americans came to hold the unique and dubious status of being the preeminent symbols of blackness in the modern world. To imagine blackness, particularly if one was talking about work and leisure, freedom and bondage, sexuality, or the connections between them inevitably meant conjuring up an image of the plantation slave. African Americans thus became what Susan Star and James Griesemer call "boundary objects," objects that are "both plastic enough to adapt to local needs and the constraints of several parties employing them, yet robust enough to maintain a common identity across sites. . . . They have different meanings in different social worlds but their structure is common enough to more than one world to make them recognizable" (1989: 393). Minstrelsy played a constitutive role in securing the plasticity of American blackness.

The blackness that was depicted on the South African minstrel stage might usefully be thought of as blackness twice-displaced for these were copies of copies of an original blackness that never existed. To understand how blackness came to be imagined and represented in African imaginations it is thus necessary to return, once again, to the black image in the white mind. The stereotyped images of New World blackness that appeared on the minstrel stage provided African people with a template from which they were able to develop a highly complex relationship to blackness. These images of the New World African, albeit presented in caricatured form, catalyzed the emergence of new forms of identity in South Africa that reimagined blackness in ways quite distant from the one-dimensional stereotypes that could be found in the racial discourse produced by whites.

Of Mines and Minstrels: Labor, Alienation, and Racial Imagery

It is more than a little ironic that minstrelsy, a form of entertainment that Frederick Douglass denounced as a product of "the filthy scum of white society" designed to "make money [while] pander[ing] to the corrupt taste of white citizens," not only was one of the first means whereby Africans in South Africa came to know blackness, but was also a conduit through which they fashioned their own identities as blacks in the modern world (Douglass quoted in Lott 1995: 15). English colonists were responsible for introducing American-style minstrel shows to South African audiences in the 1850s. After the August 1862 debut of the world-famous Christy Minstrels in Cape Town, the shows achieved a popularity previously unheard of in South Africa. Over the next three decades blackface minstrel shows became a dominant form of popular white musical and theatrical entertainment in South Africa, second only to the circus. Amateur troupes performed in all the major urban locales, and audiences were offered a wide choice of entertainment with two or more different troupes performing in each major city each night.

Minstrelsy catered to both elite and more popular audiences, as British regiments employed private minstrels for their entertainment and working-class audiences were able to enjoy shows in the numerous canteens and eating houses that proliferated in urban areas (Erlmann 1991). After the opening performance of the Natal Christy Minstrels, the *Diamond News* of July 27, 1872, carried the following report:

> The Natal Christy Minstrels made their debut at the Mutual Hall. . . . The Hall was crowded from floor to ceiling, and from ceiling to floor again. The rafters and beams of the roof were crowded with people, as well as the chairs and forms. This was a "new Rush" and no mistake. Long before the hour of performance the doors were thronged and when the doors were opened the people came in with a rush, and the ticket-takers had more work than they had counted upon. Mr. Payne, the manager, did his utmost to ensure every one his own proper place, but no manager could meet such a sudden and unexpected

rush. There were demands for admission even when the place was over full. There were crowds of people round the doors from the time of opening until the close of the performances, with the whole of which the audience was well pleased, and testified their appreciation by repeated encores and applause.

Minstrelsy had a tremendous impact on the minds and imaginations of white South Africans, and Africans on the fields quickly felt the negative effects of minstrelsy's popularity. They were frequently abused as "Christy Minstrels," "Jim Crow," or simply "Jim" (Matthews 1887: 193). It was largely due to the popularity of minstrelsy that Africans who worked in the fields were often forced to endure being called "nigger" (see the *Diamond News* of January 20, 1872; November 10, 1874; June 1, 1875; January 23, 1877). A writer to the *Diamond Fields Advertiser* of September 9, 1874, for example, complained that he and his fellow workers were "robbed right and left by the niggers squatted along the river." In the *Diamond Fields Advertiser* of May 19, 1875, another writer agreed that "the Native Question is the difficulty of the day, not only here but in the United States of America, the West Indian Islands, and wherever the Anglo-Saxon race finds itself face to face with the irrepressible nigger."

The one stock image from the minstrel stage that assimilated into the South African racial vernacular with particular ease was that of the dandy, or swell—the consummate symbol of the urban black man and thus the most distinctive and culturally loaded character of the minstrel stage. According to the historian Eric Lott, in the American context, the dandy was "an ideological fiction through which certain of the decade's conflicts were lived" (1995: 112). Although he was a creation of the white antebellum American imagination, the swell encapsulated a combination of race and class animus that was readily understood in seemingly far-flung and disparate cultural contexts. White miners, particularly those who had had experienced downward class mobility, were the most likely to vent their hostility at Africans by castigating them with the label "swell nigger" or "nigger dandy." Largely as a result of the hegemony of monopoly capital in the diamond-mining industry, white miners had first lost their status as independent diggers who owned claims and hired Africans to work them, and subsequently had become share-workers who no longer owned claims but still supervised African laborers. These diggers were frightened by the rapidity with which they were descending the class ladder and were frustrated by the loss of independence and autonomy that entailed. (see Turrell 1982; Worger 1987). One irate miner complained in the *Diamond News* of June 1, 1875, that there were "constantly in our streets a number of colored men, dressed in fine clothes, with belts for carrying diamonds and money round their waists. Many of them are great dandies in their way."

A number of parallels can be drawn between life in antebellum America and life in South Africa that help to explain their mutual fascination with blackface entertainments. Both countries witnessed the proletarianization of the craft labor force and the deskilling that accompanied more rigid practices of industrial discipline, which Lott (1995) identifies as a crucial catalyst for minstrelsy's emergence. Both also experienced the increasing functional interchangeability of working-class blacks and whites that David Roediger (1991) points to as a major impetus for the popularity of minstrelsy among working-class men. One might also draw parallels between the ways in which minstrelsy provided white immigrants in both locales with "their imagined community, their imagined home" (Rogin 1996). I contend that minstrelsy achieved such popularity because it enabled whites to sublimate the anger and rage that were a necessary component of the phenomenon Marx termed the estrangement of labor. The "nigger swell," or "nigger dandy," was a crucially important figure in this regard, as he was the figure at whom this displaced rage was directed. This parallel supplements, rather than supplants, the parallels identified by other historians.

Racial Imagery and the Phenomenon of Estranged Labor

Marx dealt extensively with the problem of estranged labor in the Economic and Philosophic Manuscripts of 1844. According to Marx, in a capitalist society the products of a person's labor, and the surrounding material world that is the aggregate of such products, becomes estranged or alienated from the worker. Thus,

> The worker becomes all the poorer the more wealth he produces, the more his production increases in power and range. . . . The more objects the worker produces the fewer can he possess and the more he falls under the dominion of his product, capital. . . . Hence, the greater the activity, the greater is the worker's lack of objects. . . . It is true that labour produces for the rich wonderful things—but for the worker it produces privation. It produces palaces—but for the worker, hovels. It produces beauty—but for the worker, deformity. (Marx [1844] 1978: 71–73)

The source of this alienation is, of course, the social property relations of capitalism. In the specific case of Kimberley, the social property relations of capitalist mining and the associated imperatives of competition, accumulation, and profit maximization resulted in the hegemony of monopoly capital, which was responsible for the alienation, proletarianization, and increased exploitation of all the workers (Turrell 1982; Worger 1987). In the discourses of white miners, however, there is a curious reversal of agent and object whereby black workers become responsible for the alienation of white workers. Instead of castigating the capitalists as the ones who enjoyed all of the material benefits of labor even though they did not produce, white miners projected the sins of the capitalist onto the black worker in the form of the swell stereotype.

Two assertions emerge as most distinctive in white miners' vitriolic denunciation of the so-called swell nigger. The first is the repeated insistence that swells do not work but they enjoy material comforts. The second is the repeated insistence that swells assail the dignity and virtue of work—particularly manual labor. In the *Diamond Fields Advertiser* of January 13, 1875, for example, a writer complained of the "hundreds and thousands of native men and women, the latter togged out in jewelry and finery, who lie about their tents all day [and] do not live from honest work. Morning and evening they are to be seen lolling on the ground, surrounded by crowds of children, and they live without putting their hands to labor." The author of an article that appeared in the *Diamond News* on June 3 of that same year argued along similar lines: "When an able-bodied man cannot give satisfactory account of how he earns his living he needs looking up. Ask any of these natives with hats stuck away upon their wooly heads and cigars in their mouths who roam about the Camp how they earn their living and they could not tell. The fact is that they do no manual labor."

In reality, of course, it was the capitalist who could not give a satisfactory account of how he earned his living and who swaggered about without doing any appreciable work. Although Cecil Rhodes never shoveled a single scoop of dirt or descended into a mine, by the time he died he had not only monopolized the world's diamonds and a large share of the world's gold, but had carved a personal empire out of the heart of Africa. He continually excoriated the so-called natives for their laziness, but he rarely put his own hands to any serious labor. According to Anthony Thomas, Rhodes went to Kimberley only for "long vacations." He spent most of his time in England, where he "played polo, rowed, or kept his neighbours awake at night by practising on a hunting horn. . . . He also became a member of the exclusive Bullingdon and Vincent's clubs, which only accepted men of wealth, dandies and bon vivants." Thomas rightly observes the irony of the fact that a man "so obsessed with the 'sin' of wasted time" followed "a regime of hunting, rowing, polo, skipped lectures and bowler-hat parades" (1996: 102–3).

It was only through the conceptual conflation of labor with capitalist enterprise—what Ellen Meiksins Wood calls a "cornerstone in the ideological justification of capitalism" (1995: 156)—that capitalists like Rhodes came to be seen as productive at all. Indeed, one of the most spectacular ideological coups of bourgeois economics was the way in which the appropriation of another person's labor came to be treated as the equivalent of performing that labor oneself. As Wood explains: "In the conventional discourse of modern economics it is capitalists, not workers, who *produce*. So, for example, the financial pages of major newspapers routinely talk about conflicts between, say, automobile *producers* and trade unions. . . . The virtues of labour and 'industry' have been displaced from the activity of labour itself to the *employment* of labour and to the productive utilization of property" (1995: 156–57, emphasis in original). Capitalists were able to lay claim not only to the fruit of workers' labor, but also to all of the virtues attendant upon it.

The vitriol directed at black miners can thus be seen as both a displacement of aggression that should have been directed at mine owners for their usurpation of the products of labor and a plea for the restoration to the worker of the virtues attendant upon that labor. Instead of protesting the owners' usurpation of the products and virtues of labor, a situation that affected blacks and whites alike, if not equally, white workers chose to vent their hostility on blacks. The baubles, trinkets, and other relatively insignificant consumer items Africans accumulated came to symbolize and to bear the responsibility for the arrogation of the dignity of labor from the white working man.

Labor, Race, and Ideology

As might be expected, there was a spirited response from certain quarters of the African community, primarily the middle classes. They not only protested that black people worked harder than anyone else while receiving the least amount of remuneration, but also made white workers responsible for undermining the dignity of labor by using the criterion of race to determine which employments were worthy and which were unworthy. A letter that appeared in the May 22, 1906, edition of *Izwi Labantu*, for example, connected whites' racism with their disdain for hard work. "Why should the white man do manual work when nature has provided the black races to do the drudgery? Hewers of wood and drawers of water has a kindly Providence placed in this country in the millions of the sons of Ham, who must ever be the political pariahs of the world. That is the line of thought that is almost universal amongst the whites of South Africa, and it is just about as silly as it is narrow and unjust." White miners' honor as workers, as whites, and as men resided in being exempt from work performed by blacks. They held onto this belief so tightly it became a spiritual ideal of sorts. In the minds of white workers, certain types of labor were hateful simply because they were associated with the common labor of blacks.

This attitude originated in the social relations of slavery, which, John Barrow observed, had a peculiar effect on the "minds and habits of people born and educated in the midst of it." He noticed that "the lower class of people particularly object to their children going as servants or being bound as apprentices to learn useful trades which, in their contracted ideas, would be considered as condemning them to perform the work of slaves" ([1801] 1968: 47). The association of labor with racial degradation became even more entrenched when officers of the colonial government wrote it into state policy. British High Commissioner Sir Alfred Milner declared: "We do not want a white proletariat in this country. The position of the whites among the vastly more numerous black population requires that even their lowest ranks should be able to maintain a standard of living far above that of the poorest section of the population of a purely white country" (Headlam 1933: 459). Given that this was the state's official position, it is no surprise that individual miners interpreted any move to equalize the status or treatment of white and black workers as the "classing of intelligent and honest white men with raw and thievish natives, which must invariably lower the moral tone and social status of the hundreds of citizens to the detriment of all concerned" (*Daily Independent*, July 16, 1880). A writer for the *Diamond Fields Advertiser* likewise asked how it could be expected that "any educated man can submit to the same disgusting degradation as the untutored Negro" (October 17, 1883). John Angove agreed that "the native labourer is to us what the Irish labourer is at home—the hewer of wood and the drawer of water" (1910: 182).

Black workers were thus well aware that it was the predatory culture of racism that gave certain types of work the mark of inferiority. In insisting that blackness be disassociated in men's habits and thoughts with weakness and subjugation to a master, African miners pointed to the impossibility of ever removing the stigma attached to productive toil without elevating the status of blackness. As an editorial in *Izwi Labantu* explained, no worker could hope for respect until "the aims of all wage earners of every colour are identical." African workers went even farther, arguing that this predatory culture had over time given rise to a hard division between drudgery, which was the "proper" lot of blacks, and leisure, which was the true vocation of the masters. Thus, Africans also claimed the right to leisure for themselves, and it is here that we can locate the transfiguration of the image of the swell from a racial caricature owned and operated by whites to a figure of critique and transcendence owned and operated by blacks.

Leisure, Consumption, and the Meanings of Blackness

It is possible to discern from contemporary accounts that African workers may have been deliberately adopting some elements of style from the minstrel stage. According to historian Christopher Ballantine, "by 1880 at least one African minstrel troupe was performing in Durban, and by the turn of the century the fashion had penetrated even to remote rural areas, where Africans formed troupes with names like the Pirate Coons or the Yellow Coons" (1993: 4). It would not be too far-fetched, therefore, to surmise that individual Africans might have cobbled together elements from various minstrel performances—both those wherein whites impersonated blacks and those wherein blacks impersonated whites impersonating blacks. Corporeal adornment was so critical to minstrelsy as a performance genre, it also makes sense that it might have inspired imitative forms of personal adornment. Furthermore, the manner in which colonialism was steadily extending its reach meant that a symbolism of wealth that borrowed heavily from American popular culture could have partially supplanted the traditional symbolism of wealth in African culture.

It is also reasonable to surmise that there might have been some connection between the alienation experienced by black workers and their affinity for certain characters they had seen represented on the minstrel stage. Black workers were no less affected by the alienating nature of capitalism than their white counterparts, and Marx could easily have been describing an African worker when he wrote the following:

> What, then, constitutes the alienation of labour? First, the fact that labour is external to the worker, i.e., it does not belong to his essential being; that in his work, therefore, he does not affirm himself but denies himself, does not feel content but unhappy. . . . Its alien character emerges clearly in the fact that as soon as no physical or other compulsion exists, labour is shunned like the plague. . . . As a result, therefore, man (the worker) no longer feels himself to be freely active in any but his animal functions—eating, drinking, procreating, or at most in his dwelling and in dressing up. . . . Certainly eating, drinking, procreating, etc., are also genuinely human functions. But in the abstraction

which separates them from the sphere of all other human activity and turns them into sole and ultimate ends, they are animal. ([1844] 1978: 74)

Direct testimonies from African workers are, obviously, hard to come by. Nevertheless, it is possible to read between the lines of narratives produced by white workers and surmise that the "animal functions" of eating, drinking, and especially dressing up became central preoccupations of African workers—particularly during their leisure hours. It was not uncommon, for example, for whites to castigate Africans for not only loafing, but loafing while dressed up in finery. As the writer of a leading article in the *Diamond News* of June 1, 1875, protested: "The bare fact that there are a large number of natives dressed in superfine clothes, swaggering about the towns and round about the various mines all day long without doing any work is sufficient to convince anyone that there is something rotten in the state of Griqualand West. Where do these men get money to buy such clothes, and to spend on wine and cigars?" Putting aside for a moment the slanderous nature of the above account and allowing for some degree of exaggeration, it is possible to surmise that leisure and personal adornment were tightly coupled and, further, that they were actualized through reenacting some version or vision of the dandy.

For better or worse the minstrel stage was a space where leisure was continually being acted and reenacted. As Saidiya Hartman explains, "the blackface mask of minstrelsy and melodrama all evidenced the entanglements of terror and enjoyment. . . . Above all, the simulated jollity and coerced festivity of the slave trade and the instrumental recreations of plantation management document the investment in and obsession with 'black enjoyment'" (1997: 23). Africans probably would not have consciously delighted in the fanciful depiction of black subjugation, but they were clearly able to suppress many of the negative elements of minstrelsy in favor of focusing on the alternative possibility it presented for imagining the black body reclaimed from the demands of work.

Whereas the white observer constantly produced the spectacle of black underproductivity so that he could both revel in it and, by way of contrast, construct himself as productive, the black worker might have read the enacted laziness of the black body on the minstrel stage differently. It must be remembered that because control over the labor process was an important means of increasing surplus in production, black workers in Kimberley were constantly under surveillance to guard against the possibility of their loafing, despite the fact that they worked upward of twelve hours a day with minimal breaks. An editorial in the paper *Imvo Zabantsundu* (Native Opinion) described Africans as "Mr. Rhodes' array of black machinery penned up in his compounds" (July 26, 1893). A contributor to the paper's April 8, 1885, edition had likewise protested, "These people, it must be remembered, are always taunted that they are lazy, and it must be discouraging and disheartening to them when they find themselves in circumstances such as these." Indeed, Thomas (1996) describes how Africans were contracted for fixed periods and confined to closed compounds linked to the mines by tunnels or fenced walkways. Over eleven thousand African workers were housed this way, twenty to twenty-five to a room in barracks patrolled by police officers with dogs. When workers returned to the compound at the end of their shift, they were stripped and subjected to invasive body searches.

The only space of freedom for blacks was in the avoidance of work. Leisure constituted the sole exercise of power in the body. Hence, the desire to emulate the clothes and mannerisms of the dandy may well have arisen out of workers' identification of the stereotype with the forbidden pleasure of stolen moments of relaxation and enjoyment. Hartman (quoting Slavoj Žižek) notes that "fantasies about the Other's enjoyment are ways for us to organize our own enjoyment. . . . Does not the Other's enjoyment exert such a powerful fascination because in it we represent to ourselves our own innermost relationship toward enjoyment?" (1997: 25). Hartman and Žižek are referring to the fantasies dominant groups have about the pleasures enjoyed by the dominated. I believe that dominated subjects might also tap into these same fantasies, albeit in very different ways. In other words, the dominated might also look to an "other" to organize their experiences of pleasure or enjoyment.

On the minstrel stage, representations of black enjoyment were orchestrated to facilitate white enjoyment. Black enjoyment was thus yoked to the needs and desires of whites. The aggressiveness with which the so-called swells pursued leisure, however, insisted on the autonomous nature of black pleasure. Adopting the persona of the swell was a means of demanding the right to pursue pleasure in ways that were not only disconnected from the wishes and desires of whites, but were also read by them as a direct and deliberate affront. Hence, rather than standing for obedience, subjugation, and despair, blackness could represent irreverent joy, raucous enjoyment, and proscribed pleasure.

The number of letters penned by white miners accusing African swells of "insolence" indicates that Africans who took on the swell persona when negotiating the public spaces of Kimberley were simultaneously making stylistic and social statements. As Houston Baker points out, "what seems passively consumed as culture as a whole, whether popular, high, commercial, mass, or otherwise, may be psychologically and affectively appropriated" (1995: 15). We might read the "insolent swagger" of the African worker as he "rolled along the sidewalks of the town, with cigar in mouth, giving inside place to no one" (*Diamond News*, June 1, 1875) as a refusal to submit to what a letter that appeared in *Imvo* called "the low type of Europeans [who] think that every nigger requires kicking, beating, thrashing, and all kinds of ill treatments" (October 12, 1909).

If we recall that the swell was an affable figure in the minstrel tradition, the menacing attributes that the swells adopted when traversing the streets and public byways of Kimberley, particularly when traveling in groups, might well be indicative of their desire to, in the words of Ralph Ellison, "change the joke and slip the yoke" (1972). The swells, above all, refused to adopt the posture of silence that was demanded of blacks in a white supremacist culture. One white digger, writing in the *Diamond News*, reported the presence of "a large number of natives dressed in superfine clothes, swaggering about the towns and round about the various mines all day," who "if spoken to, retort with the grossest abuse" (June 1, 1875). The swell persona, therefore, allowed for the cultivation and expression of a certain type of antisocial sociality that did not seek white approval but repudiated bourgeois standards of propriety.

Africans who adopted the swell persona were able to disrupt traditional social patterns whereby whites' antisocial behavior toward blacks not only was tolerated, but was a critical component of white sociality: they made black antisocial behavior toward whites a resistive form of black sociality. An article in the *Diamond Fields Advertiser* of April 26, 1878, registered its author's disgust at the manner in which black sociality undermined whites' ability to make money: "The Nigger Swell is no sooner registered than he meets with some old friends of his who, of course, advise him to leave the man who has just paid so dearly for him, and take another master, under whom he may be in company with his old companions and chums. The nigger takes their advice, and deserts his master's service." Adopting and adapting certain key attributes of an invented black persona was thus an integral component of the quest to claim public space. Rather than engaging in a politics of reversal, which would have involved actively disarticulating the connections between blackness, aggressiveness, danger, and impropriety, some African workers instead embraced and reworked these negative associations in their pursuit of heightened visibility.

When read against the practices of racial exclusion that denied Africans what George Lipsitz has called "the promises of universal inclusion through participation in market relations and consumption," the complexity of the meanings behind the acquisition of commodities becomes much more apparent (1998: 165). Access to leisure and acquisition of commodities took on enhanced social significance for Africans precisely because oppressive forms of racial power legally restricted their access to certain types of work and the wages they would have received from that work while denying them the opportunity to purchase wealth-accumulating assets. The purchase of clothes and fancy cars clearly affirms rather than challenges the dominant values of capitalism and is a limited form of resistance at best. When we consider, however, how closely the systematic effort to deny Africans access to the most superficial consumption goods was coupled with the campaign to render Africans less than human, it is possible to read a concern with personal adornment as a muted plea for recognition as a human being.

It is important to recognize that white miners' attempts to deny Africans the right to purchase depreciating assets like clothing and carriages were part of a much larger and more systematic state-sponsored campaign to impair Africans' ability to accumulate wealth and acquire financial independence. White miners' intense opposition to Africans' acquisition of clothes, carriages, and cigars cannot be isolated from the broad range of actions they undertook to deny blacks the opportunity to engage in wealth-accumulating activity. Indeed, the term *nigger swell* first emerged as a term of abuse in the course of white miners' agitation for the restriction of claim ownership to persons of European descent (see *Diamond News,* January 23, 1877; November 10, 1874; June 1, 1875; and *Diamond Fields Advertiser,* May 19, 1875). White miners were also prone to castigate Africans as "swell niggers" when trying to persuade the government of the necessity and urgency of enacting racially discriminatory labor market interventions—pass laws, laws restricting the privilege of acquiring digging licenses and registering employees to whites, and so on. The *Diamond Fields Advertiser* of November 11, 1874, for example, printed a letter from an irate white miner who railed against the laxity of the current system of pass and registration laws: "I am opposed to the pass system as it is now carried out. A few weeks ago I saw a swell nigger come in and ask to have five other swells registered to him. I have often stopped swell niggers on the kopje [fields] and have invariably been met with a pass showing they were the registered servants of Jack Swartbooi, Jack August, or some such name."

The state, acting partially on behalf of white miners and partially at the behest of mining capital, played a major role in erecting barriers to black economic self-sufficiency. The most damaging piece of legislation was that which legally denied Africans the privilege of owning their own claims. This law not only relegated Africans to the status of wage laborers, but also permanently denied them the opportunity of accumulating real capital and thereby achieving financial independence.

White wealth accumulation and black poverty were deeply implicated precisely because the same systematic policies that denied wealth-accumulating opportunities to Africans fostered the accumulation of wealth for whites. When Africans were denied the opportunity to amass assets and secure financial status, they were also denied the opportunity to pass wealth onto succeeding generations, and citizenship itself became racialized. The "sedimentation of racial inequality" (Oliver and Shapiro 1997: 5) that was the result would affect Africans well into the twenty-first century—long after they had the liberty to buy what they wished and dress as they wanted. Thus, when we place the swell persona within the context of the total ensemble of efforts to erect barriers to economic self-sufficiency and deny blacks their claims to personhood, it is possible to see that persona as a statement, however muted, about the connections between citizenship, consumption, and social power.

Minstrelsy, Mimicry, and the Meaning of Money

The symbolic importance of commodities in the lives of African people cannot be separated from what scholars have called white peoples' possessive investment in whiteness (Lipsitz 1998; Harris [1993] 1998). These two impulses must be seen as existing in dynamic interaction. In the Economic and Philosophic Manuscripts of 1844, there is a section devoted to "The Power of Money in Bourgeois Society," in which Marx characterizes the power of money as "the fraternization of impossibilities" ([1944] 1978: 105). In a particularly insightful passage, Marx discusses the manner in which money's properties and powers became the properties and powers of its possessor:

> What I *am* and *am capable of* is by no means determined by my individuality. I am ugly, but I can buy for myself the most *beautiful* of women. Therefore I am not *ugly*, for the effect of *ugliness*—its deterrent power—is nullified by money. I, in my character, as an individual, am *lame*, but money furnishes me with twenty-four feet. Therefore I am not lame. I am bad, dishonest, unscrupulous, *stupid*; but money is honoured, and therefore so is its possessor. Money is the supreme good, therefore its possessor is good. Money, besides, saves me the trouble of being dishonest: I am therefore presumed honest. I am stupid, but money is the *real mind* of all things and how then, should its possessor be stupid? . . . Do not I, who thanks to money am capable of all that the human

heart longs for, possess all human capacities? Does not my money therefore transform all my incapacities into their contrary? ([1844] 1978: 103, emphasis in original)

The dandy of the minstrel stage was marked as a distinctive character by virtue of the manner in which he adorned his body—the cast-off gentlemen's clothes that along with his mangled and comic attempts to reproduce bourgeois speech patterns confirmed the impossibility of class mobility. The dandy of the diamond fields, however, could not be so easily contained. Money opened up avenues of consumption for Africans that provided the possibility of buying whiteness by acquiring certain markers of distinction. The spectacular ways in which they adorned their bodies not only forced whites to see them, but disarticulated the automatic association of blackness with material lack. The swells' enviable position in the marketplace, in particular their access to money, which Marx called "the object of eminent possession" that gave the possessor the "property of buying everything," opened the door to a number of imaginative possibilities ([1844] 1978: 102). It is thus possible to discern in whites' obsession with the material adornment of black bodies a profound discomfort with the transformative power of money.

White miners clearly feared that the power of money to turn the individual "into something which in itself it is not . . . into its *contrary*" (Marx [1844] 1978: 104, emphasis in original) might amount to turning blacks into whites or, at the very least, niggers into "gentlemen." The repeated references to "nigger gentlemen" in letters, editorials, and articles (see the *Diamond News* for November 1, 1874; June 1, 1875; and June 3, 1875) indicate the profundity of the anxieties produced by money's alchemical powers. Thus, in addition to epitomizing the fears aroused by the potential dissolution of white bodily integrity through miscegenation, which Michael Rogin characterizes as the "hysteria" over the mixing of bodily fluids that always operated alongside "racial cross dressing," the dandy symbolized the threat money posed to the dissolution of white class integrity (1996: 25). The black miners who adopted the swell persona, embracing the material accoutrements that were a constitutive element of his character, were turning the alchemical properties of money to unanticipated advantage. Although money could by no means transform blacks into whites, it could manipulate appearances so as to disrupt any easy associations between race and status. Thus, the social relations of class society, which gave money the power to "turn *image* into *reality* and *reality* into mere *image*," had extremely contrary effects in a racially stratified society (Marx [1844] 1978: 105, emphasis in original).

The writer of an editorial in the *Diamond Fields Advertiser* of August 19,

1874, complained: "We have swell niggers drinking champagne while white men really working claims near them are scarcely able to buy bread." The *Diamond News* of November 1, 1874, urged its readers to "look at the black gentlemen, how many of them do nothing that anyone can see, except ride about in carts (which white men in pretty good circumstances cannot afford) and smoke cigars." Generally only white men with capital were allowed the privilege of riding around in carts and eschewing manual labor. Money, however, could lend anyone the appearance of living like a gentleman, if only temporarily.

Once acquired, the status symbols of whiteness could be marked with certain key stylistic markers of blackness and thereby transformed. Take, for example, the suit, which was one of the key bourgeois markers of respectability. A miner writing in the February 23, 1873, edition of the *Diamond News* complained that "the Sunday going niggers are much better dressed than the white man in England." The writer also noted the manner in which the suit was transfigured to make it something quite unlike anything worn by the typical English gentleman. "Many of them on the fields" he observed "dress like dandy Broadway swells." The element common to all of these scenarios—indeed, the element without which none of them could take place—is money. The swell persona was premised on a form of impersonation achieved through consumption that, while it exceeded the limits of simple mimicry, stopped just short of outright mockery.

It is possible to build upon the immensely productive work that Homi Bhabha has done on mimicry by placing the phenomenon within the context of capitalism and the power of money in bourgeois society. What impact did the fact that money had the power to transform image into reality and reality into image have on the "process by which the look of surveillance returns as the displacing gaze of the disciplined, where the observer becomes the observed" (1997: 156)? I suggest that the impact was quite profound. The Africans who adopted the swell persona made the choice to use the cash wages they earned to acquire material goods that at the time symbolized a degree of status and success deemed inappropriate for blacks. Although their decisions certainly leave them open to the charge of commodity fetishism, when placed in the context of intense white opposition to the accumulation of assets of any kind by Africans, we can see the desire of blacks to own luxury items as entailing an implicit challenge to white supremacy.

To adopt the swell persona, then, was to take a stance toward whiteness and bourgeois respectability that entailed mockery as well as mimicry. Spending money on the same clothes and carriages that were markers of status and respectability in the white community can be read as indicative of a desire to become white—what Frantz Fanon (1967) called narcissist mimicry. It can also, however, be read as the adoption of a deliberately mocking stance toward whiteness. Africans acquired the commodities that symbolized whiteness with relish and ease, resolutely exposing the vulnerability of whiteness.

The dandy persona was an ideal vehicle for effecting this reversal precisely because it was the outgrowth of a performance genre that already admitted the possibility of racial crossing and impersonation. Once the doors to racial impersonation had been opened, it was impossible to fully police who went in and how. On the minstrel stage the swell enacted the hilarious scenario of white transforming into black by means of masking and costume. On the diamond fields and in the streets and public spaces of Kimberley, however, the so-called swell nigger embodied the real physical horror of black transforming into white through the medium of money rather than the artifice of masking.

Whites became fascinated with minstrelsy precisely because it countenanced treating race as a field of play and racial identities as costumes that could be put on and taken off at will. Their intention, of course, was that blackness would be the only identity available for this kind of fantasy and play. In actuality, however, the same social forces and pressures that made minstrelsy compelling to whites in the first place were the ones that opened up whiteness as a field of play for blacks. The consumption patterns of the so-called swell nigger only become meaningful, therefore, when they are viewed in the context of the myriad of other assaults to whiteness that were part and parcel of capital accumulation and monopolization in the mining industry.

The social relations of capitalism that made the imperatives of competition, accumulation, profit maximization, and increasing labor productivity the regulators of all economic transactions continually reduced the social and economic distance between blacks and whites. For example, mining capitalists justified subjecting white workers to the same humiliating body cavity searches as Africans by arguing that "the unscrupulous, villainous white scoundrel uses the black, who but for him might be honest" (*Diamond Fields Advertiser*, November 11, 1874). Mine owners like S. Marks, who testified before the Select Committee on Illicit Diamond Buying in 1882, rationalized using black labor instead of white by arguing that they had tried white labor and found it wanting. "I engaged fifty white men and it would not answer," Marks declared. "They worked one day and got drunk the next. You can always count on the Kaffirs" (Parliament of the Cape of Good Hope 1882).

On the one hand, capitalism is based on the premise that money can buy anything. "He who can buy bravery is brave, though a coward. . . . From the standpoint of its possessor it therefore serves to exchange every property for every other, even contradictory property" (Marx [1844] 1978: 105). On the other hand, capitalist societies were marked by the most virulent forms of racism, which dictated that one property in particular, whiteness, should not be easily acquirable. No white South African was comfortable with the possibility that one who could buy whiteness was white, even though black. Thus, white miners were forever reiterating their contention that blacks' innate racial characteristics made it impossible for them ever to attain the status of whiteness through their material possessions. A writer for the *Diamond News* of June 1, 1875, for example, scoffed at the many black miners who, though "great dandies in their way, . . . carried their clothes and limped in high heeled boots very uncomfortably, having more the appearance of Apes in fashionable attire than men accustomed to fine linen and broadcloth." The writer's deliberate characterization of these Africans as apes in fashionable attire suggests that it is not so much that blacks' attempts to impersonate whites were futile, but that their attempts to impersonate human beings were futile. We are meant to see not simply an apish person in a fashionable suit, but an actual ape in a human suit. The entire discourse is premised on the idea that it is impossible not only for blacks access whiteness, but also for them to access the status of humans. The confidence of such writers' assertions, however, was continually being undermined in other elements of their discourse, which is shot through with descriptions of Africans drinking champagne while whites eat bread, Africans riding in carts that white men can't afford, and Africans dressed in linen and broadcloth while whites wear rags.

The disintegration of white bodily integrity, which also had an impact on the enforceability of racist laws, was likewise an issue. An editorial in the *Diamond News* of June 1, 1875, pointed out that the degree of racial amalgamation in South Africa hindered the effectiveness of many of the racially specific laws the white diggers wished to see passed: "We know that the diggers are opposed to any coloured people having licenses either to hold claims or to sort debris. That restriction, of course, cannot be attempted. In South Africa, colour runs so gradually from white into black that it is difficult to detect the point at which white leaves off and black begins."

Thus, within a social context where racial identities were insecure, the acquisition of consumer durables became highly charged politically and emotionally. Working-class men were able to use clothing as a means of accessing an image of blackness through which they could express their longings for freedom, autonomy, and selfhood. In the words of Jean and John Comaroff, clothing "made available an expansive, expressive, experimental language with which to conjure new social identities and senses of self, a language with which to speak back to the whites" (1997: 235). Working-class men were not the only ones who used images of African Americans to negotiate their identities and speak back. Images of New World Africans also provided a template for middle-class African men to assert their identities as blacks and as men.

Kimberley in the Black Atlantic World

If one were to go by the accounts of the digging classes or the mining capitalists, one could easily conclude that rural migrants were the only Africans in Kimberley. As Thomas notes, "virtually the only blacks that feature in the (white) digger literature were the 'naked,' 'laughing,' 'singing' Kaffir labourers who performed the menial heavy work on the mines and were often recruited from tribal areas far outside the territory. Apart from an occasional disparaging reference to 'darkey swells,' the literature . . . makes no mention of an aspiring black middle class" (1996: 83). In reality, African society in Kimberley was amazingly diverse, and the town became the focal point for a small but growing class of educated Africans. Because an African man with education could find employment as a translator, clerk, or messenger, or in the Posts and Telegraphs, the town became a mecca for the highly "Westernized" graduates of the Eastern Cape mission schools. Through their protest actions and cultural activities, these men articulated an emergent black modernity forged out of the unique sense of being both inside and outside the West. It was through this emergent black modernity, which they articulated in both textual and nontextual forms, that they were able to launch a critique of racial subjection that was in concert with and inaugurated them into what sociologist Paul Gilroy has called the "Black Atlantic World" (1993).

Although black South Africans did not have a tremendous impact on the processes Gilroy describes, their contribution does merit investigation. Its importance lies in the manner in which they took an image that was universally seen as a repository of negative value—that of the enslaved African American—and actively struggled to attach entirely new and different meanings to it. When Africans on the diamond fields were abused as "nigger," the intent of the insult was to liken them to those whom many people thought were the lowest creatures on earth. Any corporeal entity identified as black was available for symbolic use; it was "an abstract empty vessel vulnerable to the projection of others' feelings, ideas, desires, and values" (Hartman 1997: 21). The captive black body in America, however, was especially favored in this regard. The status of blacks and blackness everywhere was shaped and compromised by the existence of slavery and by the images of the African American that were produced and circulated to defend the peculiar institution.

The word *nigger* had such tremendous transnational valence because it referenced simultaneously a particular group of people and a broader social relationship between the inferior and the superior. The social relation between the dominator and the dominated encapsulated in the word was one of absolute and permanent dominance. A nigger was a nonperson available for any kind of abuse. A nigger did not exist as a being for itself; it was a being only for others. A nigger could not own anything—not even its own worthless nigger self or its nigger progeny. Thus, when Africans in Kimberley attempted to forge a different relationship to blackness through a positive identification with African Americans and what they represented, it was not an insignificant act. It represented an attempt to challenge white supremacy by insisting not only on seeing blackness on the whole differently, but on doing so through a positive elevation of African Americans and the struggles for freedom from white supremacy they inaugurated. Thus, the image of the nigger was inverted—instead of standing for subjugation it would stand for freedom; instead of standing for weakness it would stand for power; instead of standing for the utter absence of will it would stand for willful social action.

According to Gilroy, the fact that modernity yoked together terror and racialized subjection engendered a variety of nontextual forms of critique. Black musical expression, Gilroy contends, through its unique ability to capture the sublime, played a central role in forging a distinct counterculture of modernity. "By posing the world as it is against the world as the racially subordinated would like it to be, this musical culture supplies a great deal of the courage required to go on living in the present. It is both produced by and expressive of that 'transvaluation of all values' precipitated by this history of racial terror" (Gilroy 1993: 36). Gilroy thus defines the Black Atlantic world primarily by the unique movements and flows that characterize it, paying particular attention to "the circulation of ideas and activists as well as the movement of key cultural and political artifacts: tracts, books, gramophone records, and choirs" (Gilroy 1993: 4).

It was by means of performance, particularly of Negro spirituals, that Kimberley's African bourgeoisie forged its connection to the Black Atlantic world. After Orpheus M. McAddo and the Virginia Jubilee Singers introduced spirituals to South African audiences during their nearly decade-long international tour, that form of music became the primary nontextual means whereby the African bourgeoisie articulated its critique of modernity. A few short months after the Jubilee Singers premiered, African students at mission schools began to form musical ensembles modeled on their example. Their repertoire typically was a blend of spirituals, gospel hymns, African choral compositions, and traditional music. Negro spirituals soon became "a staple of the repository of black choirs, both professional and amateur" (Hamm 1988: 7). The African Native Choir, formed in 1892 and modeled directly on the Virginia Jubilee Singers, was the first international venture involving black South African performing artists (Coplan 1985). By the early 1900s, American gospel hymns were part and parcel of African music education. By 1908, the British Zonophone Company had issued eight discs of African American hymns sung by a group of South African traditional leaders (Cockrell 1997).

Spirituals were one of the first forms of American popular culture to enter global circulation. The Fisk Jubilee Singers, parent company of the Virginia group, undertook tours to England, Scotland, Wales, and Ireland during the early 1870s, performing for elite and popular audiences alike. Paradoxically, although spirituals were the way in which slaves had spoken to the world of the unspeakable horrors of racial terror, their global popularity was precipitated by the worldwide popularity of America's premier form of popular entertainment—the minstrel show, the cultural form that did the most to deny the very horrors that the spirituals rendered so poignantly.

Both minstrelsy and spirituals had emerged in response to the brutalities of slavery, and their histories were deeply intertwined. Familiarity with minstrelsy helped to prepare South African audiences for Orpheus M. McAdoo and the Virginia Jubilee Singers, who toured South Africa between 1890 and 1898, and the positive reception of their musical repertoire cannot be separated from the immense popularity of minstrelsy in South Africa. One critic described the Virginia Jubilee Singers as "Christianized Christies," in direct reference to the Christy Minstrels, but averred that they were "devoid of the vulgarities and forced humor of that class" (*Transvaal Advertiser*, February 2, 1891). W. E. B. Du Bois later lamented the fact that when the Fisk Jubilee Singers performed in New York, "the metropolitan dailies sneered at the Nigger minstrels" ([1903] 1989: 206).

The Virginia Jubilee Singers, their music, and what they symbolically represented soon became embroiled in larger debates occurring between mission-educated Africans and South African industrialists, missionaries, and government officials over whether African people were destined to be citizens or subjects in the land of their birth. Mission schools were the points of convergence for these debates because in South Africa, as in the United States, they had virtually the sole responsibility for educating blacks and played a pivotal role in shaping race relations and determining the trajectory of the racial order. Most white South Africans seeking to protect the status quo were united in their belief that blacks should not be trained for the higher professions. In an 1894 lecture delivered at the YMCA Hall in Pietermaritzburg, Professor R. D. Clark proclaimed that were it up to him, he would not approach the education of Africans "with theology and the Latin classics." Rather, he declared, what the South African native needed was "a good American shovel" and "continuous and consciously directed toil" (Clark 1894). A correspondent to the *Cape Argus* agreed with Clark that "education totally unfits the Native (by virtue of his own inherent character) for the sphere Nature has placed him in and fitted him for" (July 4, 1894).

Many white South Africans who held leadership positions in church, government, and industry looked to the example of segregated industrial schools for blacks like Hampton and Tuskegee in the United States (Brownlee [1896] 1977; Kidd 1904; Verschoyle 1900). American missionaries and the directors of industrial schools were likewise eager to see their ideas spread to Africa. General Samuel Armstrong, director of Hampton Institute, mentor to Booker T. Washington, and close associate of Orpheus McAdoo "felt that his methods might have particular relevance for African youth" and made offers of admission to African students (King 1971: 6). Ultimately, advocates for the global dissemination of the Hampton-Tuskegee model realized that their efforts would be considerably enhanced if they sent missionaries, particularly African American missionaries, to evangelize in Africa. American educators felt that African American culture, specifically Jubilee ensembles, had the potential to aid in the global dissemination of the segregationists' model of racial politics. Indeed, the lectures on African American culture and educational achievements that McAdoo typically included as a preamble to his show promoted the Hampton-Tuskegee model of race relations whereby "in all things purely social" the races were "as separate as the fingers on one hand" (Washington [1901] 1965: 148). Thus, although McAdoo and the Virginia Jubilee Singers came to South Africa as entertainers rather than missionaries, their performance was immediately implicated in ongoing debates about race, citizenship, and education taking place both at home and abroad.

South Africa's governing elite sought to use African Americans to promote an image of blackness as meaning satisfied subservience to white overlords. White officials in charge of government, education, and religion were becoming increasingly concerned about what they perceived as the uppity demeanor of educated Africans. *School kaffir* became a term of abuse directed against what the *Cape Argus* of October 3, 1894, called "spoiled youngsters who think that because [they] were brought up at a mission they deserve to be called princes." A writer for the *Christian Express* who characterized "educated natives" as "conceited and too ambitious" argued that education was responsible for the fact that "many a good native has gone wrong. . . . He comes back to the Cape suffering from what is vulgarly known as a swollen head and chafes at the old trammels. He becomes possessed of the idea that he is absolutely civilized up to, if not above, the level of those under whose mild authority he is placed" (March 7, 1899: 35). South African colonial officials and educators were confident that the Virginia Jubilee Singers would help convince educated Africans that it was wiser to achieve success within the racial order than to attempt to overturn that order. Therefore, the governing bodies of mission schools such as Lovedale, Fort Hare, and Headlam did not, for the most part, object when their students formed their own Jubilee ensembles, most of which were self-consciously modeled on the Virginia group. The African Native Choir was put together by two white entrepreneurs (Hamm 1988).

Despite their best efforts, however, the governing establishment in South Africa was unable to control the symbolic uses to which black South Africans put the Jubilee Singers and images of African Americans. Members of the African elite appear to have listened enthusiastically to McAdoo's lectures, and a number of them expressed the desire to study in the United States. They were motivated, however, not by a desire to learn how to accommodate themselves to white supremacy, but by a desire to enable themselves to more effectively fight against it. *Izwi Labantu,* a paper with a predominantly African readership, praised the efforts of ten African students who had been admitted to Lincoln College and Tuskegee. "We hope that more of our young men will emulate this example and proceed to England and the United States for the education denied them in this country," the editor opined (August 27, 1901). Africans who professed a desire to study in the United States and attain the position of their "brethren from America" did not take to the idea that they should desist from attempting to overturn South Africa's racial order (*Imvo Zabantsundu,* October 16, 1890). "A great future awaits the black man of South Africa," a writer in the *South African Spectator* of May 4, 1901, declared. "Because a man is black he need not be banned and ought not be socially and legislatively damned," insisted an angry writer to the *Christian Express* of March 1, 1895.

Rather than seeing the Virginia Jubilee singers as living confirmation of the virtues of capitulating to the status quo, many black South Africans focused on the way in which African Americans successfully negotiated the contradictions faced by all black people forced to live in a white supremacist world. *The South African Spectator* noted that "for polite manners, for polish and for correctness of demeanor and general conduct on the streets, no one excels the American Negro. . . . However otherwise he has suffered as the victim of slavery, he has acquired a polish in bondage" (October 11, 1902). Paradoxically, at a time when it was widely believed that American blacks had contributed nothing to advance civilization, black South Africans were embracing and imitating American Negro spirituals for their unique ability to articulate the existential dilemmas of blacks in the modern world. "Look to the American Negro as an example," admonished the *South African Spectator* of October 11, 1902. The symbolic identification that black South Africans made with the Virginia Jubilee Singers stemmed from of their mutual feelings of marginality. Rather than showing Africans the virtues of segregation, African American spirituals were instrumental in forming a dialogue between two marginalized and dispossessed groups of black people. South Africans thus used the experiences of black Americans to help them rewrite their own genealogy as African people. African Americans past and present were pointed to as examples of how people of African descent could formulate claims for inclusion as equal citizens within the national community.

Black South Africans were strongly influenced by how scholars like Du Bois explained the articulation of race and nation. Du Bois's *Souls of Black Folk* provided a blueprint for the creation of an idea of blackness that was ideologically and politically compatible with the idea of the modern nation-state. Like Du Bois, instead of contesting the claim that "African" could and should be viewed as a race, black South Africans attempted to transform blackness into a catalyst of positive political unification; thus, the manner in which they imagined black people as a race was conceptually analogous to the ways in which nations were imagined. Also like Du Bois, they sought to use race in a way that avoided the exclusive focus on blood and genetics that had been employed to justify the exclusion of African people from the frameworks of national citizenship; instead they maintained an idea of race that emphasized the metaphorical and familial.

Thus, the *South African Spectator* favored the descriptor *Black* because "this word Black applies to some millions of people who count among them some of the best men the world ever produced" (June 29, 1901). This conception contrasts strongly with the ways that white discourses rigidly separated the Bantu from the Negro from the Hottentot. The conceptions of race promulgated by African American thinkers were the impetus behind South African blacks' efforts to deemphasize the material processes of racial categorization that obsessed people like Howard Pim, president of the Native Affairs Society of the Transvaal, who advocated the establishment of a permanent bureau of statistics as a department of the Union government to "watch and classify" the African and Coloured populations (1910: 15).

Against continual English attempts to conceive of black bodies solely as problems to be overcome, the African bourgeoisie attempted to place those bodies at the center of national discourse in ways that suggested Africans were integral to the very formation and maintenance of the nation-state. The idea that black people did not exist in opposition to the ideals of the nation, but actually embodied them, was another that originated with Du Bois and was effectively used by black South African intellectuals. "It is all very well for politicians to be complaining about the existence of blacks," a writer to *Imvo Zabantsundu* asserted, "for this is what might have been expected in Africa— a black man's country. We should have thought that coming to a black man's country, Europeans would accommodate themselves to their surrounds and try to make worthy neighbors of the Natives instead of fretting and fuming over their large numbers and legislating with a view to rid them off the face of the earth" (December 15, 1892). He was supported by a fellow editorialist who pointed to the fact that those Africans who had held the franchise in the Cape had not been a danger, but had been critical to the workings of the democratic process. "We have exercised these rights in a manner that brought satisfaction to all corners and not a single instance can be pointed out of Natives abusing these rights. . . . Natives have always been able to return men of ability and weighty influence" (*Imvo Zabantsundu*, March 16, 1909).

The writings of African Americans not only helped black South Africans to suggest an alternative way of constituting the national community that placed black bodies in symbiosis, rather than conflict, with the larger whole, thus pointing to an alternative cultural identity for the nation-state. They also provided a framework for the political praxis of black leadership. However that framework took for granted certain fundamental notions about gender that shaped the paradigms and modes of discourse in ways that implicitly and explicitly placed black masculinity at the center of the project to secure equal citizenship.

Narratives of Gender, Race, and Nation

The image of the educated African proffered by white missionaries and government officials derided African men by suggesting that their quest for education and fully participatory citizenship had an emasculating effect. Cecil Rhodes described the compromised masculinity of black intellectuals in these terms: "Their present life is very similar to that of the young man about town who lounges about the club during the day and dresses himself for a tea-party in the afternoon" (Verschoyle 1900: 381). These stereotypes were also present in popular fiction. *Sitongo*, South Africa's first popular novel in English, deals with the dangers inherent in giving Africans a liberal education. In the preface to the second edition, author James Ensor explained that he was inspired to write the book by the evidence he had taken in his capacity as one of the shorthand writers for the Commission on Native Laws and Customs, which had been appointed by the Cape government to submit recommendations on how to rule large numbers of Africans while making their labor available to sustain state and private economic activity. The protagonist of the tale, a recipient of a mission education, is a "leader of fashion" at his college and mostly amuses himself by "flirting and falling in love" (Ensor 1884: 128, 133).

White leaders' attempts to place black people outside the political community were rationalized by the invocation of images suggesting that educated black men did not possess the qualities of true men. True men reveled in selfless acts of bravery and self-sacrifice, whereas the "semi-civilized school Kaffir" was simply interested in "increasing his wants in dress" (*Cape Argus*, October 3, 1893). True men were dedicated workers who labored diligently and without pause, whereas "educated young natives loaf about their father's kraals without doing any work because they reject manual labor as degrading and they cannot get the class of employment they want—teaching and preaching" (*The Glen Grey Act and the Native Question* 1903: 20). Male citizenship was thus defined in opposition to womanhood, specifically white femininity and the figure of the coquette—a fickle creature, easily seduced by luxury, whose selfishness, vanity, and manipulativeness posed a danger to herself and to the integrity of men. Likening African men to white women was a way of placing them in the category of disorderly persons who subverted social stability.

The animus that lurked behind and motivated these stereotypes was the profound anxiety over white masculinity and the manner in which sexuality mediated the relations between race and nation through the mechanism of population. One of the most striking aspects of the social commentary produced in South Africa between 1885 and 1910 is the manner in which the image of the disappearing savage who was melting away was replaced by that of the multiplying savage whose fecundity threatened to swamp and overpower European civilization. James Bryce lamented that "so far as numbers go, the country is a black man's country" ([1897] 1969: 345). Edward Dallow likewise maintained: "Supposing the natives to have passed the civilization test, . . . under this test the numbers gaining admission to the franchise might in no very distant time endanger the supremacy of the white race. The scarcity and slow increase of the white race as compared with the numbers and fecundity of the black make this no unreasoning fear" (1909: 9). W. Wybergh, an essayist for the political journal *The State*, agreed: "Those who say that in the long run the natives are or will be fit to share our civilization are saying in so many words that they will dominate it, for in numbers they exceed ourselves" (1909: 460).

Thus, white ideologues produced black masculinity as a profoundly Janus-faced phenomenon. On the one hand, blackness epitomized a compromised masculinity that was incapable of social reproduction. On the other hand, blackness epitomized a rampant, out-of-control sexuality that threatened to swamp and overwhelm the white race. These contradictory images and impulses, rather than undermining each other, actually existed in a dynamic of duality and interdependence. Both images symbolically and figuratively intertwined the sexual and political marginalization of black men and dictated that gender would mediate the relationship between race, nation, and participatory citizenship.

The stereotypes produced by whites thus profoundly influenced the philosophy and practice of black intellectual and political leadership. The problem of being black and a citizen was represented as a problem of coming into manhood, and educated Africans explained and opposed white supremacy in ways that both presupposed and favored a concern with black masculinity. For example, a writer for the *South African Spectator* of June 14, 1902, opined:

> Nowhere on earth is the intelligent and educated black man more likely to be misunderstood and unappreciated. Nowhere is he more likely to become the victim of senseless buffoonery and the coarse jests and unmerited insults of the shallow brained fools who regard the black man as being in his proper place only as the half naked savage, or that less manly type, the grotesque and rigged variety, which would seem to be the product of the labor conditions hereabouts, and who confronts one at every turn. Of course, there are those who would regard this as being unduly lugubrious. It is, however, a fact which may be easily corroborated, although, of course, none but he who has fallen a victim to these experiences can appreciate them.

The struggle to revise the meanings inscribed in the social and political constitution of blackness became synonymous, therefore, with resolving the dilemma of black manhood. Advancement of the race would be tied to the personal advancement and achievements of black men, and black leadership was defined by and through a racialized code of masculinity. Black intellectuals sought to render intellectual achievement an alternative route to masculine self-realization and actualization and posited an indissoluble link between race pride, authenticity, and masculinity. Claims to an authentic African identity were animated by a profound concern about the status of African masculinity.

The assumption of a posture of courtly self-respect was promoted as the essence of a determined racial identity, which could retain its integrity only if its masculinity was unchallenged. Thus, a writer for the *South African Spectator* of November 10, 1902, argued:

> We should aim at the production of good black men and not attempt to make impossible white men out of good black men and thereby waste excellent raw material. To civilize and enlighten from habits of savagery and ignorance is preferable to that form of transformation which is effected by masquerading in borrowed and ill fitting plumes; affecting mannerisms is grotesque and unbecoming and unnecessary. The educated and intelligent and manly black man has a place to fill in our civilization.

"Race men" like the one quoted here tied the advancement and achievement of black people as a whole to their personal achievements as men, particularly their educational achievements. As Walter Rubusana, a Congregational minister who helped to found the newspaper *Izwi Labantu*, noted, "Every nation is uplifted by its educated members. Africa will also be helped by educated Africans who will work hard and give themselves, with their little education to the nation" (quoted in Switzer 1993: 179). The responsibility for providing a framework for African political praxis thus devolved on the educated class. *Imvo Zabantsundu's* June 7, 1910, edition likewise editorialized, "Christianity, education, and civilization are harbingers of more intellectual, more moral, and more civil freedom to any race."

The African bourgeoisie developed and deployed a rhetoric about manhood that provided a set of rules for stigmatizing disorderly men, justifying citizenship for deserving men, and elevating exceptional men to positions of leadership and political authority. Restraining disorderly women and men was a crucial component of their own identities as race men. Working-class African men, frequently characterized as disorderly, were the most likely to find themselves on the receiving end of the various self-help strategies middle-class men used to translate their world views into practice. Although members of the African elite disapproved of the callous way in which working-class men were treated, particularly in the mining compounds, they accepted a number of the dominant stereotypes about them. Gwayi Tyamzashe, a well-known African minister, concluded, "The very low opinion that Europeans have of the natives of this country is not altogether groundless" ([1874]

1972: 21). A middle-class correspondent to the *Diamond Fields Advertiser* of March 14, 1896, longed for the day when the uneducated working-class African would be "sufficiently educated to discover his foolishness, which is so immense that he does not even know that he knows nothing." The manner in which middle-class Africans stereotyped working-class men is also indicative of the ways in which civic manhood was defined against femininity and male worth was assessed in opposition to female vices. These stereotypes echoed whites' stereotypes of educated Africans: discourses produced by educated Africans depicted working-class black men as coquettish in their behavior and criticized them for excessive vanity, materialism, and lack of self-control.

Black women were yet another class of disorderly persons, the control of whom was integral to the exercise of masculine authority. Narratives produced by race men frequently yoked together sexual compromise and political compromise, epitomized in the figure of the weak-willed black woman, and especially the so-called Coloured woman, whose sexual promiscuity borne of a lack of race pride led her to acts of sexual betrayal in pursuit of whiteness. "'My son's father was an Irishman' is the proud boast of many Coloured females," the writer of an editorial in the *Spectator* of November 10, 1902, complained. "There are infinite possibilities for the race but they will need to get rid of some of their preconceived notions and false ideas of inferiority before they can make much headway" he concluded. An editorial in the paper's April 4, 1901, edition asserted: "We are unable to determine by what process of reasoning the son of a black woman becomes superior to his mother because his father is a white man."

The perception that people of mixed ancestry might have aspirations toward whiteness or assimilation into white culture thus brought them under severe censure from the African bourgeoisie. The writer of an article in the March 20, 1906, issue of *Izwi Labantu* criticized a move on the part of the African Political Association to secure political rights for the Cape Coloured community that were distinct from those of the "Bantu," or blacks: "The expression 'coloured' when used to distinguish the brown or yellow from the black or white is unfortunate . . . as they weaken the position of these two classes whose political rights should be identical no matter what their social relations may be." Thus, political and sexual betrayals were presented as operating in unison. Miscegenation was perceived and presented as an act of sexual and civic cowardliness that led to the disfranchisement of African men and undermined the possibility of African political power. The extent to which African men saw themselves as the only people capable of containing the threat of sexual and political betrayal is exemplified by Tiyo Soga, whom

Switzer describes as the "prototype African nationalist of the colonial era" (1993: 161). Soga, who had married a Scottish woman, exhorted his children:

> For your own sakes never appear ashamed that your father was a Kafir, and that you inherit some African blood. It is every whit as good and as pure as that which flows in the veins of my fairer brethren. . . . I want you, for your own future comfort, to be very careful on this point. . . . If you wish to gain credit for yourselves—if you do not wish to feel the taunt of men, which you may sometimes be made to feel—take your place in the world as *coloured*, not as *white* men; as *Kafirs*, not as Englishmen. (Chalmers 1878: 430, emphasis in original)

The proper role for an African woman—one that would not compromise her partner's quest for masculine self-actualization or for inclusion in the body politic—was that of supporter and helpmate. "Manly black men" could not exist without the cultivation of a class of women to support and assist them in the public sphere. Indeed, it was considered men's duty to transform unruly women into virtuous helpmates. An editorial in *Izwi Labantu* approvingly quoted an assertion of Mary Church Terrell, an African American woman: "No people need ever despair when their women are willing and active in trying to uplift a race." The writer concurred: "Until this question is answered in the affirmative we fear that the progress of the black man in South Africa is bound in shallows. The active interest of the women is essential to race growth and prosperity and the absence of vital energy so conspicuous in the average educated black man may be traced to the condition of their womenfolk" (April 10, 1906).

Male autonomy required women's selfless devotion to individual men and families as well as the larger racial or national family. Thus, after some discussion as to whether women should be admitted to the Native Congress it was decided that they should form a partner association working under the name of the Native Women's Victoria Guild of South Africa because "Without the aid of women all efforts for the national uplift will fail. There is more reliance to be placed in women in such matters than in men if they can be sufficiently interested. . . . Such associations offer a splendid opportunity for organization among women and serve a variety of useful purposes in bringing them together for mutual encouragement, cooperation, and assistance in working out their own and their children's future" (*Izwi Labantu*, July 24, 1906).

Had it been established, the association would have addressed itself to "questions of domestic economy, the management of children, the home, and family life," thus demonstrating its members' investment in the symbolic economy of home and family that was so critical to the interpolation of white subjects into citizens in the public sphere. These ideologies can be traced back to the thought of British missionaries like Henry Calderwood, who argued:

> In the matter of Caffre Christianisation and civilization, there is no question of greater importance than that of female influence, which certainly requires more attention than it has yet received. . . . In Africa we are laying the very foundations of society. The amenities of civilized life are wholly absent in a barbarous state. But who is so likely as a pious, judicious, educated, and good-tempered woman to create and foster these very amenities, which are at once the fruits and means of civilization. These must grow up in the family, and gentle female influence is, and ought to be, most potent there. (1858: 198)

Thus, in a way that reflected the Victorian ideology of the family and the woman at home, the responsibility for safeguarding the moral and spiritual uplift of African communities devolved onto women. An important component of being a man, however, was the forging of sexual contracts that ensured the subordination of women and insulated political society from their disorderly nature and sexual passion. Male selfhood was brought about through female self-sacrifice, actualized in the marriage contract, which guaranteed female domesticity and subordination. Women were required to sacrifice their own subjectivity for the immediate good of their families and the ultimate good of the race. The work of biologically reproducing future generations would fall to women while educated black men, in concert with their peers, would give birth to the new nation.

Paradoxically, although femininity was the pole against which men defined themselves, the definition of a true race man derived from the appropriation of some of the traditional virtues associated with white upper-class femininity. The commitment to civilize lower-class African men by demonstrating to them the virtues of piety, religious feeling, and self-sacrifice, for example, effectively took the virtues of the propertied European woman and bestowed them on the middle-class African man. The manner in which middle-class African men distinguished themselves by virtue of their commitment to family—both their individual families and the larger racial family—echoed the traditional stereotype of the selfless white mother, utterly devoted to her family and community. Finally, the venerated position that race men held as symbolic fathers of the race who transmitted black racial identity to posterity can also be seen as an attempt to usurp the unique ability of the white woman to propagate her race. Just as only white women could give birth to whites babies and thereby guarantee both the purity and the continued reproduction of the white race, only true race men could forge the social bonds that created civil society and ensured the continued social reproduction and renewal of the black race.

Also paradoxically, black political culture, born of an association between men that excluded women, was not by any means an autonomous production of black men. White patriarchs also played key roles in its evolution. Thus, black political culture was the bastard child of white and black patriarchs. The work of Stanley Trapido (1982) and Colin Bundy (1979) on the history of the free African peasantry at the Cape demonstrates that African peasants had a unique relationship vis-à-vis whites who wielded political and economic power. White merchants and traders were instrumental in pushing for the political incorporation of the more elite sections of the free African peasant strata. Peasants had a considerable amount of purchasing power and therefore were the economic lifeblood of merchants. As for the political class, African producers were essential to their economic and political survival. Groups like the Glen Grey Thembu Association (1884) and the South African Native Association (1885) were the primary political links between white candidates and black voters at the local level.

The founding of the newspaper *Imvo Zabantsundu* is one example of the mutual interdependence of white merchants and politicians and the African petite bourgeoisie. *Imvo* was the first and for a considerable time the only forum within which educated Africans could learn about and debate political issues. Prominent Cape attorney Richard Rose-Innes and two well-known local merchants, J. J. Weir and T. J. Irvine (a former member of the Cape legislative assembly), assisted J. T. Jabavu, a small farmer in the Peddie district, and provided security for him to set up the paper. Jabavu had been the election agent in the campaign that won Richard's brother James Rose-Innes a seat in the legislative assembly (Switzer 1993). The paper was "never short of advertising copy inserted by local shopkeepers and traders" (Hogan 1980: 289). For Jabavu and the other men of his class, white liberals were important allies, helping them to interject African concerns into the democratic process.

Fights between white patriarchs could turn one black brother against another, as was demonstrated by the divisions that appeared within the African bourgeoisie after the passage of the 1892 Franchise and Ballot Act. The act raised the property qualification from fifty to seventy-five pounds and imposed a literacy test. Although it was a deliberate move to disfranchise African voters, Jabavu prevented any organized opposition to the act because his liberal allies Rose-Innes, J. W. Sauer, and J. X. Merriman were members of the coalition government—a government that operated under the premiership of Cecil Rhodes and included members of the Afrikaner Bond. As a result of the legislation 4,921 Africans and Coloureds in twenty-five constituencies lost their voting rights the following year. Jabavu's inactivity in the face of such a direct attack on political rights caused many to question his leadership.

In 1892 an alternative African political organization, the South African Native Congress, was formed under the leadership of Jonathan Tunyiswa, a teacher at the Mount Coke Methodist Mission in King Williamstown. The congress became further estranged from Jabavu in 1897 when he followed Sauer, Merriman, and others in the liberal coterie that joined the Afrikaner Bond against Rhodes after the debacle of the Jameson Raid. The same year that Jabavu defected to the Bond, the Native Congress established its own newspaper, *Izwi Labantu*. Rhodes funded the launching of the paper, and his Progressive Party continued to fund the paper thereafter. Thus, we can read some of the concern to assert an autonomous black masculinity as having been engendered by African elites' knowledge that the autonomous political culture to which they hoped to give birth might be compromised by its unacknowledged white patriarchy.

The ability to claim social autonomy has traditionally marked the parameters of conventional masculinity no matter the racial context; thus, it was inevitable that the attempt to claim an autonomous black identity would reference masculinity. Cultural and political reclamation became deeply implicated with the recuperation of black manhood so that many of masculinity's most deeply problematic features were unthinkingly adopted and encouraged in the name of racial progress.

CONCLUSION

In an interview with Cary Nelson, Catherine Hall once said, "We do not have, as yet, a theory as to the articulation of race, class, and gender and the ways in which these articulations might generally operate" (Grossberg, Nelson, and Treichler 1992: 270). She observed that new theoretical insights were most likely to come from carefully working through the ways in which race, class, and gender are complexly articulated to one another in precise historical contexts. As she quite simply put it: "Case studies, whether historical or contemporary, which carefully trace the contradictory ways in which these articulations take place both in historically specific moments and over time [are] very important" (270). I agree wholeheartedly with Hall about the importance of historical studies, and indeed, with this project I intended to do precisely what she advocates—unpack the workings of these phenomena in a bounded historical context. After attempting to do so, however, I am less convinced of the possibility of arriving at a theory about the workings of the "holy trinity" that is generalizable both across time and across geographic, cultural, and national boundaries.

In an attempt to remain somewhat bounded, I focused in this project on figurative uses of black South African bodies in various types of British political and social commentary. In order to do this, however, it was necessary to engage with the figurative uses of slavery and New World Africans—thus incorporating the United States, albeit quite obliquely, into the narrative. Thus, despite my best attempts to impose limits on my scope of inquiry, I was nevertheless faced with trying to unpack and say something meaningful about three vastly different geographic regions and national cultures, each with its own complicated history. These regions differ not only in their figurative uses of blackness, but also in their definitions of what constitutes a black person. Therefore, I am loath to use this case study as a launching pad for propounding a general theory of the articulation of race, class, and gender that is capable of explaining the very different social realities of, for example, England in the nineteenth century and Brazil in the twenty-first.

The utility of historical case studies lies less in their ability to generate a totalizing theory than in their ability to suggest ways of looking at the world or at social situations that may be taken up and deployed, with modification, in other contexts. Four insights, or themes, that emerged from this study are useful starting points for inquiries into the workings of race, class, and gender in other times, places, and contexts. All of the examples that follow are taken from the North American context. This is not to privilege this particular site or to suggest that all theories of race must ultimately point to a way of describing and understanding America's complicated racial history. I have simply chosen these examples because of their familiarity—both to myself and, hopefully, to the reader.

In this volume I highlight the manner in which supposedly objective analyses mark bodies by race and gender and thereby become able to use the opacity of these bodies as a way of embedding a hidden transcript within what purports to be a neutral social scientific discourse. In particular, I show how bodies marked as both racially and sexually Other can be ideologically deployed to obscure the ways in which political power is an essential condition of capitalist appropriation. The manner in which bodies are depicted in social scientific discourse, particularly when the intent of that discourse is to explain some aspect of class or income inequality, is critical to the rhetorical production of the idea of an economy and economic forces that float free of political determinants. Focusing on the manner in which racist discourse facilitates a particular understanding of the nature of force in capitalist appropriation aids in a conceptualization of the connections between racism and capitalist appropriation that both expands and complicates existing Marxist-inspired analyses of race, racial formation, and racism.

John Solomos and Les Back have argued that although Marxism has provided an important source of theoretical influence in research on race and ethnicity, it is clear that "Marxist discussion of race and racism is searching for a new agenda." They conclude that "the challenge over the next period for those scholars influenced by the Marxist tradition will be to show the relevance of their theoretical and historical insights to the analysis of contemporary forms of racial and ethnic relationships" (1995: 408). Thus, I have looked at connections between the changing forms of "racist culture" (Goldberg 1993) and the development of capitalist social relations and have gone beyond simply stating that racism originates and is reproduced in the struggle between capital and labor. In outlining the use of racial images and ideologies to reify the separation of the economic and the political in capitalist ideology, I have provided a way of looking at the connections between racism and capitalism that complicates the basically correct argument that capital requires racism for the sake of its own reproduction (Sivanandan 1982).

A related aim of this text is to develop an analysis of race that, while acknowledging its thoroughly ideological nature, takes it seriously as an object of analysis rather than simply dismissing it as a superstructural form masking the "real" economic relations below. Scholars like Robert Miles (1989) and Mara Loveman (1999) argue that to understand more fully how race shapes social relations and becomes embedded in institutions, we should abandon it as a category of analysis. Any analyst who insists on looking at the manner in which race endows action with meaning runs the risk of becoming trapped on its ideological terrain. Analytically speaking, race is nothing more than a red herring. As Miles puts it: "I recognize that people do conceive of themselves and others as belonging to 'races' and do describe certain sorts of situations and relations as being 'race relations,' but I am also arguing that these categories of everyday life cannot automatically be taken up and employed analytically by an inquiry which aspires to objective or scientific status" (1982: 42).

The value of this approach lies in the manner in which it opens up a broader set of possibilities for understanding contemporary racial ideologies. It is particularly useful for analyzing how those ideologies are constructed in the United States, the country where free-market ideology has had the greatest political and social purchase. Douglas Dowd describes American economists as "servants rather than analysts of the economic system" (2000: 198). Indeed, it is in the discourses produced by American economists that we find the reification of separate economic, political, and social spheres most pronounced. As Dowd explains, "the mainstream economist continues to take all the main elements of [social] processes as 'given,' as outside the scope of analysis: political and social institutions and all realms of change, . . . the structure and functions of business and individual income, and wealth and power" (2000: 197).

American culture is also responsible for producing some of the most reprehensible and damaging stereotypes about women of color—particularly black women. Hortense Spillers wryly observes: "Let's face it. I am a marked woman, but not everybody knows my name. 'Peaches' and 'Brown Sugar,' 'Sapphire,' and 'Earth Mother,' 'Aunty,' 'Granny,' 'God's Holy Fool,' a 'Miss Ebony First,' or 'Black Woman at the Podium': I describe a locus of confounded identities, a meeting ground of investments and privations in the national treasury of rhetorical wealth. My country needs me, and if I were not here, I would have to be invented" (2000: 57). Spillers is correct that American ideologues so needed a particular type of black woman that they went ahead and invented her.

Three images from the North American context that immediately come to mind in this regard are the welfare queen/mother, the crack whore/mother, and the emasculating matriarch. Wahneema Lubiano has described the welfare-dependent black woman as "the synecdoche, the shortest possible shorthand, for the pathology of poor, urban, black culture. Responsible for creating and maintaining a family that can only be perceived as pathological compared to the normative (and thus allegedly 'healthy') family structure in the larger society, the welfare mother is the root of greater black pathology." Lubiano goes on to observe that the welfare queen is profoundly Janus-faced:

> The flip side of the pathological welfare queen . . . is the other kind of black woman, the one whose disproportionate overachievement stands for black cultural strangeness and who ensures the underachievement of "the black male" in the lower classes. . . . There we have it. Whether by virtue of *not achieving* and thus passing on bad culture as welfare mothers, or by virtue of managing to *achieve* middle-class success via education, career, and/or economic success, . . . black women are responsible for the disadvantaged status of African Americans. (1992: 335–37, emphasis in original)

Dorothy Roberts makes a similar observation about the so-called crack mother.

> The pregnant crack addict was the exact opposite of a mother: she was promiscuous, uncaring, and self-indulgent. She was also Black. In the focus on maternal crack use, which is stereotypically associated with Blacks, the media left the impression that the pregnant addict is typically a Black woman. Even more than a metaphor for a woman's alienation from instinctual motherhood, the pregnant crack addict was the latest embodiment of the bad *Black* mother. The monstrous, crack-smoking mother was added to the iconography of depraved Black maternity, alongside the matriarch and the welfare queen. Crack gave society one more reason to curb Black women's fertility. (1997: 157, emphasis in original)

One avenue for studying these images is to look at how they operate to ideologically obscure the processes whereby new and different forms of political power are introduced into the production process via increased control over labor at the same time that political influence is purportedly being removed from the economy. We know, for example, that there is some overlap between the wider dissemination of these images and the emergence of rhetoric touting the advantages of the "New Economy," which is characterized by "intensified control over the labor process, and the development of an enlarged, more flexible workforce on a global scale that has increased inequality everywhere" and a "public policy [that] supports the intense exploitation of the majority who are ground down by the reorganization of work" (Tabb 2001: 20). Furthermore, given that in the past ideological renderings of women's bodies have worked to write the exploitation of women's labor out of the narrative of capitalism while obscuring the political forces that determine the balance of power between capital and labor, we might draw a connection between these various renderings of black female bodies and the fact that

> although women have found their way into the labor market in increasing numbers since the 1960s, they have continued to take their places largely in the ranks of the lowest paid employees. These are the women most likely to be arrested. . . . The women's prison population in the U.S. has quadrupled since 1980, largely the result of a war on drugs that has translated into a war on women and the poor generally. African-American women have been hardest hit by this increase. They are 14.5 percent of the women in the U.S. population, but they constitute 52.2 percent of the women in prison. (McClellan 2002: 35)

At the same time all of this was developing, we were hearing more and more about the virtues of the free market, untrammeled competition, getting the government out of the economy, and so on. Thus, it would be interesting to see if connections might be drawn between seemingly unrelated phenomena like the proliferation of derogatory images of the bodies of women of color and the fact that "the fastest expansion of jobs and value-added in the US Economy in recent decades has been in those sectors . . . that are notorious for their low productivity gains, and that are associated with the accumulation of money capital rather than the expansion of production" ("The New Economy: Myth and Reality" 2001: 14). This way of thinking about the connections between economic processes and the construction of racial and gender ideologies preserves the valuable insights of Marxist theories, particularly those that look at the relationship between racism and the process of capital accumulation, without being economically reductionist.

A second theme emerging from this study that might provide a way of organizing future research is that of the changing cultural meanings of work and their relationship to changing ideas about race. Gilroy has argued that "class analysis must be opened up so that it can be supplemented by additional categories which reflect different histories of subordination as well as the historical and moral elements Marx identified as determining different values for different types of labour power" (1987: 19). This text explores how the identification of production with the economic activity of the capitalist became deeply rooted in Western culture. It also examines how the general devalorization of labor that is the corollary of capitalism became racialized as there were, in most people's minds, indissoluble links between labor and blackness and between blackness and degradation. This way of looking at the connections between race and class complicates existing studies, such as that of Manuel Castells (1983), that examine how race functions to create distinct divisions and strata within the working class. It also provides a more complex explanation for why racism has had such a divisive impact on class organization and radical political action.

In contemporary America, for example, we are witnessing a curious reversal whereby the valorization of labor has as its corollary the denigration of the black body as hopelessly lazy and unproductive. Thus, labor has been uncoupled from blackness, and its status has presumably been raised. However, as Ellen Willis points out, the desire to avoid being characterized as lazy, with the implicit association of that characterization with black bodies, has resulted in the uncritical acceptance of the gospel of work—even when it is contrary to white workers' interests.

> Instead of debating blacks' purported shiftlessness, Americans might more profitably ask whose purposes are served by the current glorification of work—which is to say, any job, however mindless, deadening, useless, or even harmful, that someone will pay a pittance for—as the index of moral and spiritual worth. Or by the stigmatizing of the desire for some time of one's own as degeneracy akin to a craving for heroin. What law of nature decrees that the poor should accept endless work as almost literally its own reward? . . . Or that any activity that doesn't generate profits or is publicly supported (like child rearing by poor single women) doesn't count as work—and should probably be regarded as a sneaky attempt to avoid the real thing? (1999: 54)

We are still struggling with one of the main cultural contradictions of capitalism—that the virtues of production and industry have been displaced from workers to capitalists, thus making the productive use of property rather than the activity of labor itself worthy of admiration. The devaluation of work has, quite naturally, made workers concerned to elevate its status. In racially stratified societies, where tasks and duties are allocated on the basis of color, workers have tended to focus on elevating the status of labor by denigrating particular classes of workers, rather than by trying to recapture the virtues of labor from capital. It would be interesting and useful, therefore, to trace these changes across time and space. How, for example, might these dynamics play out in radically different capitalist societies that have slavery as part of their heritage—for instance, the United States, Brazil, and South Africa?

A third theme explored in this study is that of the transnational nature of blackness, in particular how the meanings of blackness transmute and transform across national contexts. Images of slavery, particularly slavery in North America, played a key role in constructing cross-national imaginings of the "essential" black subject. The status of African Americans and race relations in North America have historically operated as reference points for other societies wherein "social relations between people have been structured by the signification of human biological characteristics in such a way as to define and construct differentiated social collectivities" (Miles 1989: 72). Taking seriously the variant meanings of blackness in different geographical locations and among different groups of people during the same historical period as well as its meaning across historical periods gives some insight into recent debates over what Pierre Bourdieu and Loïc Wacquant have termed the "quasi-universalization of the U.S. *folk-concept* of 'race'" (1999: 48, emphasis in original). According to Bourdieu and Wacquant, the transnationalization of American ideas about whiteness and blackness is tantamount to a species of "cultural imperialism" that is attempting to forge a "new planetary commonsense" (1999: 47).

Bourdieu and Wacquant are mostly correct in their criticisms of those instances when American conceptions of race, which reflect the "peculiar schema of racial division developed by one country during a small segment of its short history" have been elevated to the status of social scientific constructs and subsequently universalized as a template on which analyses of race in widely divergent countries and contexts are to be developed (Wacquant 1997: 223). In their critique of what they term the "dehistoricization that almost inevitably results from the migration of ideas across national boundaries" (Bourdieu and Wacquant 1999: 49), however, they overlook the fact that there is a lot to be learned from looking at how ideas, concepts, and images get translated and mistranslated across time periods and national contexts.

For example, Bourdieu and Wacquant are highly critical of the ways in which European scholars have taken up the American concept of the underclass, arguing that: "the 'underclass' is but a fictional group, produced on paper by the classifying practices of those scholars, journalists and related experts in the management of the (black urban) poor who share in the belief in its existence because it is well-suited to give renewed scientific legitimacy to some and a politically and commercially profitable theme to mine for others" (1999: 49). They go on to observe that the notion of an underclass actually came to America via Europe. In Europe, however, the term was employed much more critically. It was not deployed to stigmatize the "antisocial" behaviors of the poor, but rather operated as a form of critique by describing the processes whereby the lower segments of the working class in wealthy, industrialized countries became marginalized. Noting how "profoundly the detour through America can transform an idea: from a structural concept aiming to question the dominant representation of society" to a behavioral category that makes the "most disadvantaged responsible for their own dispossession," they conclude that "the imported concept adds nothing to the knowledge of European societies" (1999: 49–50).

While I agree with Bourdieu and Wacquant that imported American notions about the underclass can tell us very little about the causes and consequences of poverty in Europe, precisely for the reasons they enumerate—the vastly different histories, agents and methods of government, and political status of marginalized populations—I believe that looking at the processes whereby these ideas get translated and mistranslated can tell us a great deal about the workings of race and class in both European and American societies. As George Lipsitz explains, "whether in politics or in performance, the meaning of 'mistakes' may have less to do with their transgressions of particular codes than with what they reveal about a broader field of action in which they are not 'mistaken'" (1994: 168).

Looking at the political contests and contexts wherein the applicability of ideas about and images of poverty and race circulate transnationally, we can learn a great deal about how these ideas manifest themselves locally in the form of unequal power relations. In order for this to happen, however, we must not only criticize the ways in which these concepts are taken up and used or misused, but also seek to answer several questions: Who gains and who loses from these acts of appropriation? What global elements are taken up locally? Which ones are left out and why? How are the accompanying images and ideologies transformed in the process of translation? Interesting and valuable insights can be found not through the universalization of North American racial categories, but rather in the analysis of both the processes whereby texts, images, categories, and ideologies about race and class are put into international circulation and the selective remembering and forgetting of the original historical conditions that produced them.

Finally, this study has shown the value of seeking out different, more counterintuitive ways of thinking about the relationship between citizenship, race, and consumption. Paul Gilroy has argued that "race can be shown to be relevant to the politics of consumption as well as to the politics of production" (1987: 25). Indeed, it has become quite fashionable in academic discourse on the so-called underclass to stigmatize and criticize black youth for their excessive consumerism. Cornel West has even characterized it as one of the main symptoms of the "nihilism" that threatens to overrun black communities and engulf them in "self-destructive wantonness" (1993a: 5). Attitudes toward consumption must be placed within the larger context of white supremacist culture. In particular, they must be analyzed as existing in a dialectical relationship with the systematic effort to deny blacks the opportunity to engage in wealth-accumulating activity. In this way, social attitudes about status and consumption that seek to limit the acquisition of certain luxury items to whites and state policies that racialize citizenship can be seen as dual manifestations of the "possessive investment" in whiteness. Although no one would deny that black youth, indeed all youth, are negatively affected by consumerist culture, we might take our analysis beyond a statement of that simple fact to a consideration of what kinds of social statements are being made through consumerism.

We might also try to problematize the ways in which whiteness, consumerism, and identity become linked while we look at how they interact with the notions that black people have about consumerism and identity, instead of focusing obsessively and exclusively on the latter. Take, for example, the manner in which many of the status symbols traditionally associated with WASP culture—Burberry Tweeds, Gucci, Polo, luxury automobiles, Moet champagne, and diamond jewelry—have been appropriated by rap artists and given a distinct "ghetto" aesthetic. Sean "Puffy" Combs, Master P, and Russell Simmons all own property in the Hamptons. Can we read this as an example of signifying on whiteness, making an ironic commentary on the values inherent in bourgeois culture? And might some of the hysteria surrounding the consumption habits and the associated posturing of ghetto youth be the result of a sublimated fear for the ability to exclusively possess the status symbols associated with whiteness?

Take, for example, luxury automakers' contradictory stance on the "minority" consumer. On the one hand, market research has demonstrated that Asians, Blacks, and Hispanics are the fastest growing market for luxury automobiles (Miller 2002). On the other hand, a 1999 Federal Communications Commission study found that both Lexus and Volvo engaged in an advertising-industry practice known as "no urban dictates," whereby "advertisers exclude stations that target minority audiences" in an effort to "control product image" (Ofari 1999). We might also take the proliferation of urban legends such as a recent one alleging that Tommy Hilfiger had appeared on Oprah and professed his disappointment and dismay about the popularity of his clothes among African American consumers as demonstrating black people's acute awareness about the ways in which status, consumption, and whiteness continue to be deeply implicated. As Vron Ware explains, "urban myths presumably circulate as long as they correspond to contemporary pre-occupations and fears" (1992: 3). Thus, we might supplement the many studies on race and education that implicitly valorize whiteness by placing the blame for African American educational underachievement on peer pres-sure to avoid "acting white" with studies that investigate the full range of meanings that whiteness holds in the black imagination. Can we read the current obsession of rap artists with Mafia images as a way of signifying on whiteness and acting white? Might the excessive consumption of certain sta-tus goods also signify acting white?

Social science would benefit tremendously from the undertaking of forms of analysis that reverse the direction of the gaze and make blackness the priv-ileged position from which whiteness is interrogated. As David Roediger wryly observes: "Contemporary dismissals 'of African-American testimony regarding whiteness abound. . . . Mainstream scholarship provides little to challenge [views] regarding the implausibility of African-American expertise about whites. In the hysteria over what gets called 'political correctness,' for example, much is sometimes made of the supposed animosity directed at white scholars who write and teach about people of color. But the con-verse—the almost utter failure to encourage or even notice studies of white-ness by scholars of color—draws no notice" (1998: 7). Postcolonial stud-ies and postcolonial scholarship have not as yet made much of an inroad among, for example, specialists in African American studies. As specialist in African American studies and literature Barbara Christian noted, "in their at-tempt to change the orientation of Western scholarship they, as usual, con-centrate on themselves and [are] not in the slightest interested in the worlds they had ignored or controlled. Again I was supposed to know *them*, while they were not at all interested in knowing *me*" (1996: 152). The fact that the two paradigms have thus far been speaking past one another does not mean that they are doomed to do so forever. As Gary Olson and Lynn Worsham correctly observe, "much of the scholarly work regarding issues particular to the United States are in fact issues of postcolonialism" (1999: 116). Ato Quayson and David Theo Goldberg (2002: xi) have likewise argued that there are "family resemblances" between postcolonial scholarship and scholarship done in ethnic and racial studies. One such resemblance is obviously their mutual concern with understanding the history and contemporary workings of race and racism.

A great deal of work in the social sciences is done in the comparative vein—for example, comparing race relations in two locales (Fredrickson 1981; Hanchard 1994; Marx 1998). While this work is quite valuable, it is unable to capture the ways in which racial discourses operate as forms of what Stuart Hall calls "transculturation" or "essentially transnational and transcultural 'global' processes" (1996: 247). Postcolonial analysis has the potential to suggest research paradigms, particularly in the study of race and ethnicity, that decenter dominant discourses and perspectives. The value of the paradigm I have outlined here lies, I believe, in the ways in which it centers on the transnational nature of race and class discourses.

One of the central aims of this text has been to take seriously Catherine Hall's admonition to remember Empire differently. Such a project, she explains, begins "from the recognition of interconnection and interdependence, albeit structured through power, rather than a notion of hierarchy with the 'centre' firmly in place and the 'peripheries' marginalised" (1996: 66–67). My intent in mapping out the diverse ways in which the political and institutional histories of the colonies and the metropole were mutually constituted has been to definitively demonstrate the manner in which these interconnections and dependencies both invoked and produced certain concepts of race and gender, many of which are still operative, albeit in altered form, today. If it is indeed the case that colonial discourses about the racial Other are continually being projected forward into the postcolonial present, such that "historical colonial fantasies . . . exercise a hegemonic role in the representation of blackness," then the reworking of the history of empire takes on even more significance (Carrington 2002: 91). I fully agree with Vron Ware that "a critical awareness of how the past is continually reconstructed and referred to ought to be inseparable from debates on post-colonialism. . . . It is essential to bring an informed historical perspective to an analysis of contemporary social relations which have been formed and contested throughout centuries of racial slavery and colonization" (1996: 142). That critical awareness of the past facilitates a better understanding of "the postcolonial condition as racial exclusion" (Olson and Worsham 1999: 116).

Conceiving of the postcolonial condition in this way is particularly valuable for bringing ethnic and racial studies, particularly those produced by American scholars, into closer dialogue with postcolonial studies. As Michael Dyson points out, American scholarship on race is suffering from "a problem of linguistic and rhetorical and ideological avoidance, of not acknowledging the degree to which this society's racist policies and practices are part of a deeper project of colonial and imperial expansion. . . . Even as those scholars of color begin to interrogate its practices, this discourse is put into a narrowly racialized frame that pays attention to black/white differences and so on without linking them to an international context of colonialism" (1999: 116). If it is indeed the case that "the sociology of 'race' all over the world is dominated by U.S. scholarship" (Loveman 1999: 894), a rethinking of the U.S. race problematic that does not code debates about race solely in terms of U.S. domestic territory alone has the potential to assist in the dismantling of those dominant structures that insist on a universalization that emanates from a singular historical tradition. Were this to become standard academic practice, we could pave the way for scholarship that truly demarginalizes the margins while decentering the center.

REFERENCES

Abrahams, Yvette. 2000. "Colonialism, Dysfunction, and Dysjuncture: The Historiography of Sarah Baartmann." Ph.D. diss. University of Cape Town.

Adams, Buck. [1884] 1941. *The Narrative of Private Buck Adams.* Reprint, with an introduction by Gordon A. Brown, Cape Town: Van Riebeeck Society.

Addison, Joseph. [1712] 1965. *The Spectator.* Edited by Donald Bond. Oxford: Clarendon.

Alexander, Nikol, and Drucilla Cornell. 1997. "Dismissed or Banished? A Testament to the Reasonableness of the Simpson Jury." Pp. 57–96 in *Birth of a Nation'hood: Gaze, Script, and Spectacle in the O. J. Simpson Case,* ed. Toni Morrison. New York: Pantheon.

Anderson, Benedict. 1991. *Imagined Communities.* London: Verso.

Angove, John. 1910. *In the Early Days: Reminiscences of Pioneer Life on the South African Diamond Fields.* Kimberley: Handel House.

Ashcroft, Bill, Gareth Griffiths, and Helen Tiffin, eds. 1989. *The Empire Writes Back: Theory and Practice in Post-Colonial Literatures.* London: Routledge.

———. 1995. *The Post-Colonial Studies Reader.* London: Routledge.

Ashworth, Henry. 1854. *The Preston Strike: An Inquiry into Its Causes and Consequences.* London: W. & F. G. Cash.

Aveling, Thomas. 1850. *The Missionary Souvenir.* London: Paternoster Row.

Bahri, Deepika. 1996. "Coming to Terms with the Postcolonial." Pp. 137–64 in *Between the Lines: South Asians and Postcoloniality,* ed. Deepika Bahri and Mary Vasudeva. Philadelphia: Temple University Press.

Baker, Houston. 1995. "Critical Memory and the Black Public Sphere." Pp. 5–38 in *The Black Public Sphere,* ed. Black Public Sphere Collective. Chicago: University of Chicago Press.

Baldwin, James. [1955] 1998. *Notes of a Native Son.* New York: Library of America.

Ballantine, Christopher. 1993. *Marabi Nights: Early South African Jazz and Vaudeville.* Johannesburg: Ravan.

Bank, Andrew. 1995. "Liberals and Their Enemies: Racial Ideology at the Cape of Good Hope, 1820–1850." Ph.D. diss. Cambridge University.

Baraka, Amiri. 1991. *The LeRoi Jones/Amiri Baraka Reader.* Edited by William J. Harris. New York: Morrow.

Barrow, John. [1801] 1968. *An Account of Travels into the Interior of Southern Africa in the Years 1797 and 1798.* Reprint, New York: Johnson Reprint.

———. 1819. "The Cape of Good Hope." *Quarterly Review* 22 (43): 203–46.

Bay, Mia. 2000. *The Black Image in the White Mind: African American Ideas about White People, 1830–1925.* New York: Oxford University Press.

Beames, Thomas. 1850. *The Rookeries of London.* London: Thomas Bosworth.

Bennett, George, ed. 1870. *The Concept of Empire.* London: Adam and Charles Black.

Best, Steven, and Douglas Kellner. 1991. *Postmodern Theory: Critical Interrogations.* London: Macmillan.

Bhabha, Homi. 1997. "Of Mimicry and Man: The Ambivalence of Colonial Discourse." Pp. 152–62 in *Tensions of Empire: Colonial Cultures in a Bourgeois World,* ed. Frederick Cooper and Ann Laura Stoler. Berkeley: University of California Press.

Bohls, Elizabeth. 1995. *Women Travel Writers and the Language of Aesthetics, 1716–1818.* Cambridge: Cambridge University Press.

Boon, James. 1885. *Travels and Adventures in South Africa.* London: William Reeves.

Booth, William. 1890. *In Darkest England and the Way Out.* London: Funk & Wagnalls.

Bourdieu, Pierre, and Loïc Wacquant. 1999. "On the Cunning of Imperialist Reason." *Theory, Culture, and Society* 16 (1): 41–58.

Bowker, John Mitford. [1862] 1962. *Speeches, Letters, and Selections from Important Papers.* Reprint, Cape Town: C. Struik.

Bredekamp, Henry, and Robert Ross, eds. 1995. *Missions and Christianity in South African History.* Johannesburg: Witwatersrand University Press.

Brenner, Robert. 1977. "The Origins of Capitalism." *New Left Review* 104:24–58.

———. 1985. "Agrarian Class Structure and Economic Development in Pre-Industrial Europe." Pp. 1–30 in *The Brenner Debate,* ed. T. H. Aston and C. H. E. Philpin. Cambridge: Cambridge University Press.

Brown, George. 1855. *Personal Adventure in South Africa.* London: James Blackwood.

Brown, Laura. 1993. *Ends of Empire: Women and Ideology in Early Eighteenth Century English Literature.* Ithaca, N.Y.: Cornell University Press.

Brownlee, Charles. [1896] 1977. *Reminiscences of Kaffir Life and History.* Reprint, Pietermaritzburg: University of Natal Press.

Bryce, James. [1897] 1969. *Impressions of South Africa.* Reprint, New York: Negro Universities Press.

Buchanan, John. 1793. *Travels in the Western Hebrides from 1782–1790.* London: J. Robinson.

Bundy, Colin. 1979. *The Rise and Fall of the South African Peasantry.* Berkeley: University of California Press.

Burchell, William John. [1822] 1953. *Travels in the Interior of Southern Africa.* Reprint, with a forward by Isaac Schapera. London: Batchworth.

Burns, John. 1900. *War against the Two Republics.* London: Stop-the-War Committee.

Burton, Antoinette. 2000. "States of Injury: Josephine Butler on Slavery, Citizenship, and the Boer War." Pp. 18–32 in *Women's Suffrage in the British Empire: Citizenship, Nation, and Race,* ed. Ian Christopher Fletcher, Laura E. Nym Mayhall, and Philippa Levine. London: Routledge.

Butler, Josephine. 1880. *Government by Police.* London: Gay & Bird.

———. 1900. *Native Races and the War.* London: Gay & Bird.

Butler, Judith. 1993. *Bodies That Matter: On the Discursive Limits of "Sex."* London: Routledge.

Calderwood, Henry. 1858. *Caffres and Caffre Missions.* London: James Nisbet & Co.

Caldwell, Dr. "On Penitentiary Discipline." 1832. *Phrenological Journal and Miscellany* 7 (March–September): 493–515.

Campbell, John. [1815] 1974. *Travels in South Africa.* Reprint, Cape Town: C. Struik.

Carrington, Ben. 2002. "Fear of a Black Athlete: Masculinity, Politics, and the Body." *New Formations* (winter): 91–110.

Castells, Manuel. 1983. *The City and the Grassroots: A Cross-Cultural Theory of Urban Social Movements.* London: Edward Arnold.

Chadwick, Edwin. 1843. *Supplementary Report on the Results of a Special Inquiry into the Practice of Internment in Towns.* London: W. Clowes and Sons.

Chalmers, J. A. 1878. *Tiyo Soga: A Page of South African Mission Work.* Edinburgh: A. Elliot.

Chase, John Centlivers. [1823] 1967. *The Cape of Good Hope and the Eastern Province of Algoa Bay.* Reprint, Cape Town: C. Struik.

Christian, Barbara. 1996. "The Race for Theory." Pp. 148–57 in *Contemporary Postcolonial Theory: A Reader,* ed. Padmini Mongia. London: Arnold.

Clark, R. D. 1894. *The Native Problem: A Lecture.* Pietermaritzburg: P. Davis & Sons.

Cochrane, James. 1987. *Servants of Power: The Role of English-Speaking Churches, 1903–1930.* Johannesburg: Raven Press.

Cockrell, Dale. 1997. *Demons of Disorder: Early Blackface Minstrels and Their World.* Cambridge: Cambridge University Press

Comaroff, Jean, and John Comaroff. 1992. *Ethnography and the Historical Imagination.* Boulder, Colo.: Westview.

———. 1997. *Of Revelation and Revolution: The Dialectics of Modernity on a South African Frontier.* Vol. 2. Chicago: University of Chicago Press.

Combe, George. 1834. *Elements of Phrenology.* Boston: Marsh, Capen & Lyon.

———. 1851. *A System of Phrenology.* Boston: Benjamin B. Mussey & Co.

Coplan, David. 1985. *In Township Tonight! South Africa's Black City Music and Theatre.* Johannesburg: Ravan.

Corbey, Raymond. 1995. "Ethnographic Showcases, 1870–1930." Pp. 57–80 in *The Decolonization of Imagination,* ed. Jan Nederveen Pieterse and Bhikhu Parekh. London: Zed.

Cowherd, Raymond. 1977. *Political Economists and the English Poor Laws.* Athens: Ohio University Press.

Crais, Clifton. 1992. *The Making of the Colonial Order: White Supremacy and Black Resistance in the Eastern Cape, 1770–1865.* Johannesburg: Witwatersrand University Press.

Cullen, Countee. 1927. *On These I Stand.* New York: Harper and Row.

Dallow, Edward. 1909. *Notes on the South African Native Problem.* Johannesburg: The Transvaal Leader.

Davidoff, Leonore, and Catherine Hall. 1987. *Family Fortunes: Men and Women of the English Middle Class, 1780–1850.* Chicago: University of Chicago Press.

Dickens, Charles. 1850. "Cape Sketches." *Household Words* 1 (March 30–September 21): 588–610.

Dodgshon, Robert A. 1981. *Land and Society in Early Scotland.* Oxford: Clarendon.

Dowd, Douglas. 2000. *Capitalism and Its Economics: A Critical History.* London: Pluto.

Du Bois, W. E. B. [1903] 1989. *The Souls of Black Folk.* Reprint, with an introduction by Donald B. Gibson. New York: Penguin.

———. 1991. *Dusk of Dawn: An Essay toward an Autobiography of a Race Concept.* London: Transaction.

Dyson, Michael E. 1999. "Race and the Public Intellectual: A Conversation with Michael Eric Dyson." Pp. 81–128 in *Race, Rhetoric, and the Postcolonial,* ed. Gary A. Olson and Lynn Worsham. Albany: SUNY Press.

Elbourne, Elizabeth. 1991. "To Colonize the Mind: Evangelical Missionaries in Britain and the Eastern Cape, 1790–1837." Ph.D. diss. Oxford University.

———. 1995. "Early Khoisan Uses of Mission Christianity." Pp. 65–96 in *Missions and Christianity in South African History,* edited by Henry Bredekamp and Robert Ross. Johannesburg: Witwatersrand University Press.

Ellison, Ralph. 1972. *Shadow and Act*. New York: Vintage.

Ensor, James. 1884. *Sitongo: A South African Story*. Cape Town: A. Richards.

Erlmann, Veit. 1991. *African Stars: Studies in Black South African Performance*. Chicago: University of Chicago Press.

———. 1999. "Spectatorial Lust: The African Choir in England, 1891–1893." Pp. 107–34 in *Africans on Stage: Studies in Ethnological Show Business*, ed. Bernth Lindfors. Bloomington: Indiana University Press.

Fanon, Frantz. 1967. *Black Skin, White Masks*. New York: Grove.

Farwell, B. 1990. *The Great Anglo-Boer War*. New York: W. W. Norton.

Fawcett, John. 1836. *An Account of Eighteen Months Residence at the Cape of Good Hope*. Cape Town, n.p.

Fawcett, Millicent Garrett. 1925. *What I Remember*. New York: G. P. Putnam's Sons.

Fee, Elizabeth. 1979. "Nineteenth Century Craniology: The Study of the Female Skull." *Bulletin of the History of Medicine* 53 (fall): 415–33.

Fields, Barbara. 1982. "Slavery, Race, and Ideology in American History." Pp. 143–77 in *Region, Race, and Reconstruction*, ed. J. Morgan Kousser and James M. McPherson. New York: Oxford University Press.

Fladeland, Betty. 1984. *Abolitionists and Working Class Problems in the Age of Industrialization*. Baton Rouge: Louisiana State University Press.

Foucault, Michel. 1979. *Discipline and Punish: The Birth of the Prison*. New York: Vintage.

———. 1980. *Power/Knowledge: Selected Interviews and Essays, 1972–1977*, ed. Colon Gordon. New York: Pantheon.

Fowler, O. S. 1846. *Fowler's Practical Phrenology*. New York: Edward Kearney.

Frankenberg, Ruth, and Lata Mani. 1996. "Crosscurrents, Crosstalk: Race, Postcoloniality, and the Politics of Location." Pp. 347–64 in *Contemporary Postcolonial Theory: A Reader*, ed. Padmini Mongia. London: Arnold.

Fredrickson, George. 1981. *White Supremacy: A Comparative Study in American and South African History*. Oxford: Oxford University Press.

Froude, J. A. 1886. *Oceana; or, England and Her Colonies*. New York: Charles Scribner & Sons.

———. 1895. *Short Studies on Great Subjects*. New York: Charles Scribner & Sons.

Fuss, Diana. 1989. *Essentially Speaking: Feminism, Nature, and Difference*. London: Routledge.

Galton, Francis. 1909. *Essays on Eugenics*. London: Garland.

Gardiner, Allen. 1836. *Narrative of a Journey to the Zoolu Country of South Africa*. London: William Crofts.

Garwood, John. [1853] 1985. *The Million-Peopled City*. Reprint, New York: Garland.

Gavin, Hector. [1847] 1985. *Unhealthiness of London and the Necessity of Remedial Measures*. Reprint, New York: Garland.

———. 1848. *Sanitary Ramblings: Being Sketches and Illustrations of Bethnal Green*. London: John Churchill.

———. 1851. *The Habitations of the Industrial Class*. London: Seeleys.

Gibson, Alan. [1891] 1969. *Eight Years in Kaffraria, 1882–1890*. New York: Negro Universities Press.

Gilman, Sander. 1985. "Black Bodies, White Bodies: Towards an Iconography of Female Sexuality in Late Nineteenth Century Art, Medicine, and Literature." Pp. 223–61 in *"Race," Writing, and Difference*, ed. Henry Louis Gates Jr. Chicago: University of Chicago Press.

Gilroy, Paul. 1987. *"There Ain't No Black in the Union Jack": The Cultural Politics of Race and Nation*. Chicago: University of Chicago Press.

———. 1993. *The Black Atlantic: Modernity and Double Consciousness*. Cambridge, Mass.: Harvard University Press.

The Glen Grey Act and the Native Question. 1903. Alice, South Africa: Lovedale Mission Press.

Godlonton, Robert. 1836. *A Narrative of the Irruption of the Kaffir Hordes into the Eastern Frontier of the Cape of Good Hope, 1834–1835.* Grahamstown: G. Greig.

———. 1842. *Sketches of the Eastern Districts of the Cape of Good Hope.* Grahamstown: G. Greig.

———. [1852] 1965. *Narrative of the Kaffir War, 1850–1852.* Reprint, Cape Town: C. Struik.

Godwin, George. [1859] 1972. *Town Swamps and Social Bridges.* New York: Humanities Press.

Goldberg, David. 1993. *Racist Culture: Philosophy and the Politics of Meaning.* London: Blackwell.

———. 2002. "Racial Rule." Pp. 82–102 in *Relocating Postcolonialism,* ed. David Theo Goldberg and Ato Quayson. London: Blackwell.

Grant, Philip. 1866. *The Ten Hours Bill: The History of Factory Legislation.* London: Simpkin, Marshall & Co.

Great Britain Parliament. House of Commons. 1851. *Hansard Parliamentary Debates.* London: HMSO.

Green, Bryan, S. 1983. *Knowing the Poor: A Case Study in Textual Reality Construction.* London: Routledge & Kegan Paul.

Green, John. 1853. *The Kat River Settlement in 1851.* Grahamstown: G. Greig.

Greenwood, James. [1874] 1985. *The Wilds of London.* Reprint, New York: Garland.

Grossberg, Lawrence, Cary Nelson, and Paula Treichler, eds. 1992. *Cultural Studies.* London: Routledge.

Hall, Catherine. 1992. *White, Male, Middle Class: Explorations in Feminism and History.* London: Routledge.

———. 1996. "Histories, Empires, and the Post-Colonial Moment." Pp. 65–77 in *The Post-Colonial Question: Common Skies, Divided Horizons,* ed. Iain Chambers and Lidia Curti. London: Routledge.

Hall, Stuart. 1996. "When Was the Post-Colonial? Thinking at the Limit." Pp. 242–60 in *The Post-Colonial Question: Common Skies, Divided Horizons,* ed. Iain Chambers and Lidia Curti. London: Routledge.

Hamm, Charles. 1988. *Afro-American Music, South Africa, and Apartheid.* New York: Institute for Studies in American Music.

Hanaway, Mary-Anne. 1776. *A Journey to the Highlands of Scotland.* London: Fielding & Walker.

Hanchard, Michael George. 1994. *Orpheus and Power: The Movimento Negro of Rio de Janeiro and São Paulo Brazil, 1945–1988.* Princeton, N.J.: Princeton University Press.

Harris, Cheryl. [1993] 1998. "Whiteness as Property." Pp. 103–18 in *Black on White: Black Writers on What It Means to Be White,* ed. David R. Roediger. New York: Schocken.

Hartman, Saidiya. 1997. *Scenes of Subjection: Terror, Slavery, and Self-Making in Nineteenth-Century America.* New York: Oxford University Press.

Headlam, Cecil, ed. 1933. *The Milner Papers: South Africa, 1899–1905.* Vol. 2. London: Cassell & Co.

Hechter, Michael. 1975. *Internal Colonialism: The Celtic Fringe in British National Development, 1536–1966.* Berkeley: University of California Press.

Heinzelman, Kurt. 1980. *The Economics of Imagination.* Amherst: University of Massachusetts Press.

Hockly, H. E. 1964. *The Hockly Family in South Africa.* Cape Town.

Hogan, Neville. 1980. "The Posthumous Vindication of Zachariah Gqishela: Reflections on the Politics of Dependence in the Nineteenth-Century Cape." Pp. 275–92 in *Economy and Society in Pre-Industrial South Africa,* ed. Shula Marks and Anthony Atmore. London: Longman.

Hogg, John. [1837] 1985. *London as It Is*. Reprint, New York: Garland.

Hole, James. 1866. *The Homes of the Working Classes, with Suggestions for Their Improvement*. London: Longmans, Green & Co.

Honeyman, Katrina. 2000. *Women, Gender, and Industrialisation in England, 1700–1870*. London: Macmillan.

hooks, bell. 1992. *Black Looks: Race and Representation*. Boston: South End Press.

Hutchins, Francis G. 1967. *The Illusion of Permanence*. Princeton, N.J.: Princeton University Press.

"Infanticide: The Sin of the Age." 1862. *The Magdalen's Friend and Female Homes' Intelligencer: A Monthly Magazine* 3:289–96.

Jerrold, Douglas. 1851. "*London Labour and the London Poor Vol. I: Those that Cannot Work and Those that Will Not Work*, by Henry Mayhew." *Eclectic Review* 2:424–36.

Jinks, Derek P. 1997. "Essays in Refusal: Pre-Theoretical Commitments in Postmodern Anthropology and Critical Race Theory." *Yale Law Journal* 107:499–528.

Johnson, Samuel. 1775. *Journey to the Western Islands of Scotland*. Dublin: Thomas Walker.

Johnson, Walter. 1999. *Soul by Soul: Life inside the Antebellum Slave Market*. Cambridge, Mass.: Harvard University Press.

Kay, Stephen. 1833. *Travels in Kaffraria*. London: John Mason.

Keegan, Timothy. 1996. *Colonial South Africa and the Origins of the Racial Order*. Cape Town: David Philip.

Kidd, Dudley. 1904. *The Essential Kaffir*. London: A. C. Black.

King, Kenneth James. 1971. *Pan-Africanism and Education: A Study of Race, Philanthropy, and Education in the Southern States of America and East Africa*. London: Oxford University Press.

Kirk, Tony. 1980. "The Cape Economy and the Expropriation of the Kate River Settlement, 1846–53." Pp. 226–46 in *Economy and Society in Pre-Industrial South Africa*, ed. Shula Marks and Anthony Atmore. London: Longman.

Kolbe, Peter. [1731] 1968. *The Present State of the Cape of Good Hope*. Reprint, New York: Johnson Reprint Company.

Kriedte, Peter, Hans Medick, and Jürgen Schlumbohm. 1981. *Industrialization before Industrialization: Rural Industry in the Genesis of Capitalism*. Cambridge: Cambridge University Press.

"The Late Atrocious Crimes in Scotland." 1830. *Phrenological Journal and Miscellany* 6 (no. 7): 534–40.

Latrobe, C. I. [1818] 1969. *Journal of a Visit to South Africa in 1815 and 1816*. Reprint, New York: Negro Universities Press.

Lavalette, Michael. 1999. *A Thing of the Past? Child Labour in Britain in the Nineteenth and Twentieth Centuries*. Liverpool: Liverpool University Press.

Le Cordeur, Basil A. 1981. *The Politics of Eastern Cape Separatism, 1820–1854*. London: Oxford University Press.

Lester, Alan. 2001. *Imperial Networks: Creating Identities in Nineteenth Century South Africa and Britain*. New York: Routledge.

Le Vaillant, Francois. 1796. *New Travels into the Interior Parts of Africa by Way of the Cape of Good Hope in the Years 1783, 1784, and 1785*. London: G. G. and J. Robinson.

Lichtenstein, Hinrich. [1812] 1928. *Travels in South Africa in the Years 1803, 1804, 1805, and 1806*. Reprint, with an introduction by Anne Plumptre. Cape Town: Van Riebeeck Society.

Lindfors, Bernth. 1999. *Africans on Stage: Studies in Ethnological Show Business*. Bloomington: Indiana University Press.

Lindsey, Donald F. 1995. *Indians at Hampton Institute, 1877–1923.* Urbana: University of Illinois Press.

Lipsitz, George. 1994. *Dangerous Crossroads: Popular Music, Postmodernism, and the Poetics of Place.* London: Verso.

———. 1998. *The Possessive Investment in Whiteness: How White People Profit from Identity Politics.* Philadelphia: Temple University Press.

Livingstone, David. [1858] 1971. *Missionary Travels and Researches in South Africa.* Reprint, New York: Johnson Reprint Co.

Loomba, Ania. 1998. *Colonialism/Postcolonialism.* London: Routledge.

Lorimer, Douglas. 1975. "Bibles, Banjoes and Bones: Images of the Negro in the Popular Culture of Victorian England." Pp. 31–50 in *In Search of the Visible Past: History Lectures at Wilfrid Laurier University, 1973–1974,* ed. Barry M. Gough. Waterloo, Ontario: Wilfrid Laurier University Press.

———. 1978. *Colour, Class, and the Victorians: English Attitudes to the Negro in the Mid-Nineteenth Century.* Great Britain: Leicester University Press.

Lott, Eric. 1995. *Love and Theft: Blackface Minstrelsy and the American Working Class.* New York: Oxford University Press.

Loveman, Mara. 1999. "Is 'Race' Essential?" *American Sociological Review* 64 (no. 6): 891–98.

Lubiano, Wahneema. 1992. "Black Ladies, Welfare Queens, and State Minstrels: Ideological War by Narrative Means." Pp. 323–63 in *Race-ing Justice, En-gendering Power: Essays on Anita Hill, Clarence Thomas, and the Construction of Social Reality,* ed. Toni Morrison. New York: Pantheon.

Maddison, F. 1900. "Why British Workmen Condemn the War." *North American Review* 170 (March): 518–27.

Mailer, Norman. 1959. "The White Negro." Pp. 337–58 in *Advertisements for Myself.* New York: G. Putnam & Sons.

Malthus, Thomas Robert. 1806. *An Essay on the Principle of Population.* Vol. 2. London: J. Johnson.

Marx, Anthony. 1998. *Making Race and Nation: A Comparison of South Africa, the United States, and Brazil.* Cambridge: Cambridge University Press.

Marx, Karl. [1844] 1978. "The Economic and Philosophic Manuscripts of 1844." Pp. 66–125 in *The Marx-Engels Reader,* ed. Robert C. Tucker. New York: Norton.

———. [1846] 1970. *The German Ideology.* Reprint, with a foreword by C. J. Arthur. New York: International Publishers.

———. [1867] 1967. *Capital,* Vol. 1. Reprint, New York: International Publishers.

Matthews, J. W. 1887. *Incwadi Yami.* New York: Rovers & Sherwood.

Mawman, Joseph. 1805. *An Excursion to the Highlands of Scotland and the English Lakes: With Recollections, Descriptions, and References to Historical Facts.* London: T. Gillet.

Mayhall, Laura, E. 2000. "The South African War and the Origins of Suffrage Militancy in Britain, 1899–1902." Pp. 3–17 in *Women's Suffrage in the British Empire: Citizenship, Nation, and Race,* ed. Ian Christopher Fletcher, Laura E. Nym Mayhall, and Philippa Levine. London: Routledge.

Mayhew, Henry. [1851] 1968. *London Labour and the London Poor: The London Street Folk.* Reprint, with a new introduction by John D. Rosenberg. New York: Dover.

———. 1981. *The Morning Chronicle Survey of Labour and the Poor: The Metropolitan Districts.* Sussex, U.K.: Caliban.

McClellan, Dorothy. 2002. "Coming to the Aid of Women in U.S. Prisons." *Monthly Review* 54 (no. 2): 33–44.

McClintock, Anne. 1995. *Imperial Leather: Race, Gender, and Sexuality in the Colonial Contest.* London: Routledge.

McCloskey, Deirdre. 1990. *If You're So Smart: The Narrative of Economic Expertise.* Chicago: University of Chicago Press.

———. 1998. *The Rhetoric of Economics.* Madison: University of Wisconsin Press.

McIlhiney, David. n.d. *A Gentleman in Every Slum: Church of England Missions in East London.* Allison Park, Pa.: Pickwick Publications.

Mehta, Uday. 1997. "Liberal Strategies of Exclusion." Pp. 59–86 in *Tensions of Empire: Colonial Cultures in a Bourgeois World,* ed. Frederick Cooper and Ann Laura Stoler. Berkeley: University of California Press.

Miles, Robert. 1982. *Racism and Migrant Labour.* London: Routledge & Kegan Paul.

———. 1989. *Racism.* London: Routledge.

Mill, John Stuart. 1989. *On Liberty with the Subjection of Women and Chapters on Socialism.* Reprint, with an introduction by S. Collini. Cambridge: Cambridge University Press.

Miller, Joe. 2002. "Minorities Key to Carmakers' Growth." *The Detroit News,* January 7.

Miller, Roger. 1853. *Memoirs of a Useful Man.* New York: Carlton & Phillips.

Milner, Alfred. 1913. *The Nation and the Empire.* London: Constable & Co.

Mitchell, Timothy. 1989. "The World as Exhibition." *Comparative Studies in Society and History* 31 (no. 2): 217–36.

Moffatt, John. 1885. *The Lives of Robert and Mary Moffatt.* London: T. Fisher Unwin.

Moffatt, Robert. 1844. *Missionary Labours and Scenes in Southern Africa.* London: Paternoster Row.

Morgan, John Edward. 1866. *The Danger of Deterioration of Race from the Rapid Increase of Great Cities.* London: Longmans, Green & Co.

Morrison, Toni. 1990. *Playing in the Dark: Whiteness and the American Literary Imagination.* New York: Vintage.

"The New Economy: Myth and Reality." 2001. *Monthly Review* 52 (no. 11): 1–15.

Newte, Thomas. 1791. *Prospects and Observations on a Tour in England and Scotland.* London: G. G. J. and J. Robinson.

Newton-King, Susan. 1980. "The Labour Market of the Cape Colony, 1807–1828." Pp. 226–46 in *Economy and Society in Pre-Industrial South Africa,* ed. Shula Marks and Anthony Atmore. London: Longman.

O'Brien, Mark. 2000. "Class Struggle and the English Poor Laws." Pp. 13–33 in *Class Struggle and Social Welfare,* ed. Michael Lavalette and Gerry Mooney. London: Routledge.

Ofari, Kofi. 1999. "Advertisers Avoid Blacks." *Black Journalism Review* (December 26).

Oliver, Melvin L., and Thomas Shapiro. 1997. *Black Wealth, White Wealth: A New Perspective on Racial Inequality.* New York: Routledge.

Olson, Gary, and Lynn Worsham, ed. 1999. *Race, Rhetoric, and the Postcolonial.* Albany: SUNY Press.

"On the Principles of Criminal Legislation." 1833. *Phrenological Journal and Miscellany* 7 (no. 35): 109–26.

Palmer, Bryan. 1997. "Old Positions/New Necessities: History, Class, and Marxist Metanarrative." Pp. 65–73 in *In Defense of History: Marxism and the Postmodern Agenda,* ed. Ellen Meiksins Wood and John Bellamy Foster. New York: Monthly Review Press.

Parliament of the Cape of Good Hope. 1882. *Report upon the Illicit Diamond Trade on the Diamond Fields, Griqualand West.* Cape Town: W. A. Richards & Sons.

Parliament of Great Britain. 1834. *Report From His Majesty's Commissioners for Inquiring into the Administration and Practical Operation of the Poor Laws.* London: B. Gellowes.

———. [1836] 1966. *Report of the Select Committee on Aborigines (British Settlements).* Reprint, Cape Town: C. Struik.

———. 1851. *Report of the Select Committee on the Kaffir Tribes.* N.p.

———. [1851] 1971a. *Correspondence with the Cape Governor Regarding the Kaffirs on the Eastern Frontier.* Reprint, Shannon, Ireland: Irish University Press Series of British Parliamentary Papers. Vol. 23.

———. [1851] 1971b. *Correspondence with the Governor of the Cape of Good Hope Relative to the State of the Kafir Tribes and the Recent Outbreak on the Eastern Frontier of the Colony.* Reprint, Shannon, Ireland: Irish University Press Series of British Parliamentary Papers. Vol. 23.

———. [1854] 1972. *Report of the Select Committee on Granting Lands in Freehold to Hottentots.* Reprint, Shannon, Ireland: Irish University Press Series of British Parliamentary Papers. Vol. 25.

———. [1857] 1972. *Further Papers Relative to the State of the Kaffir Tribes.* Reprint, Shannon, Ireland: Irish University Press Series of British Parliamentary Papers. Vol. 25.

Pearson, Karl. 1905. *National Life from the Standpoint of Science.* London: Adam & Charles Black.

Peires, J. B. 1989. *The Dead Will Arise: Nongquawse and the Great Xhosa Cattle-Killing Movement of 1856–1857.* Johannesburg: Ravan Press.

Pemberton, Robert. [1854] 1985. *The Happy Colony.* Reprint, New York: Garland.

Pennant, Thomas. 1776. *A Tour in Scotland.* London: Benj & White.

Percival, Robert. 1804. *An Account of the Cape of Good Hope.* London: Baldwin.

Perelman, Michael. 2000. *The Invention of Capitalism: Classical Political Economy and the Secret History of Primitive Accumulation.* Durham, N.C.: Duke University Press.

Philip, John. [1828] 1969. *Researches in South Africa.* Reprint, New York: Negro Universities Press.

Pieterse, Jan Nederveen. 1992. *White on Black: Images of Africa and Blacks in Western Popular Culture.* New Haven, Conn.: Yale University Press.

Pim, Howard. 1910. "A Plea for the Scientific Study of the Races Inhabiting South Africa." Cape Town: Argus.

Plato. 1950. *Symposium.* Translated by Benjamin Jowett. New York: Liberal Arts Press, 1950.

Poovey, Mary. 1995. *Making a Social Body: British Cultural Formation, 1830–1864.* Chicago: University of Chicago Press.

"Practical Utility of Phrenology." 1834. *Annals of Phrenology* 1 (no. 18): 134–40.

Pratt, Mary Louise. 1992. *Imperial Eyes: Travel Writing and Transculturation.* London: Routledge.

Pringle, Thomas. [1835] 1966. *Narrative of a Residence in South Africa.* Reprint, Cape Town: C. Struik.

Quayson, Ato, and David Theo Goldberg. 2002. "Introduction: Scale and Sensibility." Pp. xi–xxii in *Relocating Postcolonialism,* ed. David Theo Goldberg and Ato Quayson. London: Blackwell.

Raynard, Ellen. 1860. *The Missing Link or Bible-Women in the Homes of the London Poor.* New York: Robert Carter & Brothers.

Read, James. 1852. *The Kat River Settlement in 1850.* Cape Town: G. Greig.

"Recent Attacks on Phrenology." 1823–1824. *Phrenological Journal and Miscellany* 1:20–46.

"Remarks on Phrenological Specimens, Cabinet, Etc." 1840. *Phrenological Journal and Miscellany* 2:213–18.

Ritchie, J. Ewing. 1858. *The Night Side of London.* London: William Tweedie.

Roberts, Dorothy. 1997. *Killing the Black Body.* New York: Pantheon.

Roberts, M. J. D. 1995. "Feminism and the State in Later Victorian England." *Historical Journal* 38 (no. 1): 85–110.

Robertson, G. A. 1819. *Notes on Africa.* London: Sherwood, Neely & Jones.

Roediger, David. 1991. *The Wages of Whiteness.* London: Verso.

———. 1998. *Black on White: Black Writers on What It Means to Be White.* New York: Schocken Books.

Rogin, Michael. 1996. *Blackface, White Noise.* Berkeley: University of California Press.

Rosen, Andrew. 1979. "Emily Davies and the Women's Movement, 1862–1867." *Journal of British Studies* 19 (no. 1): 101–21.

Ross, Andrew. 1986. *John Philip: Missions, Race, and Politics, 1775–1851.* Great Britain: Aberdeen University Press.

Sayer, Karen. 1993. *Women of the Fields: Representations of Rural Women in the Nineteenth Century.* Manchester: Manchester University Press.

"Second Annual Report of the Ragged School Union Established for the Support of Schools for the Destitute Poor." 1847. *Quarterly Review* 79:127–41.

Sedgwick, Adam, and William Monk, eds. 1858. *Dr. Livingstone's Cambridge Lectures.* London: Bell and Daldy.

Shapiro, Michael. 1988. *The Politics of Representation: Writing Practices in Biography, Photography, and Policy Analysis.* Madison: University of Wisconsin Press.

Sharpley-Whiting, Tracey Denean. 1999. *Black Venus.* Durham, N.C.: Duke University Press.

Shaw, James. [1861] 1985. *Travels in England: A Ramble with the City and Town Missionaries.* Reprint, New York: Garland.

Shaw, William. 1874. *Memoir.* London: Wesleyan Conference Office.

Sherman, Sandra. 2001. *Imagining Poverty: Quantification and the Decline of Paternalism.* Columbus: Ohio State University Press.

Shimmin, Hugh. [1856] 1985. *Liverpool Life: Its Pleasures, Practices, and Pastimes.* Reprint, New York: Garland.

Shippard, Sidney. 1900. "How England Should Treat the Vanquished Boers." *North American Review* 170 (no. 513): 812–26.

Sivanandan, A. 1982. *A Different Hunger.* London: Pluto.

Smith, Adam. [1759] 1976. *The Theory of Moral Sentiments.* Oxford: Clarendon.

———. 1976. *An Inquiry into the Nature and Causes of the Wealth of Nations.* New York: Oxford University Press.

———. 1978. *Lectures on Jurisprudence.* Oxford: Clarendon.

Smith, Charles Manby. 1854. *Curiosities of London Life.* London: W. & F. G. Cash.

Smith, Thornley. 1850. *South Africa Delineated.* London: John Mason.

Solomos, John, and Les Back. 1995. "Marxism, Racism, and Ethnicity." *American Behavioral Scientist* 38 (no. 3): 407–20.

Sparrman, Anders. 1785. *A Voyage to the Cape of Good Hope towards the Artic Circle and round the World but Chiefly into the Country of the Hottentots and Caffres from the Year 1772–1776.* London: G. G. and J. Robinson.

Spelman, Elizabeth. 1982. "Woman as Body: Ancient and Contemporary Views." *Feminist Studies* 8 (no. 1): 109–32.

Spillers, Hortense. 2000. "Mama's Baby, Papa's Maybe: An American Grammar Book." Pp. 57–88 in *The Black Feminist Reader,* ed. Joy James and T. Denean Sharpley-Whiting. London: Blackwell.

Star, Susan Leigh, and James R. Griesemer. 1989. "Institutional Ecology, 'Translations' and Boundary Objects: Amateurs and Professionals in Berkeley's Museum of Vertebrate Zoology, 1907–39." *Social Studies of Science* 19:387–420.

Stavorinus, John Splinter. 1798. *Voyages to the East Indies.* London. G. G. Robinson.

Stepan, Nancy Leys, and Sander L. Gilman. 1991. "Appropriating the Idioms of Science: The Rejection of Scientific Racism." Pp. 73–103 in *The Bounds of Race: Perspectives of Hegemony and Resistance,* ed. Dominic La Capra. Ithaca, N.Y.: Cornell University Press.

Stoler, Ann Laura. 1995. *Race and the Education of Desire: Foucault's History of Sexuality and the Colonial Order of Things.* Durham, N.C.: Duke University Press.

Straub, Kristina. 1987. *Divided Fictions: Fanny Burney and Feminine Strategy.* Lexington: University Press of Kentucky.

Streak, Michael. 1974. *The Afrikaner as Viewed by the English, 1795–1854.* Cape Town: C. Struik.

Strother, Z. S. 1999. "Display of the Body Hottentot." Pp. 1–61 in *Africans on Stage: Studies in Ethnological Show Business,* ed. Bernth Lindfors. Bloomington: Indiana University Press.

Switzer, Les. 1993. *Power and Resistance in an African Society: The Ciskei Xhosa and the Making of South Africa.* Madison: University of Wisconsin Press.

Tabb, William K. 2001. "New Economy: Same Irrational Economy." *Monthly Review* 52 (no. 11): 16–27.

Taylor, William. 1895. *The Story of My Life.* Toronto, Ontario: William Briggs.

Theal, George McCall. 1902. *Records of the Cape Colony.* Vol. 12. Cape Town: C. Struik.

Thirsk, Joan. 1978. *Economic Policy and Projects: The Development of a Consumer Society in Early Modern England.* Oxford: Clarendon.

Thomas, Anthony. 1996. *Rhodes: The Race for Africa.* Johannesburg: Jonathan Ball.

Thomas, E. W. 1862. "The Great Social Evil: A National Question." *The Magdalen's Friend and Female Homes' Intelligencer: A Monthly Magazine* 3:324–27.

Thompson, Phyllis. 1985. *To the Heart of the City: The Story of the London City Mission.* London: Hodder and Stoughton.

Thorne, Susan. 1999. *Congregational Missions and the Making of an Imperial Culture in Nineteenth-Century England.* Stanford, Calif.: Stanford University Press.

Topham, Edward. 1776. *Letters from Edinburgh Written in the Years 1774 and 1775.* London: J. Dodsley.

Trapido, Stanley. 1982. "The Friends of the Natives: Merchants, Peasants, and the Political and Ideological Structure of Liberalism in the Cape, 1854–1910." Pp. 247–74 in *Economy and Society in Pre-Industrial South Africa,* ed. Shula Marks and Anthony Atmore. London: Longman.

Turley, David. 1991. *The Culture of English Anti-Slavery, 1780–1860.* London: Routledge.

Turner, Edward Raymond. 1913. "The Women's Suffrage Movement in England." *American Political Science Review* 7 (no. 4): 588–609.

Turrell, Robert. 1982. "Kimberley: Labour and Compounds, 1871–1882." Pp. 45–76 in *Industrialisation and Social Change in South Africa: African Class Formation, Culture, and Consciousness, 1870–1930,* ed. Shula Marks and Richard Rathbone. London: Longman.

Tyamzashe, Gwayi. [1874] 1972. "Life at the Diamond Fields, August 1874." Reprint, in *Outlook on a Century,* ed. Francis Wilson and Dominique Perrot. Alice, S.A.: Lovedale.

Urban, Wilbur Marshall. 1951. *Language and Reality.* New York: Macmillan.

Valenze, Deborah. 1995. *The First Industrial Woman.* London: Oxford University Press.

Vanderkiste, R. W. 1852. *Notes and Narratives of Six Years Mission, Principally among the Dens of London.* London: James Nisbet.

Vaughan, Robert. [1843] 1971. *The Age of Great Cities; or, Modern Society Viewed in Its Relation to Intelligence, Morals, and Religion.* Reprint, Shannon, Ireland: Irish University Press.

Verschoyle, John. 1900. *Cecil Rhodes: His Political Life and Speeches.* London: Chapman Hall.

Volosinov, V. N. 1986. *Marxism and the Philosophy of Language*. Cambridge, Mass.: Harvard University Press.

Wacquant, Loïc. 1997. "Towards an Analytic of Racial Domination." *Political Power and Social Theory* 11:221–34.

Walker, Thomas. 1831. *Observations on the Nature, Extent, and Effects of Pauperism*. London: James Ridgeway.

Ware, Vron. 1992. *Beyond the Pale: White Women, Racism, and History*. London: Verso.

———. 1996. "Defining Forces: 'Race', Gender and Memories of Empire." Pp. 142–56 in *The Post-Colonial Question: Common Skies, Divided Horizons*, ed. Iain Chambers and Lidia Curti. London: Routledge.

Washington, Booker T. [1901] 1965. *Up from Slavery*. Reprint, with an introduction by John Hope Franklin. New York: Avon Books.

Watson, Hewett C. 1832. "Experiments by Sir William Hamilton." *Phrenological Journal* 7:434–44.

Weldon, Constance. 1984. *The Interaction between the Missionaries of the Cape Eastern Frontier and the Colonial Authorities in the Era of Sir George Grey, 1854–1861*. M.A. thesis. University of Natal.

West, Cornel. 1993a. *Keeping Faith: Philosophy and Race in America*. New York: Routledge.

———. 1993b. *Race Matters*. Boston: Beacon.

Willis, Ellen. 1999. "The Up and Up: On the Limits of Optimism." *Transition* 7 (2): 44–61.

Wood, Ellen Meiksins. 1995. *Democracy against Capitalism: Renewing Historical Materialism*. Cambridge: Cambridge University Press.

———. 1999. *The Origin of Capitalism*. New York: Monthly Review Press.

Wood, J. G. 1878. *The Uncivilized Races of Man in All Countries of the World*. Hartford, Conn.: J. Burr.

Wood, Peter. 1991. *Poverty and the Workhouse in Victorian Britain*. Wolfeboro Fall, N.H.: Alan Sutton.

Worger, William. 1987. *South Africa's City of Diamonds: Mine Workers and Monopoly Capitalism in Kimberley, 1867–1895*. New Haven, Conn.: Yale University Press.

Wybergh, W. 1909. "Native Policy: Assimilation or Segregation." *The State* (April): 455–64.